TOWTON

TOWTON

The Battle of
Palmsunday Field
1461

JOHN SADLER

Pen & Sword
MILITARY

This work is dedicated to the members of the Towton Battlefield Society

First published in Great Britain in 2011
and reprinted in this format in 2014 by
PEN & SWORD MILITARY
An imprint of
Pen & Sword Books Ltd
47 Church Street
Barnsley, South Yorkshire
S70 2AS

ISBN 978 1 78346 192 9

A CIP catalogue record for this book is
available from the British Library

Typeset in 11pt Ehrhardt
by S L Menzies-Earl

Printed and bound in England
By CPI Group (UK) Ltd, Croydon, CR0 4YY

Pen & Sword Books Ltd incorporates the Imprints of Aviation, Atlas,
Family History, Fiction, Maritime, Military, Discovery, Politics, History,
Archaeology, Select, Wharncliffe Local History, Wharncliffe True Crime,
Military Classics, Wharncliffe Transport, Leo Cooper, The Praetorian Press,
Remember When, Seaforth Publishing and Frontline Publishing

For a complete list of Pen & Sword titles please contact
PEN & SWORD BOOKS LIMITED
47 Church Street, Barnsley, South Yorkshire, S70 2AS, England
E-mail: enquiries@pen-and-sword.co.uk
Website: www.pen-and-sword.co.uk

Contents

Illustrations and Maps

Unless otherwise stated, illustrations and maps are from the author's own collection.

Abbreviations

Arrivall	*The Arrivall of Edward IV* etc
Benet	John Benet's Chronicle
Chastellain	Chastellain G. *Chronique des derniers Ducs de Bourgoyne* in Pantheon Literaire iv
Croyland	The Croyland Chronicler
CS	Camden Society
CSPM	*Calendar of State Papers of Milan*
Davies	*An English Chronicle of the Reigns of Richard II, Henry IV, Henry V and Henry VI* ed. J.S. Davies
De Commynes	Philip de Commynes *The Memoirs of the reign of Louis XI 1461–1463* transl. M. Jones 1972
EH	English Heritage
Fabyan	Robert Fabyan *The New Chronicles of England and France* ed. H. Ellis London 1809
Froissart	*Froissart's Chronicles* ed. G. Brereton
GCL	*Great Chronicle of London*
Gregory	William Gregory's *Chronicle of London* in *Historical Collections of a Citizen of London in the Fifteenth Century* ed. J. Gairdner C.C. New Series xvii 1876
Hall	Edward Hall *The Union of the Two Noble and Illustre Famelies of Lancastre and York 1548*
Hearne's Fragment	*Hearne's Fragment* in Chronicles of the White Rose
London Chronicles	*Chronicles of London* ed. C.L. Kingsford Oxford 1905
NCH	*Northumberland County History*
NPG	National Portrait Gallery
PL	*Paston Letters*
PV	Polydore Vergil *English History* (ed. H. Ellis)
RA	Royal Armouries
SAM	Scheduled Ancient Monument
SS	Surtees Society

TNA	The National Archives
Warkworth	John Warkworth *A Chronicle of the First Thirteen Years of the Reign of Edward IV 1461–1474* ed. J.O. Halliwell C.S. Old Series x 1839
Waurin	Jean de Waurin *Recueil de Chroniques D'Angleterre* eds W. Hardy & E.L.C.P. Hardy
Whethamstede	*Registrum Abbatis Johannis Whethamstede* ed. H. T. Riley
Worcester	William of Worcester *Annales Rerum Anglicarum* in *Liber Niger Scaccarii* ed. J. Hearne 2 vols. Oxford 1728
Year Book	*The Year Book de Termino Paschae 4 Edward IV* in Priory of Hexham S.S. 1 1864

Biographical Notes

Edmund Beaufort, 2nd Duke of Somerset (1406–1455)

Fourth son of John Beaufort, the 1st Earl, Edmund was involved in the French Wars and the recapture of Harfleur. Knight of the Garter ('KG' hereafter) in 1436, Earl of Dorset 1442 and Marquess a year later. In 1444 Edmund succeeded his father as 4th Earl. After Suffolk's removal and murder, Edmund became leader of the Lancastrian faction at court. Handsome and urbane (he was rumoured to have had a clandestine affair with Queen Katherine in 1427) he was, nonetheless, totally unscrupulous. Edmund was killed at the First Battle of St Albans on 22 May 1455.

Henry Beaufort, 3rd Duke of Somerset (1436–1464)

Previously Earl of Dorset, Henry was wounded at the First Battle of St Albans. A prime mover in the Lancastrian revival after the constitutional settlement of 1460, Henry fought at Wakefield and Second St Albans, where his generalship proved superior. Defeated at Towton, he maintained the war in the north, and although he capitulated in 1463, reverted the following year, and was executed following the debacle at Hexham.

Edmund Beaufort, titular 4th Duke of Somerset (1438–1471)

Younger brother of the 3rd Duke, Edmund led the Lancastrians in the Tewkesbury campaign. On the day after defeat at Tewkesbury, Edmund was taken from sanctuary and beheaded.

Thomas Bourchier (1404–1486)

Younger son of William Bourchier, Count of Eu, and Anne of Gloucester (half-brother to Humphrey Stafford, 1st Duke of Buckingham), Thomas was educated at Oxford, before entering the Church, where he rose with dizzying rapidity. He became Bishop of Worcester in 1434, Bishop of Ely in 1443, and finally, Archbishop of Canterbury in 1454. At first, Thomas was neutral in the wars, inclining to the court, though an advocate for peace. After 1459, however, he became a Yorkist partisan, crowning Edward IV and Elizabeth Woodville (he became Gloucester's emissary for the surrender of the young Duke of York in 1483). He then crowned the usurping Richard III before an effortless transition to the Tudor camp, crowning Henry VII.

George, Duke of Clarence (1449–1478)
Sixth son of Richard of York and Cicely Neville – one of four to reach maturity – George was elevated to his dukedom in 1461. After marrying Warwick's elder daughter, George joined the conspiracies of 1469–1470. Reverting his allegiance prior to Barnet, he was 'privately' executed in 1478. Brilliant and charismatic, George was also unstable, jealous and treacherous.

John de Clifford, 9th Baron Clifford (1435–1461)
The Cliffords were a long-established family, holding the lordships of Appleby and Skipton. After his father, Thomas de Clifford, the 8th Baron (1414–1455) was killed at the First Battle of St Albans, John de Clifford became a savage paladin of the House of Lancaster. He fought at Wakefield and is credited with the slaying of Richard, Duke of York's second son, Edmund, Earl of Rutland. He was, in turn, killed in the skirmish at Dintingdale prior to the Battle of Towton and his followers, 'The Flower of Craven' were decimated around him.

William de la Pole, 1st Duke of Suffolk (1396–1450)
Second son of the 2nd Earl, Michael de la Pole, William became 4th Earl and later Marquess and 1st Duke. He held joint command at Orléans after the death of Salisbury. One of Henry VI's chief ministers, he was blamed for the loss of the French territories and subsequently impeached and murdered while attempting to quit the realm.

John de la Pole, 2nd Duke of Suffolk (1442–1491)
Son of the 1st Duke and first husband of Margaret Beaufort (she did not recognise the marriage, which was annulled by Henry VI in 1453), brother-in-law of Edward IV and father of the Earl of Lincoln. While fighting for York at the First Battle of St Albans, he remained largely inactive thereafter.

John de Vere 12th Earl of Oxford (*c*. 1408–1462)
A Lancastrian by sentiment, de Vere did not fight at the First Battle of St Albans, arriving a day late. Accused of plotting against Edward IV, he was executed in 1462.

William, Lord Hastings (*c*. 1430–1483)
A stalwart Yorkist, Hastings fought at Towton, Barnet and Tewkesbury – commanding a wing of Edward IV's army in the latter two engagements. Lieutenant of Calais and a favourite crony of the king, he was much disliked

by the Woodville faction. A staunch ally of Gloucester's, after Edward's death, it may have been his doubts as to the duke's intentions that led to his summary execution.

Henry VI of England (1422–1471)
Henry came to the throne as a minor on the death of his father, Henry V. His reign witnessed the steady decline of English fortunes in France and a growing crisis at home. He married Margaret of Anjou in 1445 and was captured by the Yorkists after 1465, briefly reoccupying the throne during the Readeption, engineered by Warwick. He was done to death in 1471, while a captive in the Tower, following the Battle of Tewkesbury.

Henry Holand, 3rd Duke of Exeter (*d.* 1475)
Despite his wedding to one of York's daughters Holand came to be implicated in the disturbances of 1453 as a partisan of the Percys. He fought at Blore Heath, Wakefield, the Second Battle of St Albans, Towton and Barnet – where he was left for dead. Escaping to the Continent, he was reduced to beggary, but later returned to England, meeting a dubious end as a prisoner in the Tower.

Edward of Lancaster (1453–1471)
Only child of Henry VI and Margaret of Anjou (some questions were raised as to his legitimacy). Edward was raised in exile in readiness for an attempt to recover his father's throne. Allied to Warwick the Kingmaker by marriage, he lost his chance – and his life – at Tewkesbury.

Edward, Earl of March (1442–1483)
King of England 1461–1470 and 1471–1483. 'The Sunne in Splendour', eldest son of the Duke of York and Cicely Neville ('The Rose of Raby'), victor of Mortimer's Cross, Towton, Empingham, Barnet and Tewkesbury. He secretly married Elizabeth Woodville on 1 May 1464. Courageous on the field with a flair for both strategy and tactics, he was rightly regarded as the leading captain of his day.

Margaret of Anjou (1429–1482)
Daughter of the impecunious Rene I of Sicily, Duke of Anjou, King of Naples and Sicily, married to Henry VI of England at the age of fifteen. Beautiful and vivacious, she was strong-minded and, with her favourite, the Duke of Somerset, dominated the Lancastrian court faction. Up to 1463

Margaret was the mainspring of resistance in the north, where she had been prepared to swap the twin bastions of Berwick-upon-Tweed and Carlisle in return for Scottish arms. Kept in the Tower after the disaster at Tewkesbury and released in 1475, she spent her final years in Anjou.

John Mowbray, 3rd Duke of Norfolk (1415–1461)
It was the terminally ill Norfolk's late arrival on the field of Towton that turned the tide of battle. York's nephew, he had previously fought at the First Battle of St Albans.

Richard Neville, Earl of Salisbury (1400–1460)
Younger son of the Earl of Westmorland and Joan de Beaufort, Richard married Alice Montacute, Countess of Salisbury. KG in 1438, he received the lesser share of the family estates on the east side of the Pennines. In addition to his feud with the Percys he was at odds with the senior branch of the Nevilles (from west of the hills). Brother-in-law to the Duke of York, he was active in Yorkist councils and a senior statesman in the cause. Killed at the Battle of Wakefield in 1460, along with one of his sons, Sir Thomas Neville, whose marriage to Maud Stanhope fanned the flames of the Percy–Neville feud.

William Neville, Lord Fauconberg (*c*. 1410–1463)
Younger son of Ralph, Earl of Westmorland, brother of the Earl of Salisbury, and a veteran of the French Wars, William was knighted in 1426, Castellan of Roxburgh, KG 1440, captured by the French in 1449 and subsequently ransomed. Like York, he was owed substantial sums by the Crown. Though a staunch Lancastrian prior to 1455, he successfully led the Yorkist van at Northampton and Towton. He acquired his title by right of his wife (who lacked mental capacity) and became Earl of Kent and Lord Admiral.

Richard Neville, Earl of Warwick (1428–1471)
Known as 'The Kingmaker', mightiest of the Crown's overmighty subjects and a pivotal figure of the period. He was Salisbury's eldest son and York's nephew, marrying a daughter of the de Beauchamp Earl of Warwick. He fought at the First Battle of St Albans, Northampton, Second St Albans and Towton. Seeing himself as the power behind the throne, he was increasingly alienated from Edward IV, following the Woodville marriage. His final manipulation led to the 'readeption' of Henry VI in the coup of

1470. Richard Neville, along with his brother, Lord Montagu, was killed at Barnet in the following spring.

John Neville, Lord Montagu (*d.* 1471)
The Earl of Warwick's younger brother, an able soldier and administrator, principal architect of the Yorkist victory in the north from 1461 to 1464. Temporarily installed as Earl of Northumberland, he was later stripped of the title and, though partly compensated, joined his brother in the coup of 1470, dying with him at Barnet.

George Neville (*d.* 1476)
Brother of John, Thomas and Richard, George entered holy orders to become Bishop of Exeter and then Archbishop of York. He sided with his brother in the rising against Edward IV in 1469 and, on presenting himself to the king (as the latter was effectively captured), revealed his partisan stance by appearing in full harness rather than ecclesiastical robes.

Thomas Percy, Lord Egremont (1422–1460)
Younger son of the 2nd Earl of Northumberland, Thomas was created Lord Egremont in 1445. A violent, thuggish actor in the Percy–Neville feud of the early 1450s, he was killed at the Battle of Northampton.

Henry Percy, 2nd Earl of Northumberland (*d.* 1455)
Son of the famous 'Hotspur', who was killed at Shrewsbury in 1403. Henry gradually clawed back the family lands after his father's attainder, and was involved in the rivalry with the Nevilles. He was killed at the First Battle of St Albans.

Henry Percy, Lord Poynings, later 3rd Earl of Northumberland (*d.* 1461)
Border Warden after his father, Henry was one of the leading northern Lancastrians, fighting at Wakefield, Second St Albans and Towton, where he fell. The title was, once again attainted after his death, passing to John Neville, Lord Montagu. Edward IV subsequently restored his son, who became the 4th Earl.

Sir Ralph Percy (*d.* 1464)
Margaret of Anjou's champion in the north from 1461 to 1464. While

prone to switching allegiance, he reverted to Lancaster for the last time before the rout at Hedgeley Moor, where he died fighting.

Humphrey Stafford, 1st Duke of Buckingham (1402–1460)
Married to York's sister, Anne, Humphrey was perceived as a peacemaker. Champion of the 'Loveday' accord, he fought at First St Albans and died at Northampton. He was the son of Edmund Stafford, 5th Earl of Buckingham and Anne of Gloucester, a granddaughter of Edward III. Knighted in 1421, KG in 1429, he was active on the Royal Council from 1429, serving extensively and with distinction in France. He was created Duke in 1444.

John Tiptoft, Earl of Worcester (d. 1470)
Tiptoft held the office of Constable of England from 1462 to 1467 and again in 1470. Noted for his extensive literary tastes, outstanding library and severity, he was universally reviled. Warwick had him executed in 1470, primarily as a sop to widespread clamour.

Sir Andrew Trollope (d. 1461)
A successful career-soldier who fought in the French Wars, Trollope was appointed Master Porter of Calais and acted as advisor to York. His defection provoked the collapse of morale and subsequent 'Rout' of Ludford. Trollope may have been instrumental in the Lancastrians' winning tactics at Wakefield and fought with distinction at Second St Albans. His luck finally ran out at Towton.

Edmund Tudor, Earl of Richmond (1430–1456)
The son of Owen Tudor (d. 1461, executed after Mortimer's Cross) and Katherine of Valois, widow of Henry V, Edmund married the formidable Margaret Beaufort and fathered Henry Tudor, the future Henry VII, before succumbing to a bout of the plague.

Jasper Tudor, Earl of Pembroke (1431–1495)
Brother of Edmund, a diehard Lancastrian, he fought at First St Albans and Mortimer's Cross but avoided Towton. After an unsuccessful attempt to relieve Harlech, he fled to Brittany after Bosworth (1485), subsequently marrying Buckingham's Woodville widow.

John, Lord Wenlock (c. 1400–1471)
A venerable survivor of the French Wars, Wenlock proved a steadfast

Yorkist, fighting at Mortimer's Cross and Towton. Nonetheless, he supported Warwick in 1470 and survived to be killed at Tewkesbury – possibly felled by Somerset himself, in a fit of suspicion.

Queen Elizabeth Woodville (1437–1492)
Married to the Lancastrian knight, Sir John Grey of Groby, and then widowed, Edward IV married her in secret – to the great consternation of his supporters, most particularly Warwick, who had been seeking to broker a French alliance. Noted for her ruthless avarice and rapacity, her family were excoriated for their shameless greed.

Richard Woodville, 1st Earl Rivers (*d*. 1469)
Elizabeth's father, married to Jacquetta of Luxembourg, widow of the Earl of Bedford (Henry V's brother and regent after his death). Initially an adherent of Lancaster, fighting at Towton, he held high office under his son-in-law, earning the powerful enmity of the Earl of Warwick, who had him executed after the defeat at Edgecote.

Anthony Woodville, 2nd Earl Rivers (1442–1483)
Fought for his brother-in-law with some distinction at both Barnet and Tewkesbury, and was notable in the lists. He was also something of a poet. A victim of Richard of Gloucester's coup in 1483. Despite early reassurances from his brother-in-law, he was subsequently – and summarily – executed.

Margaret of York, Duchess of Burgundy (1446–1503)
Sister of Edward IV, she was married to the quixotic Charles the Bold, Duke of Burgundy (*d*. 1477). Margaret remained a Yorkist meddler after the death of her brother at Bosworth.

Richard, 3rd Duke of York (1411–1460)
The senior member of the Yorkist faction, with a strong claim to the throne, Richard was active in the later stages of the French Wars. A bitter opponent of Somerset, he was Lord Protector on two occasions. Claiming the throne in 1460, he was killed at Wakefield at the end of that year.

Timeline

1399	The Lancastrian usurpation; death of Richard II.
1402	Battle of Homildon.
1403	Battle of Shrewsbury.
1415	Battle of Agincourt.
1420	Treaty of Troyes.
1422	Death of Henry V.
1424	Battle of Verneuil.
1428	Siege of Orléans.
1435	End of the Anglo–Burgundian Alliance.
1437	Henry VI comes of age.
1450	Fall of Suffolk.
1453	Battle of Castillon; end of English hopes in France; Henry VI experiences mental breakdown (August); the Percy–Neville feud erupts.
1454	York appointed Protector (April); Henry VI recovers (December).
1455	York resigns as Protector (February); First Battle of St Albans (22 May); York reappointed to the Protectorate.
1456	End of York's second Protectorate (February).
1458	'Loveday' at St Paul's (March); putative attempt to kill the Earl of Warwick (November).
1459	Battle of Blore Heath (23 September); the 'Rout of Ludford' (October).
1460	Warwick and March land in Kent (June/July); Battle of Northampton (10 July); York recognised as heir to Henry VI (October); Edward of Lancaster disinherited; Battle of Wakefield (30 December).
1461	Battle of Mortimer's Cross (2 February); Second Battle of St Albans (17 February); Earl of March proclaimed Edward IV (March); Battle of Towton (29 March).
1462	War in Northumberland; Lancastrians hold coastal fortresses; Margaret of Anjou surrenders Berwick to the Scots.
1464	Battle of Hedgeley Moor (25 April); Battle of Hexham (14 May); Montagu created Earl of Northumberland.
1465	Capture of Henry VI by the Yorkists (July).

1469   Warwick plots to overthrow Edward IV; the Duke of Clarence
        marries Warwick's daughter; Battle of Edgecote (26 July);
        Edward IV regains control of the kingdom.
1470   Battle of 'Losecote Field' (12 March); Warwick and Clarence
        exiled to France (July); Warwick comes to an agreement with
        Margaret of Anjou; Edward and the Duke of Gloucester flee
        Warwick's coup (September).
1471   Return of Edward IV and Gloucester (March); Battle of
        Barnet (14 April); Battle of Tewkesbury/death of Henry VI
        (4 May); Gloucester assumes Warwick's offices as warden and
        begins his tenure in the north.
1475   July, Edward IV launches French expedition.
1478   Execution of the Duke of Clarence (February).
1482   Gloucester launches Scottish campaign, recovering Berwick
        and occupying Edinburgh.
1483   Death of Edward IV (April/June); Gloucester seizes power,
        eliminating the Woodvilles and Lord Hastings; Edward V and
        the Duke of York (the Princes in the Tower) are confined.
1483   The Duke of Buckingham's rebellion (October) crushed.
1484   Richard III rules an uneasy realm.
1485   Landing of the Lancastrians under Henry Tudor (August);
        Battle of Bosworth (22 August).
1487   Battle of Stoke (16 June).

Preface

Towton is a village about 10 miles south-west of York.
It owes what fame it has to the fact that it was once the scene
of a battle. But this was not just any battle. At the Battle of
Towton more English people were killed than on any other day
ever [. . .] while the population of Britain in 1916 was more
than 40 million, that of England in 1461 was considerably
less than 4 million [. . .] one in every 100
Englishmen died at Towton.

Martin Kettle,
the *Guardian*, 25 August 2007

My fascination with Towton can be traced to early 1960s TV productions like the BBC's *Age of Kings* and *Wars of the Roses*. Both series were based on *Henry VI* (Parts I, II and III) together with *Richard III*. That Shakespeare could be enjoyable, indeed rivetingly so, came as something of a revelation to one reared on the standard GCE (as it then was) diet of dull exam questions. An immediate debt of gratitude is therefore due to the producers and cast. As a young lad I found the frequent – virtually non-stop – bloodletting particularly appealing, if, sequentially, rather hard to follow. Who was killing who and why? The search for answers has occupied a considerable amount of time since. What follows is therefore a military study, rather than a full political and social history – already covered by a number of distinguished authors.

Thanks are due to: Rupert Harding (my editor at Pen & Sword), Dr Maureen Meikle (Sunderland University), Dr Richard Britnell (Durham University), Professor Tony Pollard (University of Teesside), Professor Gordon Batho, Chloe Rodham (for producing the maps and battle plans), Adam Barr (for the photography), Richard Groocock (National Archives), Dr Joan Harvey (University of Newcastle upon Tyne), Dr Constance Fraser, the late Professor George Jobey, Jennifer Gill and Liz Bregazzi (County Durham Record Office), Malin Holst (Towton Mass Grave Project), Philip Albert (Royal Armouries), Nicola Waghorn (National Gallery), Matthew Bailey (National Portrait Gallery), the staff of the Lit.& Phil. in Newcastle upon Tyne, Adrian Waite (of the Red Wyverns), Duncan

Brown (EH Photo Library), Anthea Boylston and Jo Buckberry (Bradford University), Winnie Tyrell (Glasgow Museums), Rosie Serdiville (Society of Antiquaries of Newcastle upon Tyne), Mark Taylor and Graham Darbyshire (Towton Battlefield Society), and my colleagues at the Centre for Lifelong Learning, Sunderland University. Lastly, and as ever, thanks are due to my wife Ruth for her unfailing patience and support. Any errors and omissions remain entirely the responsibility of the author.

John Sadler, Belsay, Northumberland,
October 2009.

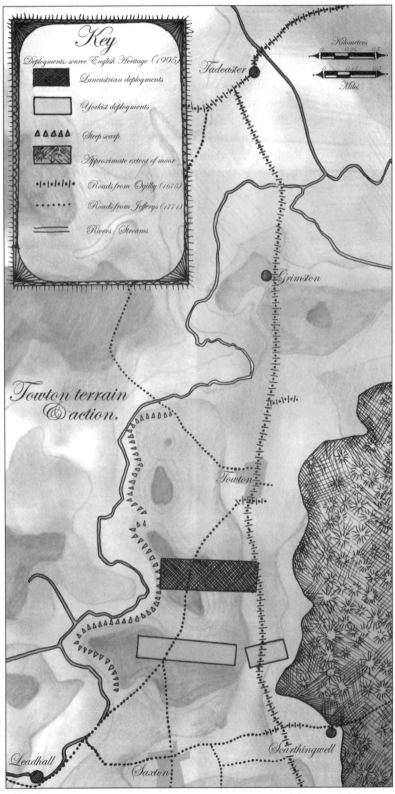

Key

Deployments: source English Heritage (1995)

Lancastrian deployments

Yorkist deployments

Steep scarp

Approximate extent of moor

Roads from Ogilby (1675)

Roads from Jefferys (1771)

Rivers / Streams

Kilometers

0   0.25   0.5

Miles

0   0.15   0.3

Tadcaster

Grimston

Towton terrain & action.

Towton

Leadhall

Saxton

Scarthingwell

Map 1

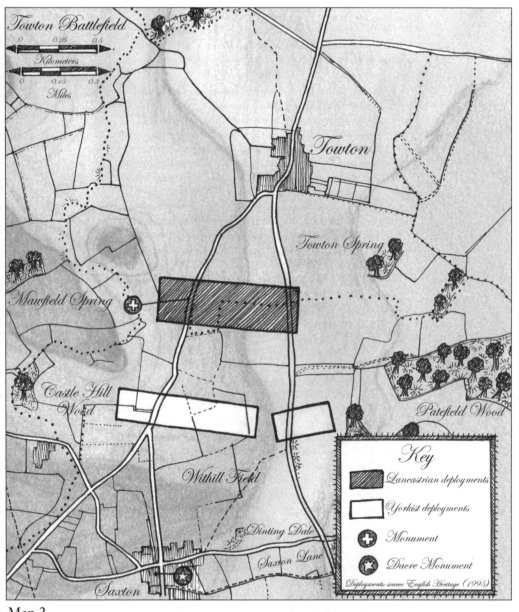

Map 2

The Rose of Rouen
(Contemporary ballad)

For to save all England the Rose[1] did his intent,
With Calais and with London with Essex and with Kent,
And all the south of England up to the water of Trent,
And when he saw the time best the Rose from London went.
[Chorus]
Blessed be the time, that ever God spread that flower!
Blessed by that royal rose that is so fresh of you,
Almighty is you blesses that soul[2], that the seed sew,
And blessed be the garden[3] that the rose grew.
Christ blessing have they all that to the rose be true.
The way into the north country, the Rose full fast he sought,
With him went the Ragged Staff[4] that many men there brought,
So did the White Lion[5] full worthily he wrought.
Almighty Jesus bless his soul, that their armies taught.
Blessed be the time, that ever God spread that flower! Etc.
The Fish Hook[6] came to the field in full eager mood,
So did the Cornish Chough[7] and brought forth all her brood,
There was the Black Ragged Staff[8] that is both true and good,
The Bridled Horse[9], The Water Bourget[10] by the Horse[11] stood.
Blessed be the time, that ever God spread that flower! Etc.
The Greyhound,[12] The Harts Head[13] they quit them well that day,
So did the Harrow of Canterbury and Clinton[14] with his Key,
The White Ship of Bristol he feared not the fray,
The Black Ram of Coventry he said not one nay.
Blessed be the time, that ever God spread that flower! Etc.
The Falcon and the Fetterlock[15] was there that tide,
The Black Bull[16] also himself would not hide,
The Dolphin[17] came from Wales, Three Corbies[18] by his side,
The proud Leopard of Salisbury gaped his eyes wide.
Blessed be the time, that ever God spread that flower! Etc.
The Wolf[19] came from Worcester, full sore he thought to bite,
The Dragon[20] came from Gloucester, he bent his tail to smite,
The Griffen[21] came from Leicester, flying in as tight,
The George[22] came from Nottingham, with spear for to fight.
Blessed be the time, that ever God spread that flower! Etc.
The northern party made them strong with spear and with shield,
On Palm Sunday afternoon they met us in the field,
Within an hour they were right fayne to flee, and eke to yield,
Twenty seven thousand the Rose killed in the field.
Blessed be the time, that ever God spread that flower! Etc.
The Rose came to London full royally riding.
Two archbishops of England crowned the Rose king.
Almighty is you, save the Rose and give him blessing
And all the realm of England rejoice at his crowning.
Blessed be the time, that ever God spread that flower! Etc.

(Anonymous (*c.*1461), *Archaeologia*, XXIX pp. 344–347)

Introduction

The boast of heraldry; the pomp of power,
And all that beauty; all that wealth e'er gave,
Awaits alike the inevitable hour:
The paths of glory lead but to the grave.

Elegy Written in a Country Churchyard – Thomas Gray

The town of Ferrybridge in North Yorkshire, lying on the south bank of the River Aire, is the kind of place only a Yorkshireman could love. A nondescript remnant of post-industrial, post-war utilitarian despondency, it requires a powerful imagination to transpose the landscape and events of spring 1461 onto such an unpromising canvas. Yet it was here the Towton campaign began in earnest – both sides disputing the span of the medieval bridge.

Discovering the field of Towton involves a fair amount of detective work – no bad thing in itself, perhaps – but surprising, considering this was Britain's bloodiest day in a long history of sanguinary conflict, including both world wars. It seems likely that more Englishmen died on that day than any other, including 1 July 1916 – the disastrous opening day of the Somme offensive. Admittedly, the modern road system – planned with no regard for history – obfuscates progress. Not until one drives north on the A162 is the route of the Yorkist army clear. Sherburn-in-Elmet is now neatly bypassed by a loop in the road. The first tangible and tantalising evidence is found just beyond the village of Barkston Ash. There, by the side of the road, at the junction of the lane leading west to Saxton, is a stump of medieval cross – the 'Leper Pot'. It is here, tradition asserts, that Lord Clifford fell. According to Edward Hall, Clifford's throat was pierced by an arrow, after he unwisely removed his bevor.[1]

On a muggy morning in late spring, passing through pastoral vistas of fields and peaceful hamlets, it seems impossible that such a savage and momentous struggle occurred in this place. Traces are few. Only a ragged cross marks the field, easily missed by the motorist. A rutted pedestrian track strikes west over fields to the edge of Bloody Meadow, identified by some rather forlorn interpretation boards. And that is it. I cannot think of another field of such significance so poorly served (Naseby, to be sure, is a similar case) – a striking contrast with, for example, North America, where a booming heritage industry ensures adequate care for sites of national importance. Members of the Towton Battlefield Society[2] – who continue to do such sterling work – deserve every praise for their doggedness, which, hopefully, will one day result in the construction of a sympathetic visitor centre.

Driving on the A162 from Barkston Ash to Towton, one ascends the rise the Yorkists would have climbed. As you arrive parallel to Dacre's Cross, Castle Hill Wood can be glimpsed away to your left. All this ground now lies under the plough and is privately owned. There is nothing in the village to associate with the battle other than the Hall – a private dwelling. Following the B1217 from the village takes us past the supposed campsite of the Lancastrian van, past the cross, now on your right just off the road, and then down to the minor crossroads, a left-hand turn takes you into Saxton, where the church and Dacre's tomb are located. If you park and begin walking down the bridlepath to your right, you are afforded a good view of Castle Hill Wood and the enticingly mysterious mounds, whose purpose no one is quite sure of.

Perhaps the most atmospheric spot is the tiny, forgotten St Mary's Chapel, which stands alone in a field on the left-hand side of the road, south of the crossroads, with the Crooked Billet Inn on your left. This is the sole surviving fragment of the lost village of Lead, associated with the Tyas family. A thirteenth-century foundation, restored before the Second World War and simple to the point of austerity, fits the landscape as though cast down by divine providence. It was probably once attached to the vanished manor house. This simple triangle of undulating farmland, enclosed within three roads – A162 in the east, B1217 in the west, and the minor road west from Sherburn-in-Elmet linking up with the latter – encloses the site of Towton or Palmsunday Field – England's bloodiest meadow.

Ground

Between the great Yorkshire rivers of Wharfe and Aire, the land rises in a Magnesian Limestone belt, extending across North Yorkshire and furnishing the stone that built York Minster. This tract is cut by lateral gorges through which race the Humber's tributaries – Ure, Nidd, Wharfe, Aire, Went and Don. Once, the land was dressed by a dense covering of ancient elms, giving the historical name Elmet – the 'Sylva Elmetae' of Bede.

When Elizabethan antiquary John Leland visited the field, some four score years after the fight, locals claimed that many of the fallen had been interred in Saxton churchyard: 'They lay afore in five pittes, yet appering half a mile of by north in Saxton feldes.'[3] The subsequent Act of Attainder referred to the battle as having occurred on 'Sonday called comynly Palme Sonday, the xxix day of Marche [. . .] in a feld bitwene the Townes of Shirbourne in Elmet and Tadcaster [. . .] called Saxtonfeld and Tawtonfeeld, in the Shire of York.'[4] Thus, there is a general consensus the action took place between the two hamlets of Saxton and Towton. The ground is elevated – not to any great extent, a mere 150 feet or so – but sufficiently so to form a distinct space. Eastwards, the land slopes away to merge into the flatness of the Vale of York. To the west it declines sharply, falling into a defile above Cock Beck. From Saxton – line of approach for the Yorkists – the ascent is clear and abrupt from Towton, and thus, for the Lancastrians, more gentle. The level ground atop is bisected by a small ravine, which declines from North Acres in the east to a sharper trough in the west, where it debouches into the vale of the Cock.

This area is known as Towton Dale, and that steep slope down to the water became the infamous Bloody Meadow – scene of the most concentrated carnage. It is possible the low ground by the river was altogether wetter and given to flooding, though there is no direct evidence to support this. These precipitous banks only level out further south by the Crooked Billet and St Mary's. Two gentry families, Tyas and Skargill, are linked to Lead and it may be, as Andrew Boardman suggests, that a portion of the Neville affinity encamped here. He offers some interesting insight on a possible heraldic provenance of the name 'Crooked Billet' – although earlier authors, particularly Dr Leadman, associate the name more with the arms of Lord Fauconberg. This place, and the delightful chapel that was in situ in 1461, have a singularly melancholic, somewhat enigmatic air. Visitors – or at least those with a romantic tendency – are left feeling that the stones have a story to tell. Meanwhile, the angle of descent to the east, at the extremity of North Acres, is generally milder, but, by the excellent vantage of the Hawthorn tree, dips more radically. From here one can obtain a clear view of the field, the cockpit, the arena of Towton where the two sides slogged it out in the whorls of bloodied slush for – if the chroniclers are to be believed – a full ten hours.

Dr Leadman, writing in 1889, refers to a peculiar strain of dwarf bush said to have been found only in the fields between Towton Lane and Castle Hill Wood – in his day, referred to as 'the Field of the White and the Red Rose'. Here, the grass was said to grow both rank and lush, manured by such great torrents of blood as were spilled on the day. Even by the late nineteenth century, this flora was becoming rare, having been extremely popular with collectors. It is described as a white rose with a red spot in the centre of each petal – the colour suffused by a darkening red as the plant ages:

> There is a patch of wild roses that bloom on a battlefield.
> Where rival rose of Lancaster blushed redder still to yield.
> [. . .] And the little sparkling river was cumbered as of yore,
> With ghastly corse [corpse] of man and horse,
> and ran down red with gore.
>
> [Extracted from *The Flower of Towton Field:*
> *A Ballad of Battle Acre* by J. R. Planche]

English Heritage's Report[5] disagrees with some writers who have suggested the ground was wholly given over to open moor in 1461. English Heritage contend the land was at least partly under the plough or winter pasture, hemmed by forestation. These were open fields devoid of hedge or boundary:

> similarly, much of Towton Parish land in the battlefield area appears to have been an open field rigg and furrow landscape. The North Acres area features a substantial bank (including old burr-elm stumps) running across it which could have been produced by ploughing – a 'headland'. Further evidence for ploughing exists in the form of medieval lynchets below Castle Hill Wood.[6]

Away from the plateau itself, Renshaw Woods in Cock Valley, appear to be of ancient provenance.[7] Towton Spring[8] and Carr Woods[9] are likewise very old. Further field evidence would seem to confirm that some extant roads are of sufficient age to have existed as track-ways at the time of the battle. The bridleway known as Old London Road, the B1217 and possibly the current A162 may well have followed a similar course in 1461 as they do today. English Heritage are of the opinion that nineteenth-century enclosures subdivided existing fields and that more recent stripping of hedges has, in part, restored the landscape to its pre-enclosure appearance. All in all, the ground may, therefore, not have really changed all that much.

This view is corroborated by Leland, to whose account Andrew Boardman refers. The great antiquary recorded that, in the general area, were to be found 'good high plains, corn ground . . . and some wood'.[10] In Towton itself only the hall, which may date to the reign of Richard II, can be traced as far back as 1461. The old Roman road, now the A162, ran through on its route to Tadcaster, swinging left beyond to climb onto the plateau then dropping sharply to cross the Cock Beck. This may have been a wooden bridge or merely a ford. It may also mark the site of that notorious 'bridge of bodies', which, in the fury of the rout, groaned with the weight of dead and dying.

The Battle

In this valley on one savage day, a greater proportion of our population died than in a whole year of the First World War. It was by far the bloodiest battle in our history, yet Towton is largely forgotten and untaught.

A. A. Gill

In the wet summer of 2008, *Sunday Times Magazine* journalist A.A. Gill visited the field of Towton, where, he noted, 'it would be impossible to walk [. . .] and not feel the dread underfoot – the echo of desperate events vibrating just behind the hearing'. Battlefields take on a particular air of melancholy. One has merely to visit the mute testimony of the war cemeteries, which mark the line of the Western Front to feel a tangible sense of loss. The German burials at Langemarck just north of Ypres are particularly gaunt, bare and austere. A nation's suffering written in stone. Towton has no such commemoration, just the cross, unannounced and generally unnoticed. This seems bizarrely inequitable, as Palmsunday Field was the largest and bloodiest fight on British soil, with only Marston Moor in 1644 coming close (in every sense, as the two fields lie close together).

During the rather better summer of 1996, builders undertaking new works accidentally uncovered the site of a mass grave and the Towton Mass Grave Project was born. The remains of some forty-three dead were recovered from the pit, a mere 6m x 2m and 50cm below the rich topsoil.[11] Here was the Holy Grail of Towton scholars, that which had eluded generations of searchers – grave evidence, mortal traces of those who had died in the carnage.

As A. A. Gill points out, Towton, for all its magnitude and drama, plays poor relation to other renowned fields, such as Hastings, Bosworth and Culloden. But Palmsunday Field remains bare, despite the dedicated efforts of the Towton Battlefield Society. Part of the difficulty lies in the nature and ownership of the ground, which does not readily lend itself to development as a heritage site. Many might prefer it stayed that way. Yet

Towton is *huge* – the biggest, bloodiest and arguably most dramatic battle fought on British soil, where the number of combatants and casualties exceeded the combined total of the three other fields mentioned above.[12]

Apart from the Ricardian element – which enjoys almost mystical status and is frequently pursued with as much grasp of historical reality – the Wars of the Roses (a term unknown to participants) has been consigned to academics and anoraks. History, as far as I can determine, is taught insofar as the curriculum encourages teaching in any recognisable form – as a series of unrelated sound-bites, focusing on themes rather than events. As one who spends some time offering historical interpretation to schools, I am not infrequently saddened by the yawning chasms. This is certainly not the fault of teachers who remain enthusiastic and competent. It is rather a systemic failing arising from a politically correct syllabus, dictated by the controlling, liberal élite.

Martin Bell, writing in *Through Gates of Fire* (2003), asserts there are only two categories of war in the twenty-first century, one being 'wars of collapsed states'. The Wars of the Roses (and here I adopt the convention bundling the range of dynastic conflicts from 1453–1487 into one generic band) could be said to represent something very similar – a series of linked campaigns of civil discord, which arose primarily because of the failure of the Lancastrian dynasty and the particular incapacity of Henry VI. One must always be wary of pushing the contemporary analogy too far, but there are parallels. In these events the Battle of Towton deserves to be a grand Wagnerian climax but it is not. It was decisive in establishing Edward IV on the throne and relegating his Lancastrian predecessor to a truncated realm by the cold waters of the North Sea, but it did not bring the overall cycle of conflict to an end. Indeed, it did not even draw a line under the 1459–1464 phase. Hostilities spluttered on for another three dismal years in Northumberland, until the extended skirmish at Hexham in May 1464 brought matters to a close.

Though Towton was a famous Yorkist victory, Edward IV ('Sunne in Splendour') had more battles to fight before he could sit securely on his throne: Empingham, Barnet and Tewkesbury – all almost equally dramatic, if less titanic in scale and duration. Nor could the Yorkists really claim to be the outright winners, any more than the Lancastrians. Henry Tudor was a rank outsider, a gifted opportunist whose nominal allegiance to the Lancastrian cause amounted to nothing more than a convenient platform, his followers equally drawn from disaffected Yorkists.

This book, then, constitutes an ambitious undertaking with two clear aims. The first is an attempt to elevate Towton to its true place in the history of England among a wider constituency. The second is an attempt to tell the story as fully as possible, seeking to create an impression of what it was like for the participants. It is, therefore, intended as a narrative. I have included a detailed run-up to the actual battle and while this covers some of the same ground as earlier works, I feel the reader is entitled to a full explanation of why so many Englishmen came together in that particular place with the primary objective of killing each other. As to the aftermath and border war (1461–1464), I have placed them among the appendices.

In this endeavour I cannot, of course, claim to be alone. From the original chroniclers through nineteenth-century antiquarians to Ramsay, Sir Charles Oman, Colonel Burne and modern writers such as Lander, Goodman, Gillingham, Professor Pollard and, most notably, A.W. Boardman (whose excellent, groundbreaking study was published first in 1994), have written on Towton. Yet the impact upon a wider readership has not been marked and cannot be compared with, say, John Prebble's account of Culloden from the 1960s. I shall attempt to bridge that gap.

A Note on Sources
Given the importance of Towton, the events are badly served by contemporary chroniclers. The fullest accounts appear on the pages of later Tudor writers, particularly Edward Hall, who provides us with a full and rather racy narrative. The difficulty is that Hall is writing in 1548 (possibly a decade or so earlier) and the gap is considerable. Obviously, he could not have interviewed survivors, but memories and second-generation accounts would still abound. If we are too precious to accept Hall as viable primary source material, then we are thrown back upon the Burgundian Jean de Waurin, whose account, though contemporary, is suspect in some details. He does, however, furnish us with a full description of the events at Ferrybridge.

Hearne's Fragment was written perhaps sixty years after the event and, though the chronicler adds some interesting details, appears to assert the battle was fought as a night action. This is patently absurd and while some medieval battles – Otterburn in 1388 springs immediately to mind – were fought by moonlight, this was in high summer not early spring. Some interesting details also emerge from the *Brief Latin Chronicle*, which is included in the Camden Society's *Three Fifteenth Century Chronicles*. Gregory, who is extremely helpful on the course of the subsequent campaigns in Northumberland 1461–1464, offers little insight. He says nothing of Ferrybridge but his pious exhortation, 'Jhesu be pou marcyfulle unto hyr soulys',[13] has a clear resonance.

Chapter 1

The Art of War in the Fifteenth Century

A rguably the first clash in the Wars of the Roses occurred in 1453, when the Percies prepared an ambush for the Neville affinity, attending the wedding of Sir Thomas Neville.[1] But first blood was not properly shed till the Battle of St Albans in May 1455 and much of that was aristocratic – in civil war, traitors carry no promise of ransom. According to Philip de Commynes:

> King Edward told me that in all the battles which he had won, as soon as he had gained victory, he mounted his horse and shouted to his men that they must spare the common soldiers and kill the lords of which none or few escaped.[2]

At Towton, the Lancastrians, as their army disintegrated, suffered very badly. However, with the rotting skulls of their own families grinning down from Micklegate Bar, it is no wonder the Yorkists were unmoved by notions of chivalry.[3]

Raising Armies

In order to provide a reliable supply of trained fighting men, Edward III developed the contract system. The monarch, as commander-in-chief, entered into formal engagements with experienced captains who were then bound to provide an agreed number of men at established rates for a given period. Consequently, protracted campaigns in France secured the reputations of captains such as Robert Knollys and John Chandos. Frequently, however, it was the magnates who acted as the main contractors, sub-contracting knights, men-at-arms and archers.[4]

To what extent the end of the French Wars – with the consequential glut of unemployed men-at-arms – fuelled the rise of aristocratic violence, remains questionable. It is certain, however, that a swelling reservoir of trained manpower provided recruits for gentry affinities. The provision of indentures and annuities was also employed by lords to bind their retainers. Humphrey Stafford, 1st Duke of Buckingham, killed at Northampton in 1460, had ten knights and twenty-seven esquires in his service. One of the former, Sir Edward Grey, was granted a life annuity of £40 in 1440. Those further down the social scale might receive annual emoluments ranging from £10 to £20.[5]

In addition to his professional retainers, a lord could call out his tenantry, some of whom would have military experience. To these he might, if numbers were sought, round up a following of masterless men, happy to receive the protection of a great man. A surviving indenture, dating from 1452 and entered into by the Earl of Salisbury and his tenant, Walter Strickland, knight of Westmorland, lists the complement Sir Walter was to muster:

> Billmen – 'horsed and harnessed', 74; mounted bowmen to the number of 69; dismounted billmen 76, with 71 foot archers, an impressive total of 290.[6]

In most companies, archers were still the predominant arm, greatly outnumbering bills by as much as ten to one.

When Sir John Paston was preparing to sail for Calais, he begged that his brother recruit four archers, 'likely men and fair conditioned and good archers and they shall have four marks by year and my livery.'[7] In short, these were to be permanent retainers, paid an annual wage. A particularly skilled archer belonging to a lord's household might command equal remuneration to a knight. In 1475 Edward IV was raising an army to intimidate France and the great magnates each contributed to his muster as follows:

> Duke of Clarence; 10 knights, 1,000 archers;
> Duke of Gloucester; 10 knights, 1,000 archers;
> Duke of Norfolk; 2 knights, 300 archers;
> Duke of Suffolk; 2 knights, 300 archers;
> Duke of Buckingham; 4 knights, 400 archers[8]

The king still had the power to issue what were termed 'Commissions of Array', which empowered his officers to call up local militias which, in theory at least, were to be the best armed and accoutred men from each village in the county. This system, though time-honoured, was much open to abuse – the comic antics of Shakespeare's Falstaff provide a fine parody.[9] Contemporary letters from the Stonor correspondence, relating to the Oxfordshire half hundred of Ewelme, comprising some seventeen villages in that county, show that the catchment yielded eighty-five recruits, seventeen of whom were archers. The village of Ewelme itself provided six men:

> Richard Slyhurst, a harness and able to do the King service with his bow, Thomas Staunton [the constable] John Hume, whole harness and both able to do the King service with a bill. John Tanner, a harness and able to do the King service with a bill. John Pallying, a harness and not able to wear it, Roger Smith, no harness, an able man and a good archer.

Those without any armour are described as 'able with a staff'.[10]

Surviving muster rolls from the period also provide an insight into local levies. One muster held at Bridport, Dorset, on 4 September 1457, before the king's officers, reveals that a man was expected to possess a sallet, jack, sword, buckler and dagger. Of those on parade that day, around two-thirds carried bows and had arrows; other weapons on show included poleaxes, glaives, bills, spears, axes, staves and harness.[11] Dominic Mancini has left us a vivid eyewitness account of the appearance of troops Gloucester and Buckingham brought into London in 1483:

> There is hardly any without a helmet, and none without bows and arrows; their bows and arrows are thicker and longer than those used by other nations, just as their bodies are stronger than other peoples, for they seem to have hands and arms of iron. The range of their bows is no less than that of our arbalests; there hangs by the side of each a sword no less long than ours, but heavy and thick as well. The sword is always accompanied by an iron shield [. . .] they do not wear any metal armour on their breast or any other part of their body, except for the better sort who have breastplates and suits of armour. Indeed the common soldiery have more comfortable tunics that reach down below the loins and are stuffed with tow or some other soft material. They say the softer the tunics the better do they withstand the blows of arrows and swords, and besides that in summer they are lighter and in winter more serviceable than iron.[12]

Attitudes to War

Civil wars do not promote chivalric conduct. Vendettas tend to mar fair play and the decline in knightly values was much bemoaned by contemporary chroniclers, although vestiges persisted. In his work, *Le Jouvencel* (*c*. 1466), chronicler Jean de Bueil gives an insight into the mind of the fifteenth-century gentleman:

> What a joyous thing is war, for many fine deeds are seen in its course, and many good lessons learnt from it [. . .] You love your comrade so much in war. When you see that your quarrel is just and your blood is fighting well, tears rise in your eyes. A great sweet feeling of loyalty and pity fills your heart on seeing your friend so valiantly expose his body to execute and accomplish the command of our Creator. And then you prepare to go and live or die with him, and for love not abandon him. And out of that there arise such a delectation, that he who has not tasted it is not fit to say what a delight is. Do you think that a man who does that fears death? Not at all; for he feels strengthened, he is so elated, that he does not know where he is. Truly, he is afraid of nothing.[13]

Fine sentiments indeed; but the scale of slaughter that accompanied fifteenth-century battle and its aftermath does not bear this out.

Thirst for revenge, fear, greed and sheer expediency were all powerful realities. Salisbury was handed to the mob after Wakefield (or so it appears) and in the same battle his nephew, Rutland, was murderously slain by Clifford. Battles such as Hexham and Tewkesbury were immediately followed by a savage round of executions.

At Shrewsbury, in 1403, the English had discovered what it was like to be on the receiving end of the missile storm. During the Wars of the Roses both sides employed the longbow and many battles opened with an archery duel. Consequently, casualties would be high and it was usually the side that fared worst in the opening exchanges that first advanced to contact. If the armourer's art had developed to a point where good-quality harness could deflect a clothyard shaft, the commons – relying on jacks – were less protected. At the Battle of Stoke in 1487 the Earl of Lincoln's ill-harnessed Irish kerns were shot down in droves.

When archers stepped forward to shoot – and at Towton, some half a million shafts may have been loosed in fifteen minutes or less – the arrow storm would literally blacken the sky (on Palmsunday Field the sky was already obscured). Winning this opening exchange was crucial. Both sides had limited options as the storm burst over their ranks. They could attempt to retreat but the arrows would likely follow; and furthermore, withdrawing in good order was a mighty difficult task. Whichever side could inflict the greatest loss of men or morale in this opening phase had very likely won the fight before even coming to contact. At Towton, as we have seen, the Yorkists won the archery duel, obliging their foes to advance, files hacked down as they stumbled over the snow.

Improved armour did not render a knight invulnerable. When Lord Clifford unwisely removed his bevor to gulp water in the extended skirmish at Dintingdale he was pierced through the throat.[14] A similar fate befell Lord Dacre. It has been estimated, again with reference to Palmsunday Field that, if each archer loosed four dozen arrows, then over a million shafts with a gross weight of 40 tons fell across the field.[15] In all probability archers, like billmen, remained posted with their own companies, rather than being formed as a separate arm. Most likely, at the commencement of the fight, all would advance a few paces from the line to shoot and then retake their places for the mêlée that was bound to follow. As a contemporary chronicler observed: 'After the third or fourth, or at the very most the sixth draw of the bow, men knew which side would win.'[16]

Strategy

Strategy tended to be based on the offensive; conversely, tactics often assumed the defensive. Command was most frequently exercised by the magnates themselves: York at St Albans and Wakefield; Warwick at Second St Albans and Barnet; Henry Beaufort, 3rd Duke Somerset, at Wakefield, Second St Albans, Towton, Hedgeley Moor and Hexham. Divisional commanders would often be family or high-ranking members of the commander-in-chief's affinity. Thus, Richard of Gloucester commanded a wing of his brother's forces at Barnet and Tewkesbury; Oxford and Exeter led divisions of Warwick's army at Barnet. Commanders might and did rely on the advice of seasoned professionals such as Sir Andrew Trollope, though some of the older generation of protagonists – York, the 2nd Duke of Somerset,

Buckingham and Fauconberg – had all seen service in the French Wars. Their sons and successors, for the most part, had not.

Campaigns were of short duration, avoiding the need to keep forces victualled and in the field through the harshness of winter. Commanders tended to seek a decisive encounter. Rarely was the offer of battle refused (Warwick at Coventry in 1471 is an obvious if rare exception). When one side faced hopeless odds the temptation was simply to flee the realm: as did the Yorkist leaders after Ludford Bridge; Warwick and Clarence after Empingham; and Edward IV in 1470. As Professor Hicks points out, in each case the exiles made a successful return bid. To force the issue, then, was the preferred course. Once strong forces were in the field then attempts at mediation invariably foundered. If a ruling monarch was unable to prevent his enemy effecting a lodgement, then it was essential to move quickly to destroy his forces before he could recruit sufficient contingents – thus Richard III hastened to confront Henry Tudor. Consequently, major engagements dominated the conflict. Long sieges (Harlech being an exception, and the sieges of the Northumbrian Castles 1461–1463) were rare. Territory was neither held nor ceded; manoeuvre to contact was the norm. Where a magnate raised his flag of rebellion, he would seek battle before forces owing loyalty to the Crown might fully muster. Warwick sought to bring the army of Henry VI to a decisive encounter at Northampton before the northern Lancastrians could add their strength to his muster.

Grand Tactics

Subtlety was lacking. In most campaigns the two sides simply squared up. Somerset's flanking manoeuvre before Second St Albans evidences a rare degree of strategic and tactical innovation: to stake all on the outcome of a single battle was high risk.[17] Once forces were committed, a commander had little prospect of influencing events. The soundest tactics could be undone by the fog of war – witness Edmund Beaufort at Tewkesbury. A want of intelligence regarding enemy numbers could lead to disaster – York's end at Wakefield being a salutary lesson. Knights and men-at-arms dismounted to fight on foot. Horses were sent to the rear, to be mounted only when the enemy was in rout. Pursuit of a beaten foe was rigorous and merciless, the slaughter indiscriminate. A wealthy captive in the French Wars could be the making of a yeoman's fortune but a lord whose lands stood to be attainted by the victors had no commercial value. Personal animosities were a constant factor. In their very hour of triumph, Edward IV and his affinity would have seen the ghastly remains of their relatives, fixed on high, as they rode triumphantly into York.

Hobilars or light horsemen – sometimes called 'prickers' – were deployed for scouting and vedette work, but once battle was joined, there was little direct control a commander could exercise. Armies were still marshalled into three divisions or 'battles': the van or vaward; main battle; and rear or rearward. Deployment was in linear formation – knights and men-at-arms dismounted and ready, archers moving to the fore to shoot, all beneath the banner of their captain or lord. Battle was a most hazardous enterprise. In the fifteenth century a commander had limited forces at his disposal. A single, significant defeat in the field would likely ruin his cause and not infrequently his person. Defeated generals fared badly in the Wars of the Roses: Somerset at St Albans; York at Wakefield; Northumberland at Towton; the younger Somerset at Hexham; his brother at Tewkesbury; Warwick at Barnet; Richard III at Bosworth; and Lincoln at Stoke. Communications were dependent upon flags. Supply and victualling remained a constant headache and the spectre of treachery omnipresent.

With the impetus and fury of an opening arrow storm, both sides would tend to move swiftly to contact but, on several occasions – such as Salisbury's stand at Blore Heath – defensive tactics worked well. Warwick's complex network of defences proved a veritable Maginot Line at Second St Albans and the Lancastrian entrenchments at Northampton failed miserably – primarily, it has to be said, due to treachery abetted by adverse weather. Treachery and subornment were random cards that could wreck any strategy – Lord Grey at Northampton, and Trollope's defection at Ludford Bridge precipitated a rout in each case. Warwick chose to blame the disaster at Second St Albans on the treachery of his Kentish captain, Lovelace; 'False Perjured Clarence' betrayed first his brother, then his father-in-law, finally and fatally his brother.

Good intelligence was, as always, vital. All armies fielded scouts or 'scourers'. Bad intelligence, such as York's failure before committing to battle at Wakefield, could prove fatal. Once the decision to engage in battle was taken and the army marshalled accordingly, it was a difficult business to reverse. In the dangerous game of cat and mouse that unfolded during the Tewkesbury campaign, Margaret of Anjou several times avoided contact, leaving Edward's army drawn up in battle array but without an enemy in sight! The king also had his scouts, however, and by dint of gruelling marches in the heavy heat, followed by a dash through the short spring night, he succeeded in frustrating a Lancastrian attempt to cross the Severn at Gloucester and brought Somerset to bay at Tewkesbury.

Although contending armies deployed in line opposite each other, this neat arrangement could go awry, depending on weather and terrain, as in the fog of Barnet. A commander with a good eye for ground might try to deploy an ambush party for a flank attack. Somerset attempted this at Towton and Edward the same at Tewkesbury. Such tactics were not new. A Scottish flanking move at Otterburn in 1388 had proved decisive, as did Prince Henry's attack at Shrewsbury fifteen years later.

Late medieval captains were, for the most part, literate and familiar with the tenets of their trade. Many, if not most, would have read the classical authors, such as the late Roman theorist Vegetius, whose *Epitoma Rei Militaris* was revised in the fifteenth century by Christine de Pisan. She also wrote the *Livre des fais d'armes et de chevalerie*, subsequently translated and popularised by Caxton as *The Book of the Fayttes of Armes and Chyvalrye*. At this time the continental system of 'lances' was not popular in England. Companies were led by captains and formed up according to their chosen arms. Banners were important as morale boosters, signalling devices and rallying points. The use of liveries did, at least, promote some degree of uniformity. In practice this consisted of a loose tunic or tabard, which the soldier wore over his jack or harness in the lord's colours. The Percys, for instance, fielded a livery of russet, yellow and orange with the badge of the Percy Lion rampant sewn onto the shoulder. The system could still produce moments of confusion – perhaps most tellingly in the fatal mist of Barnet, where Lord Montagu's men mistook Oxford's badge of the star and stream for King Edward's sun and stream with disastrous consequences.

Arms and Armour

The late fifteenth century witnessed a final flowering of the armourer's art – fine plate armours that could resist even the deadly arrow storm. Italian harness of this era was skilfully and beautifully constructed to maximise deflection. Defences for the vulnerable areas at the shoulder, elbow and knee were strengthened, fashioned ribs on exposed parts were constructed to deflect a killing blow.[18] German armourers moved this concept towards the angular perfection of the Gothic style, with its emphasis on uncompromising lines, swept by heavy fluting. A harness of this period might weigh around 60 lbs (30 kilos) and would not greatly inhibit the mobility of a robust man, trained since boyhood to move and fight in armour.[19]

Medieval knights, even when fighting on foot, frequently bore a less onerous load than the average 'Tommy' of World War One, burdened with rifle and pack, ammunition bandoliers, wire and tools. The Italian and German styles came together in Flanders – a flourishing centre of manufacture, where Italian armourers produced a hybrid style that featured the flexible, fluted plates of the Gothic combined with the more rounded pauldrons (shoulder defences) and tassets (thigh guards) of their native style. Much of this armour was sold in England, as evidenced by its regular appearance in funerary monuments. For head protection the stylish sallet form of helmet was popular from mid-century onwards. The rear of the elegantly curved brim swept downwards into a pointed tail to provide extra deflection to the vulnerable areas at the back of the head and neck. Usually provided with a fixed or moveable visor, the sallet was accompanied by the bevor, which afforded protection to the throat and lower face. Although knights could move freely, even in full plate, thirst and heat exhaustion were constant threats even in winter campaigning. That swift end meted out to Butcher Clifford by an alert archer, was the penalty for unstrapping a bevor in the heat of battle. Dressing for war was best achieved at leisure, before the enemy was in the field, as a contemporary author, writing *c.* 1450 explains:

> To arme a man. Firste ye must set on Sabatones [armoured over-shoes] and tye hem up on the shoo with small points [laces] that woll not breke. And then griffus [greaves – plate defences for the calves] and then cuisses [thigh defences] and ye breche [leggings] of mayle. And the Tonlets. An the Brest and ye Vambras [upper arm defences] and ye rerebras [lower arm] and then gloovis [plate gauntlets]. And then hand his daggere up on his right side. And then his shorte sworde on his lyfte side in a round rynge all naked to pull it out lightli [the sword is carried without a scabbard, hung

in a ring for quick release]. And then put his cote upon his back. And then his basinet [bascinet – a form of helmet in use prior to the sallet] pyind up on two greet staples before the breste with a dowbill bokill [double buckle] behynde up on the back for to make the basinet sitte juste. And then his long swerd [sword] in his hande. And then his pensil in his hande peynted of St George or of oure ladye to bless him with as he goeth towarde the felde and in the felde.[20]

While knights and men-at-arms would wear full harness, archers tended to favour padded jacks or brigandines, as the account from Dominic Mancini, quoted earlier, suggests. This fabric garment was finished with plates of steel or bone riveted between the inner and outer layers or, as in the cheaper version, simply padded and stuffed with rags and tallow. The ubiquitous jack was far cheaper, lighter, and for many purposes more practical. Some were fitted with sleeves of mail to afford protection to the arms. Though archers traditionally eschewed leg harness, billmen and men-at-arms would wear whatever they could afford or were able to loot – a seasoned campaigner augmenting his kit from the spoil of dead and captives. As an alternative to the expensive sallet, the foot might rely on the basic 'kettle' hat.

One of the most popular knightly weapons of the age was the fearsome poleaxe – a heavy axe blade on a stout ash shaft, some 4 to 6 feet long, a hefty 'beak' or hammer head on the reverse of the blade, and the head tapering to a wicked spike. This tool was designed to defeat the armourer's art by 'opening up' a harnessed opponent, in the manner of a crude but deadly can opener! Popular in the tourney and judicial duel, the blade was secured by steel strips or 'languets' intended to frustrate the action of lopping off the head. The doomed Somerset, cornered at First St Albans, fought valiantly and brought down a quartet of Yorkist opponents before a blow from a poleaxe felled him. Swiss peasants had already proven the worth of their halberds and English bills had contributed to the glorious victories in France. The horseman's lance, grown heavier than the original Norman spear, was carried couched under the arm and used for thrusting. The weight was such the weapon had to be held with the point angled across the saddle, a difficult business that could only be accomplished with plentiful training. When used on foot, the shaft was generally cut down in length to make for easier handling.

At this time the knight's sword reached the apex of its development prior to its eclipse by the rapier in the following century. Blades were designed for both cut and thrust. Long and elegantly tapering, with a full grip that could be hefted in one or two hands, in section resembling a flattened diamond; simple quillons, curved or straight, a wheel, a pear or kite-shaped pommel. This was the hand-and-a-half or 'bastard' sword – the very 'King of Swords'. Such precision instruments were extremely expensive and consequently reserved for the gentry. The commons carried a simpler, lighter and considerably cheaper sidearm – a short, single-edged blade with the quillons curving around up to the hilt to provide a form of crude knuckle guard. Gentlemen and commons both bore daggers. The long-bladed rondel with tapering triangular blade, hardwood grip, disc guard and pommel, was a popular style. Ballock knives, whose wooden handle featured two rounded protuberances of suggestive form, rather resembled the later Scottish dudgeon dagger. As handy as a tool as a weapon, daggers were carried by all ranks and might be used to stab an opponent or plant vegetables as the situation required. In battle the thin-bladed knife could be used to deliver a coup de grâce to an armoured enemy, either thrust directly through the eye slit of the steel visor or into the more vulnerable areas of armpit or genitals.

The Arrow Storm

Only later, during the sixteenth century, did the term 'longbow' come into usage. A plainer expression – 'bow' or 'livery bow' – was more commonplace during the fifteenth. Retained or liveried archers normally carried their own bows, but in the long continuance of the French Wars, the Office of Ordnance began issuing standardised kit on campaign to replace those lost or damaged. Thus, quantities of bows were manufactured to a standard or government pattern, like the infantry musket of following centuries. Yew was the preferred timber, though ash, elm and wych-elm were also favoured. The weapon was usually between 5 feet 7 inches (1.675 m) and 6 feet 2 inches (1.850 m) in length. The cross section corresponded to a rounded 'D' with a draw weight of between 80 and 120 lbs (40–60 kilos). A modern target bow has an average draw of around 45 lbs (22.5 kilos).

Arrows were crafted from a variety of woods. Roger Ascham, tutor to Elizabeth I and a noted sixteenth-century authority, advocated aspen as the most suitable, though ash, alder, elder, birch, willow and hornbeam were also utilised. The shafts were generally around 2 feet 6 inches (75 cm) in length, fletchings formed from grey goose feathers. Arrowheads came in a variety of forms: flat, hammer-headed, barbed or wickedly sharp needle-pointed piles or bodkins, designed to punch through plate and mail. Livery-quality arrows were issued to retainers, 'standard' grade was just that and 'sheaf' arrows came in bundles of two dozen.[21] At each extremity the bow was tipped with cowhorn, grooved to take a linen string and, when not in use, the stave was carried unstrung in a cloth cover. To draw, an archer gripped the bow with his left hand, about the middle, where circumference of the wood was around 4½ inches (11.25 cm), then he forced the centre of the bow away from him to complete the draw, using the full weight of his body to assist, rather than relying on the strength in his arms alone. Such strength, stamina and expertise demanded constant drill. Practice at the butts was compelled by statute. The bow could kill at 200 yards. Every archer wore a leather or horn 'bracer', strapped to his wrist to protect against the vicious snap of the bowstring.

Properly deployed, bows proved a battle-winning weapon. At Homildon in 1402 a Scottish army had been routed by archers alone. Many who fought for Lancaster or York would have already seen active service in the French Wars. Few who suffered the deadly hail of an arrow storm could have forgotten the experience. If gentlemen, secure in fine plate, enjoyed greater protection than their predecessors, the rank and file were less fortunate. As we have seen, when the armies faced each other at Towton, cunning Fauconberg took advantage of poor visibility to advance his Yorkist archers before they loosed, the mass of shafts slamming into the tightly packed Lancastrians. Having shot, his men then smartly stepped back while Somerset's archers, gauging the range, shot into empty ground! Their arrows were swiftly returned by their opponents and so galling were the Yorkist volleys that the Lancastrians had no recourse other than to advance to contact.

The Gunner's Art

By the early years of the fifteenth century artillery was steadily becoming the dominant arm in siege warfare. In April 1464, as Edward IV was preparing to march north, he caused his siege train to be made ready and this included 'the great ordnance of England' – the bombards

'Dijon', 'London', 'Newcastle', 'Edward' and 'Richard Bombartel'.[22] This new science of gunnery had begun to surpass that of the military architect. Henry V had deployed his train against the walls of Harfleur in 1415 and had subsequently breached the formidable walls of Le Mans after a few days.[23] 'Bombard' was a generic term, used to describe a large siege gun; in this era there was, as yet, no standardisation of calibres.[24]

These monsters were fired from ground level and from behind a hinged, timber shutter rather like a very much larger version of the archer's mantlet. This provided some cover for the gunner, his mate and matrosses. Most guns loaded at the breech, having a removable block, shaped not unlike a commodious beer mug. By the 1460s trunnions were coming into use and even the heavier pieces were being equipped with wheeled carriages; elevation was achieved by the use of wedges.[25] Transportation was an area of major difficulty. Large teams of draught horses or oxen were required, a section of pioneers had to be added to the train, their task to level and fill the generally appalling roads over which the guns must pass. Larger pieces were still manufactured on the hoop and stave principle (hence the term 'barrel'), though casting in bronze was, by mid–century, commonplace.[26] Another arm, growing in significance and potency, was the smaller handgun or 'gonne'. These were little more than miniature cannons lashed onto basic wooden stocks. Such 'hagbutts' were held underarm, or over the shoulder, rather than pressed into the shoulder as with a modern firearm. Once loaded with powder and shot, the gun was fired by means of a lit length of slow match, the burning end of which was applied to a touchhole, drilled in the side of the breech.

Although artillery had radically diminished the status of castles as centres of resistance, guns remained frightfully expensive to procure and difficult to move. The various sieges of the Lancastrian-held strongholds in Northumberland between 1461 and 1464 were conducted with an artillery train in attendance, but only once were the great guns deployed in earnest, at Bamburgh, in the closing stages of the final year's campaigning. Here the ordnance was brought into play with considerable reluctance. Bamburgh was a major bastion against the Scots and slighting such a key fortress was best avoided.[27] In 1473, John de Vere, Earl of Oxford, launched a lightning strike against the Yorkist regime by seizing St Michael's Mount in a coup de main. With no more than a couple of companies of foot, the Earl captured and held the fortress. Perhaps the most prolonged and celebrated siege of the Wars of the Roses was the investment of Harlech, which resisted for the best part of seven years – holding out even when Jasper Tudor, as castellan, fled to Ireland.

Field fortifications featured in a number of the battles. Salisbury, caught with inferior numbers at Blore Heath by Lord Audley's Lancastrians in September 1459, sought to consolidate an already strong defensive position by digging a ditch to cover his rear and erecting a palisade to the front. The labour proved worthy of the effort. Nearly a year later, in a miserable July, it was the Lancastrians at Northampton who placed their faith in a wet ditch and timber palisade studded with guns. They were doubly unfortunate. Unseasonal rainfall flooded the gun pits and soaked their powder; treachery surmounted the fieldworks. Warwick also placed great trust in elaborate entrenchments when preparing to meet Queen Margaret's host by St Albans, scene of his earlier triumph, in February 1461. A number of prepared positions were dug, augmented by a liberal sowing of caltraps – the anti-personnel and anti-equine devices of their day with an array of spiked nets, hinged mantlets and other elaborate contrivances. Bad intelligence, slow thinking and possibly yet more treachery confounded the whole complex scheme, turned by a flank attack.

The Face of Battle

Time and romance have, over the intervening years, cast a shroud of pageantry over the harsh realities of medieval combat. The truth is somewhat less attractive. Though lacking the scale and widespread devastation of modern conflicts, fifteenth-century warfare was every bit as frightful. As discussed, many battles opened with an archery duel, regular volleys thudding into tightly packed ranks, inflicting numerous fatalities and wounds. These preliminaries probably lasted a short time before the side that was suffering the most was compelled to advance. The movement would be ordered rather than swift, the sergeants bellowing commands to keep the ranks dressed. Cohesion was all important. Those divisions that could maintain both order and momentum stood the best chance of breaking a more chaotic foe. A commander with an eye for ground would always seek the position of best advantage, though elements in the topography, adverse weather, mist and darkness could combine to upset the best laid plans and, as at Barnet, each side might find themselves equally confounded. Once battle was joined in earnest the combat became an intensely personal affair – a hacking, stamping mêlée of bills and other polearms, swords, and axes.

Men, half blind in plate, soon assailed by raging thirst and swiftly reaching exhaustion, would become disorientated. Dust and the steam from thousands of sweating men would further obscure any wider view. Few would be killed by a single blow; but a disabling wound, bringing the sufferer to his knees, would expose him to a further flurry – pierced through the visor or groin by daggers, hacked by bills, stamped on, kicked and slashed. Not a swift death, nor an easy one. Illustrations from the period show the field heaped with the press of the slain, garnished by a slew of severed limbs. Blood would run in great rivulets, splattering the living.

Once a side broke in rout, casualties would begin to mount. Armoured men trying to flee towards horses tethered at a distance would be easy prey. Those less encumbered or not enfeebled by wounds might survive the race, others would not. The victors, their horses brought forward by grooms, would be swooping and circling like hawks. Abbot Whethamstede, who may have been an eyewitness, graphically chronicles the fate of some of Warwick's men, fleeing from the debacle at Second St Albans:

> The southern men, who were fiercer at the beginning, were broken quickly afterwards, and the more quickly because looking back, they saw no one coming up from the main body of the king's army, or preparing to bring them help, whereupon they turned their backs on the northern men and fled. And the northern men seeing this pursued them very swiftly on horseback; and catching a good many of them, ran them through with their lances.[28]

The Towton mass grave, excavated during the 1990s, has provided a grim insight into the sheer nastiness of fifteenth-century warfare. Some forty-three skeletons were unearthed. Most had suffered a series of horrific head injuries, puncture wounds and calamitous fractures with evidence of specific and deliberate dagger thrusts to the back of the skull – either a coup de grâce or cold-blooded execution. In either event the victim would have been stripped of head protection at the fatal moment.[29]

By modern standards the available medical services were both rudimentary and sparse. The perceived presence of evil humours was the source of copious bleedings; quacks cast horoscopes and peddled bizarre potions. Wounds, sensibly, were cauterised with hot pitch. Anaesthesia, with solutions mixed from herbs, was by no means unknown, however, and surgical techniques perhaps more sophisticated than might be assumed. Gerhard von Wesel, travelling in England in 1471, has left an eyewitness account of the army of Edward IV as the survivors of Barnet trudged wearily back into London: 'Many of their followers were wounded, mostly in the face or the lower part of the body, a very pitiable sight.'[30] These, it must be remembered, were the victors.

Campaigns tended to be highly mobile and of relatively short duration. Adequate logistical provision for keeping large bodies of men in the field was a singular problem, as was the need to raise cash. In common with other periods, men undoubtedly died from disease and want. Dysentery was a major killer, as were cholera and typhus. Plague also stalked armies. The late medieval era has been described as 'the golden age of bacteria'[31] with perhaps thirty-odd outbreaks occurring prior to 1487. French mercenaries in the service of Henry Tudor were blamed for introducing the 'sweating sickness' that, in 1485, killed off two mayors of London with six aldermen in barely a week.

Chapter 2

The House of Lancaster and the Path to Conflict 1400–1455

Kings and kingship were the foundation of English civil government in the medieval period. The king stood at the head of the social and economic pyramid, supported by a sophisticated legal and fiscal framework that had been evolving since the Conquest.[1] Should the king, however, behave in an authoritarian and unjust manner, he remained king – the subject owed him an absolute duty of obedience. In such an instance, which had arisen in the rule of Edward II and latterly, that of Richard II, there was no certainty about what should be done to bring the monarch to account. Removal of the king was contrary to God's law.

By far the most influential people, in political terms, were the magnates, the great landowners. Not only did they control vast acres but they provided the military 'muscle' the Crown required to enforce its will. There was no standing army as such (unless we include the Calais garrison). The magnates, with their household men and retainers, formed the nucleus of any military force the monarch needed – either to deal with civil discord or to fight abroad. Throughout this period the nobility, if the Crown was weak, might elect to settle their disputes by force of arms rather than through the medium of the courts – the Courtenay/Bonville, Percy/Neville, Stanley/Harrington feuds are merely some instances. The plain fact was that the administrative authority of the king, in terms of available force, was upheld by privately raised contingents he did not directly control.[2]

Many historians, taking a traditional view, have, following Tudor chroniclers, seen the roots of the Wars of the Roses as lying in the fact of the Lancastrian usurpation of 1399. More recent writers have inclined away from this, preferring to see the conflict more as the consequence of administrative failures of the 1450s and a consequential rise of aristocratic discord. Richard II, son of martial Edward, the Black Prince and grandson of Edward III, came into his inheritance while still a minor. His reign witnessed a resumption of both the French and Scottish Wars and in both cases the English cause faltered. A preference for unsuitable favourites, pressing economic needs and an inability to develop a firm affinity among the nobility spread disaffection. His attempt to sequester those vast estates of the Duchy of Lancaster on the death of his uncle, John of Gaunt, provoked a rising led by the exiled Henry Bolingbroke, Earl of Derby, old Gaunt's heir. Richard was dispossessed, dying very soon thereafter and Derby became Henry IV. The new king was thus a usurper and the crown sat uneasily. Henry V, by contrast, is considered one of medieval England's most able and successful rulers. This great warrior-king succumbed, not to the swords of his enemies, but to the commonplace scourge of dysentery, his vision tantalisingly close but incomplete. He left a legacy of success, a French widow and an infant son.

The Lancastrian Administration

Henry VI has been harshly judged by many writers. One of the charges laid at his door was fiscal incompetence. During the reign of Richard II, the annual income of the Crown stood at around £120,000; by the 1450s this had declined sharply to no more than £40,000.[3] In part, Henry himself was to blame for his failure to manage his own household expenses, but his core revenue was also plummeting and this was due to factors beyond his control. The yield from Crown lands – a major source of revenue – had tumbled and customs dues had dwindled. A slump in agriculture and a trade recession, which had begun to bite from the 1350s, fuelled the economic collapse. The king was not the only sufferer. A similar decline threatened to impoverish the magnates and it has been suggested that the financial pressures created by recession prompted the lords to compete more vigorously for Crown appointments.[4] A further agricultural slump in the years 1438–1440 caused yields to fall yet further. It has been suggested that the Wars of the Roses were fought, not because magnates were recruiting soldiers, but because they could not afford to pay those already in their employ.[5]

During the king's minority from 1422–1437 his uncle John, Duke of Bedford, maintained the policies of Henry V. He and Cardinal Beaufort broadly agreed that the correct course was to maintain the steady acquisition of territories and establish the full authority of the English Crown in France. Until the collapse of the Burgundian alliance in 1435 and Bedford's death, this appeared entirely feasible – English armies continued to win battles, though the emergence of Joan of Arc and defeat at Orléans showed that victories were by no means assured. The role of the late king's other surviving brother, the mercurial Humphrey, Duke of Gloucester, was restricted to that of protector, defender and chief councillor – a rather shapeless remit. His authority only lasted while Bedford was engaged in affairs overseas and he was unable to exercise full sway over a council that was increasingly dominated by Cardinal Beaufort, Bishop of Winchester.

Henry VI remained childless. Excessive chastity and distaste for the lures of the flesh may have been contributing factors, but a king without an heir was failing in his dynastic duty and therefore vulnerable. This weakness was exacerbated by the fact that, should Henry die childless, the Duke of York was heir presumptive.[6] The House of Lancaster had not, of course, obtained the throne by legitimate or constitutional means. Henry Bolingbroke, son of John of Gaunt (third son of Edward III), had usurped the crown from his cousin, Richard II (son of Edward, Prince of Wales). Gaunt's innocuous younger brother, Edmund of Langley, Duke of York, took little part in national affairs. His son, Richard, Earl of Cambridge, married Anne Mortimer, descended from the old king's second son, Lionel of Clarence, and was executed for his part in the abortive Southampton Plot. Nonetheless, the fact remained that this branch of the family could claim seniority over John of Gaunt's line and York was the dead traitor's son.

In 1437 the real difficulties of the reign were not entirely apparent. Despite internal divisions, the council had done much to maintain the English position in France and maintain the rule of law at home. Bedford and Beaufort had seen themselves as legatees of Henry V's policies. They had striven, not without success, to maintain these but a holding policy cannot be indefinite: at some point a new direction must be forthcoming and this could only emanate from the person of the king himself. It was time for Henry VI to take control of the affairs of state.

The Adult Rule of Henry VI 1437–1453

A question that has dogged historians is the extent to which, if any, Henry VI ruled in his own right. Was he a contributor to the gradual collapse of the regime or was he a hapless pawn in the hands of a venal cabal? It may be assumed that Henry's active role declined after his breakdown in 1453 and was minimal after the end of the second protectorate in 1456. The king was certainly old enough to wield the sceptre after 1437. Princes came into their own at a young age. Despite this devolution of power onto the royal person, the council appears to have reasserted a measure of control in 1441– possibly due to the young king's continuing inexperience or – far more serious in implication – a perceived inability to rule. Recent scholars, such as John Watts, followed by Carpenter, have put forward the notion that Henry showed a marked disinclination for kingship. This was potentially disastrous in a society where the king stood at the apex of the social and economic pyramid. It therefore became necessary for a group of magnates, based around the household – initially guided by Cardinal Beaufort then, successively, the Dukes of Suffolk and Somerset – to rule by proxy. The façade of royal administration was preserved, remarkably so. Current thinking suggests the differences between York and Somerset did not arise until after the crisis of 1450 and that York was a functioning member of the English polity throughout the 1440s.[7]

At this time of mounting difficulties, with the position in France unravelling, England had a boy king, a divided Council and a resentful Parliament, whose willingness to continue levying taxes was waning. Cardinal Beaufort, with Suffolk and others of his affinity, was in favour of a pragmatic approach – peace with honour. It appeared obvious to the peace faction that England was no longer able to add to her French territories. The pendulum had swung too far the other way: it was more a matter of clinging to such gains as could be salvaged. Henry VI had, in fact, been crowned King of France in Paris on 2 December 1431– a good show no doubt but something of a sham, for the true King of France was always crowned at Rheims, where he was anointed with St Remy's Holy Oil. In the circumstances a negotiated peace was the only viable option and Cardinal Beaufort was adopting a pragmatic approach. In this he was undoubtedly correct: both he and Suffolk, whose role was expanding, appeared to agree. Humphrey of Gloucester, in remaining loudly bellicose, fast became an anachronism.

It was rapidly becoming clear to those around the young Henry that he was not likely to espouse his father's martial stance. His finances were becoming parlous.[8] Fresh campaigns, such as that in Guyenne during 1439, proved difficult to fund – the glory days were clearly over. In this new mood of pragmatism, Beaufort attempted further negotiations at Calais in 1439 and offered to release the captive Duke of Orléans, languishing since 1415. This was expressly contrary to the late king's policy. Humphrey of Gloucester, the king's volatile uncle, managed to get the initiative blocked in council. The commons were still loud for the war and Duke Humphrey achieved a measure of popular acclaim, but he and his supporters were blinding themselves to current realities.

In the early 1440s, Cardinal Beaufort's influence waned (dented by the failure of the Gravelines initiative) and Suffolk assumed a more pivotal role. If the duke was not a great man and prone, like many of his contemporaries, to some level of venality, he was in a very difficult position – trying to carry out a policy that should properly have been directed by the king, but hamstrung by a king who appeared disinterested. The Duke of York was sent to France as Lieutenant for a further five-year term in 1440. There is no direct evidence, at this time, that York was in any way disadvantaged or that he was anything other than a functioning member of the English civil government. He does not appear to have been at odds with Suffolk. Before the Cardinal's death in 1447 something of a rift had opened between the duke and him.

Buoyed by his great personal wealth, Beaufort still had an eye for opportunities to confer estates upon his nephews, Edmund of Dorset and John of Somerset. Unlike York, these Beaufort siblings did not inherit any vast patrimony. In 1442 Somerset was given an independent command and turned loose on Maine and Anjou. Beyond robbing York and Shrewsbury of resources, little was achieved: John received his dukedom but died in May 1444, possibly by his own hand. Whether this ill-judged intervention prompted York to conceive an active resentment of the Beauforts at this stage is unclear – quite possibly it did not. He was owed substantial arrears but, due to the Crown's crippling indebtedness, most officers were awaiting payment. The Beauforts may have been compensated sooner but it does seem likely that York's resentment was effectively backdated after 1450. It was only then that the cracks became all too visible and harmony disappeared.

By way of a dynastic marriage, the best the young king of England could achieve was the hand of the sixteen-year-old Margaret of Anjou, daughter of Duke Rene of Bar and Lorraine, the titular, if impecunious, King of Sicily – unable even to fund a dowry. This young and spirited princess arrived in England during April 1445. Her sea passage, though her fleet was magnificent, was turbulent and she required several days of rest at Portsmouth. She had yet to meet her new husband, though already officially married a month since at Nancy, with Suffolk standing as proxy for the absent groom.

Suffolk may, during the negotiations at Tours, have offered to trade Maine as an expedient to win the truce. Subsequently, Henry, in the course of personal correspondence with Charles VII, offered to return the district, the effective date of handover to be 22 December 1445.[9] There was no direct military pressure that could account for this retreat – English forces were still tying down Gascony, Anjou, Maine and Normandy. The decision appears to have been dictated by pure pragmatism. Such realpolitik could not be publicised – neither Council nor Parliament would have stood for what appeared as mere appeasement. Consequently, the king did not broadcast his intention and even Suffolk, upon whom the brunt of public opprobrium fell, sought to distance himself from the surrender by offering a formal disclaimer.

Despite these and later strenuous denials, Suffolk was widely suspected of foul play when Humphrey of Gloucester expired suddenly in custody and gained higher stature in death than he had ever enjoyed in life. The legend of 'Good Duke Humphrey' probably arose posthumously and even York, who was later to assume the mantle of opposition, remained supine at the time – he was even a beneficiary of the dead man's estate. The plain fact was that with matters in France at such a critical pass, Gloucester's stirring of the commons was intolerable. York, whatever he may have broadcast later, expressed no reported concerns at the time.

In the event, abandonment of Maine achieved nothing. The Fougères incident[10] merely provided Charles VII with the pretext he had been seeking to recover Normandy. The increasing burden of taxation imposed by English rule had alienated local opinion to the extent that many of the Norman towns simply threw open their gates to welcome their countrymen as liberators. Though popular outrage focused on Suffolk, the fault was by no means his alone. Collapse of the

Anglo-Burgundian entente, the fiscal burden and the king's lack of effective leadership had combined fatally to damage the English position.

England no longer had the means or the stomach to continue the fight as subject towns and provinces groaned under a harsh and arbitrary rule. Money was a continual worry. The mounting cost of maintaining a losing war was massively exacerbated by the king's difficulties in controlling his personal finances. Henry's annual income amounted to some £33,000. Even as early as 1433 his indebtedness stood at £164,000– a sum that by 1450 had rocketed to £372,000.[11] Since his marriage, expenditure on the king's household had increased more than threefold, from £8,000 to some £27,000 per annum, with Parliament expected to make up the shortfall.

Swelling anger against 'these traitors' focused on an influential cabal, a 'gang of three' – the king's principal advisors: Suffolk, William Ayscough, Bishop of Salisbury (Henry's spiritual advisor) and Adam Moleyns, Bishop of Chichester. The latter was done to death by a disgruntled mob in the course of violent disturbances at Portsmouth in January 1450. Unrest swiftly spread to the capital[12] and though order was restored, the spirit of protest could not be extinguished, the lords joining the popular protest. On 28 January Parliament successfully ousted Suffolk, who found himself in the Tower. Two formal indictments were laid – first, that he was guilty of treason by virtue of his dealings with the French; second, that he was guilty of widespread corruption. In a bid to stave off an inevitable conviction, advisors managed to fix the sanction as five years of exile. On 30 April 1450 the duke took ship from Ipswich. He was not destined to reach sanctuary on the Continent. A carefully prepared ambush at sea had been laid and Suffolk found himself a prisoner aboard *Nicholas of the Tower* – he can have had few illusions as to what would follow.

Suspicion of the deed fell on the men of Kent, though the catalogue of the murdered Duke's enemies was so extensive as to make identification problematic. Reprisals against the entire county were rumoured, which served only to spark another bout of disturbances. Jack Cade[13], brandishing the rebels' manifesto, 'Complaint of the Commons of Kent', led an army of citizens as far as Blackheath, and the government appeared impotent, its paltry forces scattered and the king seeking refuge at Kenilworth. It seemed as though Henry's government could now collapse completely in the face of such determined unrest.

However, the Kentishmen soon angered Londoners and the tide began to ebb as swiftly as it had surged. Concessions were made and a Royal Commission established to examine local grievances. Fresh disturbances bubbled through the summer but did not explode into large-scale violence; a semblance of calm returned. The crisis of 1450 was one of the most serious to afflict the Crown in the medieval period.[14] For a decade the magnates around the throne, including York, had managed to rule in the king's name, masking the vacuum that existed. The final collapse in Normandy fractured the illusion – the commons were suddenly jolted into the realisation that there was an emptiness at the heart of the English polity. On 11 August the port of Cherbourg, the very last English toehold in Normandy, capitulated without any attempt at relief.[15]

Richard of York – Unlikely Rebel

It was, perhaps, York's good fortune that his tenure across the Irish Sea distanced him from the crisis. He was able to escape the rush of opprobrium that descended on Suffolk and those closest to the throne as Normandy was lost. This providential distance afforded him the opportunity to create a platform and it is, from now, that he appears as the inheritor of Good Duke Humphrey, in whose fall he had – at the very least – been complicit. The nobles were reeling from the collapse of the edifice so carefully tended during the preceding decade. The gentry and commons had reacted with violent outrage to the nobility's failures. York, having spent little of his life within his own estates, lacked a solid affinity. A number of his retainers – men like Fastolf and Oldcastle – had served him in France and suffered pecuniary loss when Normandy fell. Somerset, despite having been the defeated general, managed to attach himself to the king's household and, effectively, replace Suffolk. His job would be that much harder because the pretence of direct royal command had faltered. Before York returned in September 1450, Somerset had taken steps to begin the return to stability.

Having assumed Gloucester's mantle, York's platform was essentially anti-household, broadly populist, drawing support from some magnates but also gentry and bourgeois. As the king was still childless, York stood to be recognised as heir-presumptive. In fact,

Somerset was nearer in blood but debarred by statute. Somerset was hamstrung in that he was adopting a mode of governance that had already failed, and failed badly. York stood for 'collective conciliar action'[16] and also for the continuance of the French Wars. He was the man who might have saved English possession in France. In practice this was unlikely but it added to his manifesto. Somerset, like Suffolk, acted as the king's proxy, and like his predecessor was, to an extent, a hostage of the household. His authority was never absolute and this was particularly noticeable in the rash of local magnatial disputes that flared after 1450, and which contributed to bringing him and the court faction into disrepute.

In Parliament the duke had a number of sympathisers – Sir William Oldhall from his affinity was elected speaker and certain reforms did reach the statute books. However, this support only obtained for as long as the House was in session. York, whose eye for timing was never good, sought to engineer the passage of a bill whereby the king would formally recognise the duke as his heir. This proved a step too far and Parliament was promptly dissolved.[17] Somerset, meantime, had acquired the office of Captain of the Calais garrison, a significant appointment – one that placed him in control of the country's largest standing force. That there was need for a strong hand to enforce law and order was amply demonstrated in 1451, when a simmering rivalry that had been brewing in the South West during the 1440s boiled over into open discord. Leadership in that corner of the kingdom had, for generations, been the preserve of the Courtenay Earls of Devon. Latterly, they had been offered a challenge by Lord Bonville of Chewton. William Bonville was a capable officer who had served both Henry V and his brother, the Duke of Bedford, in France, where he had risen to high office as seneschal of Gascony. Since returning he had occupied himself energetically in local matters and had married a Courtenay, the 12th Earl's aunt.

This move, outwardly politic, did not ingratiate him with the Earl, as the Courtenays were themselves divided. Worse, Henry VI appointed Thomas Courtenay as Steward of the Duchy of Cornwall, an office previously awarded to Bonville. Throughout the 1440s the feud festered. Bonville was perceived as Suffolk's creature, therefore favoured by the court faction, so, inevitably, the Earl gravitated towards York's affinity.

In September 1451 matters reached a head when the Earl, with his confederate, Lord Cobham, took up arms and marched against Bonville, bottling him up in Taunton Castle, which they then besieged. The administration was ignored while the nobles made private war. It was York who, on his own initiative, relieved Taunton, calmed the Courtenay faction and brought the warring parties to their senses. While this was highly effective policing, there may also have been a private motive insofar as York would not wish to see Devon, his ally, brought to account and incarcerated.[18]

Such a signal success emboldened the duke who, still finding himself thwarted by Somerset, resolved to enforce his right by more direct means. The situation was exacerbated by yet more defeats in France. Having regained Normandy and at so little cost, Charles VII naturally turned his eyes south to the ripe plum of Gascony. Bordeaux was presently threatened as the French swept through the province and the castellan agreed to lower his flag should relief not arrive by 14 June 1451. None came and the city surrendered – three centuries of English domination came to an end. The loss of Bordeaux constituted a disaster of the first magnitude and there appeared no hope of its recovery. Sir William Oldhall was detailed to act as his master's tool in laying the foundations for a possible coup, though he quickly developed a bad case of cold feet and sought sanctuary, from whence he did not fully emerge until 1455.[19]

York had canvassed support from both commons and gentry by widespread circulation of his manifesto; however, he had again misread the mood of the country. Aside from areas under his direct control, or that of his affinity, there was no general uprising. He commanded respect, there was sympathy for the perceived wrongs done to him, but he simply did not have a sufficient power base among his fellow magnates. As he made his camp at Dartford the duke could count only upon Devon and Lord Cobham. Even the prominent Nevilles were to be found in the king's great army mustering at Blackheath. The confrontation of March 1452 did not result in a fight. York was heavily outnumbered but neither his brother-in-law, Salisbury, nor his nephew, Warwick, wished to see him defeated.

York was not minded to compromise. It is likely that, behind the scenes, he believed the Nevilles leant his way and he insisted on Somerset's removal and indictment as conditions precedent to any accord. By the end of the meeting at Blackheath, the duke was convinced the meeting, with the king's acquiescence, had agreed to these terms: consequently, he disbanded his forces and the matter appeared settled. In this he was mistaken. York, whatever his qualities, was not a skilled politician. Somerset certainly appears as the more astute and York found himself treated, if not as a traitor, then as something very close – humiliated when the royal train returned to London, compelled to ride before the royal party as though a mere felon. Both of his followers, Devon and Cobham, were kept for a period in detention, though the duke himself was restored to liberty on 10 March 1452, amid rumours a large force of Welsh adherents was set to march on London and procure his liberty, by force if necessary.

In France, matters took a turn for the better when, in the autumn, Bull Talbot recovered Bordeaux. And in the spring, the English Queen was at last with child. But by the summer of 1453 the brief English recovery ended for good when Talbot, fighting valiantly, was overwhelmed and killed, his small force decimated at Castillon on 17 July.[20] This was bad but, even worse, while at Clarendon, the king suffered a complete mental collapse. Try as they might, members of the court faction could not hide the king's breakdown and without his sovereign power behind them their authority evaporated. The crisis of 1450 had exposed the weakness at the core of the English polity. York, previously acquiescent, shifted his stance, leaping onto the bandwagon with regard to popular discontent with the Lancastrians, but his intervention appeared abortive. What had now changed was that there was a clear division: the outward amity of the 1440s disappeared; York had rewritten his role during the late 1440s and early 1450s; the rift was palpable; lawlessness was mounting; and the realm inexorably drifting closer to civil strife.

The Gathering Storm 1453–1455

In Derbyshire a slew of gentry families – Blounts, Gresleys, Vernons and Longfords – were openly feuding. In Warwickshire Richard Neville, as Earl of Warwick, was experiencing difficulties exercising sway over his late father-in-law's wide lands. In East Anglia Lord Scales created friction. There was trouble in East Anglia. The Courtenay/Bonville fracas had erupted. In Gloucestershire the Talbots and Berkeleys were at odds and the Duke of Exeter was sparring with Lord Cromwell. The events in Warwickshire had been causing tension between the Earl of Warwick and the Duke of Buckingham. The earl was also at odds with Somerset over various portions of the Beauchamp inheritance.

When, in the north, Percy adherents sought to ambush a Neville wedding party, the affair may appear as little more than a local – and largely bloodless – brawl. Nonetheless, it could be said to represent the first significant armed clash between these two pre-eminent northern magnates, who were also active in the wider movement to reform – and ultimately remove – the Lancastrian administration.[21] Some commentators have seen the Percy/Neville feud as the catalyst that led mere factionalism to degenerate into civil war.

A policy (begun by John of Gaunt) of buttressing the power of the Nevilles as a counterweight to the Percys was continued by Henry VI; and the expanse of the Nevilles' affinity was, not infrequently, at the expense of the Percies.[22] The prestige of the Nevilles was particularly high in County Durham, where the influence of their rivals was noticeably weaker. William, Lord Fauconberg ('Little Fauconberg'), the Earl of Salisbury's brother, together with others of the Neville affinity – George, Lord Latimer, Edward, Lord Abergavenny and his son Sir Thomas – are consistently named in commissions of the peace. Richard, Earl of Salisbury, inherited the bulk of the Neville holdings in Yorkshire, centred on the valuable estates of Middleham and Sheriff Hutton. The worth of this legacy, Salisbury being the son of the Earl of Westmorland's second wife, sparked a deep division with the senior branch, which retained the title and lands in the north-west. Undisturbed by this family rift, Salisbury went on to steadily build up the scale of his holdings. His own eldest son, another Richard, added the dazzling Beauchamp inheritance and the earldom of Warwick to his titles and was to mature into a key political figure, bringing the power of his name to its ultimate zenith before crashing to ruin: 'Warwick the Kingmaker'.

The three ridings of Yorkshire were parcelled out, in terms of land ownership, between four of the greatest magnates of the realm, including the Crown as Duchy of Lancaster, the Percies, Nevilles and the Duke of York, Salisbury's brother-in-law. The Percy holdings east of the Pennines were interspersed with those of Salisbury and York, though the latter showed scant interest in his northern estates.[23] Having taken the years from 1416–1440 for the Earl of Northumberland to recover the bulk of his father's lost inheritance, Salisbury, who had been elevated to his earldom in 1429, had had ample time to consolidate his hold on manors in Cleveland, Westmorland, Cumberland and the important lordship of Raby.[24]

Most aggressive of the Percy brood was the Earl's second son, Lord Egremont, who had threatened the life of the Sheriff of Cumberland, Thomas de la Mare, an adherent of Salisbury.[25] Egremont, who had gained his lordship in 1449, at the age of twenty-five, typified all the adverse traits of his name:

> quarrelsome, violent and contemptuous of all authority, he possessed all the worst characteristics of a Percy for which his grandfather [Hotspur] is still a byword.[26]

Salisbury's sister, Eleanor, was married to Northumberland, but the ties of blood counted for little in a game with such high stakes. Both families possessed mature and ambitious patriarchs, each with a brood of young, restless and potentially lawless sons, and no shortage of available manpower.[27]

When Thomas Neville married Maud Stanhope, this proved a provocation too far for the volatile Egremont. The bride had been married before, to Robert, Lord Willoughby of Eresby, who had died the previous summer. She was also, and significantly, the niece and co-heiress of Ralph, Lord Cromwell, a choleric character himself but one who had acquired the leases on two choice manors at Wressle and Burwell in Lincolnshire, previously in the hands of the Percys. In February 1440 Cromwell had purchased the reversionary interest. Northumberland, whose line had spent lavishly on Wressle, had litigated in vain. When Cromwell married his niece to a Neville he was adding insult to injury.[28] Tension had been mounting throughout the early summer of 1452. In June the king had summoned both Egremont and John Neville. By the end of that month, Neville was laying plans for an ambush of his own. On 2 July, Henry dissolved Parliament and journeyed north to confront his quarrelsome vassals. He proposed that Percy and his affinity should gird themselves in readiness for service in Gascony, where their martial spirit might be more usefully deployed, but the proposal came to nothing.

Percy v Neville

The king established a commission of oyer and terminer, the membership of which included both the rival earls, Viscount Beaumont and some fourteen others.[29] A fortnight later, the commission was reissued but to little effect. Salisbury who, unlike Northumberland, sat in the Council, undoubtedly used his influence to pack the membership with allies, whose ranks included such Neville stalwarts as Sir James Pickering, Sir Henry Fitzhugh and Sir Henry le Scrope of Bolton.[30] Despite the commission's excellent credentials it proved ineffective amid a rising tide of disorder and, by the end of July, a new and perhaps less overtly partisan body was set up under the guidance of Sir William Lucy, a knight of Northamptonshire and Council member – his leadership supported by a senior legal adviser. Immediately, Sir William set to work, summoning Ralph Neville, Sir John Conyers, Sir James Pickering, Sir Ralph Randolf, Sir Thomas Mountford, Richard Aske, Thomas Sewer and John Alcombe. On 10 August nine Percy adherents were summoned, together with both Sir Ralph and Sir Richard Percy.[31]

Undeterred by the failed ambush at Heworth, Richard Percy and a band of unruly adherents now embarked on a spree of vandalism, culminating in the kidnapping of Lawrence Catterall, the bailiff of Staincliff Wapentake, who was roughly dragged from his devotions in Gargrave Church on 9 September. He was subsequently incarcerated, first in Isel Castle and later at Cockermouth. Obviously the luckless man had, in some unrecorded way, offended the Percys.[32] The unrest continued. On 25 September a brace of Percy retainers – John Catterall and Sir John Salvin – pillaged the house of William Hebdon, vicar of Aughton. This may have been in reprisal for John Neville's plundering of the Earl of Northumberland's property at Catton.[33]

On 8 October King Henry wrote plaintively to both earls, enjoining them to exercise some degree of control over their headstrong siblings. At this time the king's mental health was already causing concern. Henry had no history of instability and his queen, supported by the court faction, was not inclined to advertise his recent mental decline. The exact nature of the king's malady has never been definitively diagnosed, though catatonic schizophrenia has been favoured. Whatever the cause, the plain fact was that Henry's deteriorating mental condition contributed to his administration's grip on law and order. By 17 October Egremont had assembled perhaps half a hundred harnessed retainers, who mustered at Topcliffe. Rather less than half of these were from the Percy heartland of Northumberland or the City of Newcastle.[34] Heedless of the feeble royal admonitions, both sides were squaring up for a further brawl and a confrontation of sorts probably occurred at Sandhutton on 20 October. Here, Salisbury and Warwick, joined by Sir John and Sir Thomas Neville, were bolstered by such trusty friends as Sir Henry Fitzhugh and Sir Henry le Scrope. Not to be outdone the Percy affinity was led by the Earl and Lord Poynings, Lord Egremont and Sir Richard Percy. The stand-off seems to have amounted to little more than bravado on both sides but the magnates themselves had now clearly shown their hands in the fracas. Battle lines had been drawn, even if few blows had yet been struck.[35]

As the tempo of strife rose, the king's grasp on reality declined. By now it was impossible to hide the truth about his condition. Matters were further stirred by the birth, on 13 October of a son, Edward of Lancaster. With this, York's hopes of securing the succession from a childless monarch vanished like the mist. Increasingly vociferous, the duke, as the senior magnate, was clamouring to be appointed as regent during the term of the king's illness – a demand the queen and Somerset were equally determined to resist. On 25 October the Council convened at York with both Salisbury and Warwick in attendance. Both Northumberland and Lord Poynings were pointedly absent.[36]

The Duke of York had married Salisbury's sister, Cicely, the celebrated 'Rose of Raby'. His career in the public service had been worthy if undistinguished. His efforts to secure Normandy had been wasted by Somerset's subsequent mishandling. Much of his endeavours had been self-financed and the duke was owed substantial sums by the Crown. His posting to Ireland was, in all but name, a form of exile, yet he had done good service in that unruly province. As a man he was:

> a somewhat austere, remote and unsympathetic figure, with little capacity of inclination to seek out and win support from his fellow noblemen or from the wider public.[37]

York had no love for Somerset, whom he perceived, almost certainly correctly, as the main block to his inclusion in the king's inner circle. The loss of the French territories had led to the confrontation at Blackheath. It was here that Salisbury and Warwick undertook the roles of honest brokers. None can have been impressed when the promises made were contemptuously put aside. The king's breakdown dramatically altered the balance of power and York, fully supported by his brother-in-law and nephew, assumed the office of Protector of the Kingdom. Despite his Beaufort blood, Warwick maintained a separate quarrel with Somerset, over ownership of a portion of the vast Beauchamp inheritance. The duke's greed surpassed his judgement – making an enemy of the earl was outright folly with the balance of power so delicately poised. No sooner was York in office than his former rival was consigned to a sojourn in the Tower.[38]

Meanwhile, Lord Cromwell, notoriously litigious, had been at odds in the courts with Henry Holand, Duke of Exeter. The matter had become so heated between these two choleric peers that, in July 1453, both had been temporarily incarcerated. With the Neville marriage, Cromwell found an ally in Salisbury. Exeter, inevitably, sought common cause with the Percys.[39] On 27 March 1454 the Duke of York was formally installed as protector and, less than a week later, his brother-in-law was appointed Chancellor. Secure in this high office, Salisbury summoned Egremont and Richard Percy to attend upon his convenience on pain of forfeiture and outlawry.[40] Whereas the Percys might disdain the king's feeble complaints, Salisbury, in the mantle of Chancellor, could not be ignored. York's appointment marked a period of more decisive governance, though the Nevilles were clearly, as ever, motivated by self-interest. Sensing the mood, Sir Thomas Neville of Brancepeth (not Salisbury's son but a younger brother of the Earl of Westmorland and no friend to his cousins), took the opportunity to 'take up' the property of Sir John Salvin at Egton in Eskdale. This was accomplished with a body of two dozen armed retainers who lifted 'gear' (valuables and household goods) worth some £80.[41]

In May 1454 York, as Protector, sent a strongly worded summons to the Earl of Northumberland, ordering him to appear before the Council on 12 June. Lord Poynings and Ralph Percy were summoned to appear ten days beforehand. Already, on 3 April, Exeter had been removed from his lucrative and prestigious post of Lord Admiral.[42] Not unsurprisingly, the Percys were not minded to follow the path of humility. On 6 May they showed what respect they had for the new Chancellor by vandalising his house in York and roughing up one of his tenants, John Skipworth. Many of those now involved in this fresh rash of disturbances had been 'out' upon Heworth Moor the previous summer. By the middle of May, Egremont was mustering his affinity at Spofforth and there, on the 14th, he was joined by Exeter, bridling at his humiliation. Riotous behaviour broke out in the streets of York, alarming the burgesses, especially after the mob had brutally assaulted the Mayor and the Recorder. A wave of anarchy now swept through the North Riding, while Exeter, not to be outdone, busily stirred up trouble in Lancashire and Cheshire.[43] Needless to say, the invigorated Council, supported by York as protector, was not minded to remain inert while these troubles flared. Sir Thomas Stanley, the Duchy of Lancaster's Receiver for the counties of Lancashire and Cheshire, ably assisted by Sir Thomas Harrington, saw Exeter off in short order. The Protector himself entered the City of York on 19 May – the rioters fled the streets.[44]

Exeter, whose thuggish traits matched those of Egremont, was, nonetheless, one of King Henry's closest blood relations, tracing his line through John of Gaunt. It is conceivable he perceived in this localised brawl the chance to light a fuse that might unseat York.[45] On 21 May, with Egremont and his affinity, Exeter reappeared in York and set about further intimidation of the much abused mayor and burgesses. Disorder flared once again through the shire. Egremont was sufficiently inflamed to solicit aid from James II of Scotland. The Scots had recently violated the previous year's truce and the herald dispatched to Edinburgh to register the Council's protest was kidnapped at Spofforth. This smacked of rebellion and the rebels, as they could now be termed, planned to lure the Protector into an ambush beneath the walls of York.[46]

York summoned both the ringleaders to appear on 25 June and used the interval to consolidate his position and build up local forces. By the 15th of the month he was reinforced by Warwick and Lord Greystoke. A week later Lord Clifford, the Earl of Shrewsbury, and Sir Henry Fitzhugh added their retinues. A number of summonses had been issued and several individuals suffered forfeiture or even outlawry – Exeter, Egremont and Sir Richard Percy all failed to appear.[47] For all their violent posturing, the rebels had completely failed to achieve any serious objective. Exeter crept back to London. By 8 July he was in captivity, and by the 24th he had been safely incarcerated in Pontefract Castle. The snake might appear to be scotched but was still writhing. With the Percies still at large, York did not feel sufficiently secure in the north to return to the capital.[48] Matters continued in this tense vein until the autumn, when a further confrontation took place, this time at Stamford Bridge, some 7 miles east of York, and held by the Nevilles. Whether any actual fighting occurred is doubtful but the Percy faction was confounded by treachery, when one of their own bailiffs – Peter Lound with around 200 followers – deserted. The Nevilles, led by Thomas and John, pounced on their discomfited enemies and captured both Egremont and Sir Richard Percy.

If the Nevilles felt they had cause for satisfaction, their triumph was shortlived for, in December 1454, Henry VI recovered his wits and was deemed able to pick up the reins of government: the office of Protector was thus redundant. On 7 February Somerset was freed from the Tower and reinstated to all his many offices. A month later Salisbury bowed to the inevitable and resigned as Chancellor. A mere seven days after his departure Exeter was set at liberty. Somerset and the queen would be in the mood for retribution rather than compromise. A further and greater trial of strength now appeared inevitable.

What had changed since the earlier showdown at Blackheath was that York was not now entirely isolated – true the Courtenays, disgruntled at the duke's handling of their feud with Bonville, had switched their allegiance to the court faction. Now, however, York had the powerful support of the Neville earls – Salisbury and Warwick with their large affinities. Somerset had blundered in allowing the alienation of the Nevilles who, with York, now believed the duke with Wiltshire, Exeter, Beaumont and Northumberland, was at the head of a faction intent upon their destruction. The situation was considerably more volatile than that which had obtained in 1450. The scene was thus set for armed confrontation.

Chapter 3

By the Sword Divided
1455–1460

S omerset and the revived court party were minded to deal decisively with their Yorkist opponents. As the winter of 1455 turned to spring, York and his affinity remained safe in the north, building their strength. Somerset could not allow this process to continue and we may assume that his was the guiding hand behind the decision, taken on 21 April, to summon a council, ostensibly to seek resolution of the current impasse. A date, one month hence was fixed and the notice contained the provision 'that they should meet to discuss the safety of the king against anyone who would threaten it'.[1] This contained a clear intimation that more than a whiff of treason was in the air. York cannot be blamed for concluding that attending without a substantial show of strength would be to invite a similar fate to that of Humphrey of Gloucester. The duke thus resolved on a bolder strategy – possibly urged by his nephew, the Earl of Warwick – that the Yorkists should head south, down the track of the Great North Road and confront the royal train before it reached Leicester. In so doing, they would free the person of Henry VI from the evil counsellors around him, particularly Somerset, for whom York nursed a particular animosity. Beaufort's mishandling of affairs in France was blamed for the collapse of English fortunes there. He had behaved deceitfully and cynically after Blackheath and had gleefully humiliated his rival, York.

Matters had, of course, changed for the Yorkists since Margaret of Anjou had provided her husband with a male heir. Henry's long hiatus in conforming to dynastic duty might have given York grounds for optimism – the birth of Edward of Lancaster appeared to confound any hopes the duke might have entertained. Worse, with the court faction thus immeasurably boosted, York was simply a rival claimant; the queen and Somerset would be far safer if he were dispensed with altogether. As they set off for Leicester it would appear that Somerset and Henry were unaware that York was on the march and under arms. Perhaps, even at this stage, they expected him to arrive humbly like Gloucester before him.

The northern army that now followed the banners of York, Salisbury and Warwick, numbered perhaps 3,000 men – not a huge force but large enough should a trial of arms ensue.[2] Within the English polity civil government, matters were now more finely balanced than they had been at Blackheath. Warwick and Salisbury were fully alienated and had nailed their colours to the Yorkist mast, and the duke could count on Devon as before. His redoubtable uncle, Sir William Neville, Lord Fauconberg, was with the king but his sympathies were likely elsewhere. Somerset could rely on his son, Henry Beaufort, Earl of Dorset, Northumberland, Lord Clifford of Skipton, Jasper Tudor, Earl of Pembroke and a particular royal favourite, James Butler, Earl of Wiltshire. The veteran Duke of Buckingham, though attached to the court faction, was a respected moderate who constantly sought to broker an accord.

Once it became clear that York was advancing under arms, a sharp reminder was sent to him that failure to disband his forces forthwith would be deemed an act of treason. No reply was forthcoming and, on 21 May – the day fixed for the council hearing – the king, together with Somerset and a substantial body of retainers, marched north from the capital. Three days earlier a general summons had been sent to the magnates to lend their banners to the royal cause. Some time had passed since Blackheath and Somerset's perceived misgovernment had alienated many peers whom, while they would baulk at outright defiance, were in no rush to comply. York did, finally, write, intimating that he was unfairly excluded from the council and that the detested Somerset must be removed from office forthwith. This correspondence, begun on 20 May, was initially addressed to Canterbury, as Chancellor, protesting at the Yorkist peer's exclusion from an earlier council meeting at Westminster and affirming their loyalty to the king. The following day a copy of this letter was sent to the king with a covering note.

The king received this communication while at Kilburn, the duke being already in Royston. Nonetheless, despite having fewer numbers, Henry marched on to Watford, while York moved up to Ware. From there he dispatched a further communication, which largely reiterated the content of the previous message: there could be no reconciliation while the hated Somerset remained at the king's table. Barely a score of miles now separated the two forces. Finally, the threads that had wound through the English polity for several decades were about to coalesce: the process of dissent, begun by the mercurial Gloucester, was finally to burst into armed dispute.

It cannot be ascertained if the king and Somerset, with the lords they had in attendance, intended to fight from the outset, as some commentators have suggested. This seems unlikely – with no more than 2,000 men their force was small. It is probable the Duke of Somerset was anxious to avoid any confrontation in the south near London, where Yorkist sentiment ran high, but may well have clung to the belief he could face York down as the court faction had done at Blackheath. The duke, however, had imbibed the bitter lesson of that humiliation: for him there was no question of backing down or even temporising. In the warm spring dawn of 22 May, the king received intelligence that the northerners were approaching St Albans. Thus, before continuing his march, King Henry summoned an urgent meeting of his officers. Somerset showed no desire to avoid a fight. The northern Lancastrians, Percy and his affinity, were not shy of a showdown with their detested Neville rivals. It was the moderate, Buckingham, who sought, by cautious counsel, to deflect the hotheads, advising a more conciliatory approach aimed at negotiation rather than confrontation. This was sage advice – Buckingham, loyal to the king, had no personal quarrel with York.

At this point Henry, who preferred to avoid the prospect of bloodshed, heeded Buckingham's advice and appointed him commander-in-chief. There was sound logic in this: Buckingham was related by marriage to York and was known as an honest broker, his presence at the head of the king's forces would surely reassure the northerners that battle could be avoided. But negotiations stalled and battle became imminent.

By 9 a.m. both armies were circling the town and the king was first to enter, planting his royal standard in the market place while his forces consolidated their grip on the streets.

The First Battle of St Albans

For the first time, Englishmen were now to fight each other in earnest. The Lancastrians appear to have been caught slightly off guard by the Yorkists' sudden push towards the barriers, but the narrow road and the town gates were sufficient to slow the attackers, denying them the advantage their numbers might otherwise confer. It seemed as though the defences would hold up indefinitely but the Earl of Warwick, having wisely judged the tactical stalemate, now led the uncommitted portion of his forces in an outflanking move. The attackers swarmed over the town ditch, filtering through the gardens to break through the ribbon of houses onto the street and gain the market square.[3]

The commons were perhaps fortunate, the gentry less so, being particular targets for their enemies. Warwick's retainers cut down Lord Clifford; the Earl of Northumberland fell shortly after. Henry Beaufort, Earl of Dorset, was taken and spared, though badly wounded – as were Buckingham and the captured Tudor. The Earl of Wiltshire – who was to demonstrate something of a genius for survival – made good his escape.[4] Lord Fauconberg, who had, at least nominally, been in the king's host, departed unmolested.

One man for whom there could be no expectation of clemency was Edmund Beaufort, 2nd Duke of Somerset. The man who would control the civil government of England coughed up his life's blood over the cobbles of St Albans, though his son, at least, survived.

Soon, the only Lancastrian left alive in the square was the reigning monarch. Even his standard-bearer, Sir Philip Wentworth, had joined the stampede to escape. The king, wounded by an arrow, was led from the bloodied streets, taken first to a tanner's dwelling to have his wound dressed, and then conveyed to the more suitable surroundings of the Abbey. Presently, his Yorkist subjects craved an audience to beg forgiveness for so inconveniencing their sovereign; expressing the desire he should share their relief at his favourite's demise! In the circumstances, Henry proved sufficiently politic to ameliorate his previous harsh and uncompromising attitude to the rebels, who were now a ruling junta, and gave them his dispensation.

The Protectorate

The Duke of York now appointed himself Constable and the plum of Calais went to Warwick. Viscount Bourchier replaced Wiltshire as

Treasurer. With Somerset dead, the blame for the fray could be laid alongside his corpse. A Bill of Attainder, passed on 18 July, fully cleared the Yorkist faction of any treasonable conduct. It would naturally seem that the bloodletting at First St Albans had effectively polarised the two factions and that the future battle lines had now been irrevocably drawn. This may not necessarily be the case: Christine Carpenter argues that the final split may have come later and that, between the years 1455–1458, a broad sweep of the nobility was working to find a constitutional settlement. York had a very narrow base, dependent upon the Nevilles, and even Salisbury and Warwick may not have been completely committed to an unswerving Yorkist stance. St Albans had witnessed the destruction of both Somerset and Northumberland, thus any local rivalries had been resolved in their favour.

Calais and the Pale[5] was a problem of far greater magnitude. The garrison was necessary but also very expensive. In the three years from mid 1451 to 1454 the wages bill topped £17,000. When, in 1450, York had ousted Somerset and assumed his office of Captain, the mood of the garrison was so sour that the duke was denied entry – truculence that soon flared into outright disobedience. York had been too distracted by other matters to effect a settlement with the troops, who received neither their arrears nor an assent to dispose of the wool they'd seized to make good the deficiency. Now it was Warwick's turn to encounter the same impasse – the only difference being that the arrears had accrued steadily in the interval. Protracted negotiations, aimed at ending the deadlock, followed and the matter was not resolved until January 1456.[6] Warwick did not formally enter into his command until that summer and by then York had lost his tenous grip on power in England. Henry VI, addressing Parliament, formally withdrew the duke's authority as Protector. The Yorkists were not yet marginalised, their control of the council did not waver, and the king lacked sufficient allies.

Margaret of Anjou, with Somerset gone, was the natural focus for any resurgent court faction. Dynamic and utterly determined to secure her son's rightful inheritance, she feared York's dynastic ambitions. The duke's faction held sway among the mercantile classes in London, so the queen shifted her court to the Midlands, to the heartland of the Duchy of Lancaster and the lands of Prince Edward's earldom of Chester. This was a carefully and cleverly calculated move: it enabled Margaret to escape the confinement of a pro-Yorkist capital and build up new centres of influence in the shires.

Loveday

Henry joined Margaret at Kenilworth and steadily the queen clawed back the reins of power, using the king's authority to stuff the offices of state with her nominees. Laurence Booth, Margaret's able chancellor, was created Keeper of the Privy Seal.[7] When the prince bishop,[8] a Neville, died in 1457, Booth was appointed to the powerful and prestigious See of Durham. Soon the Yorkists had lost the offices of Treasurer and Chancellor, Shrewsbury replacing Bourchier, and it was he who, with Exeter and Henry Beaufort (now Duke of Somerset), who set out to assassinate the Earl of Warwick. Wiltshire was another who enjoyed a fresh spell in office as Treasurer. Ominously for the Yorkists, the thuggish Egremont was soon, like his old ally Exeter, at liberty, while his brother, Lord Poynings (now 3rd Earl of Northumberland), was appointed as East March Warden, a traditional Percy sinecure.

A lone but powerful voice for moderation and reconciliation was that of the Duke of Buckingham, who appeared to have a constant ally in the king himself. Henry, like the duke, was equally concerned to avoid further bloodshed. The carnage in the streets of St Albans had clearly taken its toll of his brittle personality. It is an element of Henry's tragedy that he was a dove in an age of hawks. Had he been a man of blood and iron – like his illustrious father – then history would, undoubtedly, have given him a more glowing obituary. The culmination of the peacemakers' efforts was a singular ceremony of reconciliation, which took place in St Paul's on 24 March 1458 – 'Loveday'. The title is ironic, as there was little of love in the air when the principal antagonists – Somerset, paired with Salisbury, Northumberland with Warwick and York with Margaret – joined hands in a symbolic series of gestures. Previously, the Yorkists had conceded that they would endow a chantry in St Albans to celebrate masses for the souls of the dead and pay compensation to both Percy and Clifford.

As an effort to paper over the cracks, Loveday was a fine show: those not prone to cynicism might have discerned the dawn of a new era; others might have noted the numbers of liveried soldiery that followed in the magnates' trains. There might be gestures of peace but the capital was an armed camp, with the mayor and burgesses sweating mightily lest some spark ignite a conflagration that would transform the streets of London into a second St Albans. However, as Christine Carpenter points out, Loveday may, in fact, mark the point at which factional discord slid into the abyss of civil war. The ceremony clearly recognised that two separate factions existed and that one could not prevail without the destruction of the other. There were two clear sources of authority surrounding the supine king and a sustained trial of arms the only remedy. Fear of this polarisation irrevocably pushed the Nevilles towards York.

In the Channel, the Earl of Warwick, secure in the Captaincy of Calais, pursued his swashbuckling career as a privateer. Queen Margaret, fretting that the Nevilles should cling to so important a post, continued a policy of withholding the garrison's salaries. Warwick was ready for this – the deficiency could be made good through piracy. Far from bringing down opprobrium, the Earl's naval forays met with widespread approval.

Blore Heath and Ludford Bridge

Later in 1458 Warwick deigned to answer a royal summons to explain an assault on Hanse ships. In London the earl's party became involved in a fracas with royal retainers; this swiftly degenerated into a brawl and the Neville party claimed they were obliged to fight for their lives to break free and escape by water. From now on, Warwick held his post in Calais in defiance of the king – battle lines once again being drawn. Moderation was the first casualty, the middle ground completely eroded. Buckingham, no admirer of Warwick, and with whom he was personally at odds,[9] refused to shift his loyalty from the throne. When Margaret summoned a council to Coventry in June, prominent Yorkists were pointedly excluded, including George Neville and Bourchier. Richard, Duke of York, was fully aware of this manoeuvring and prepared to resist what he perceived as the inevitable application of force to reduce his affinity. He planned to gather his strength in the Yorkist heartland at Ludlow; Warwick would bring a strong detachment from the Calais garrison[10], while Salisbury would muster his northern retainers.

Even at this stage, York did not necessarily intend to fight. However, he and his fellowship were painfully aware that only a strong show of force would deter the Lancastrians, who now viewed themselves as being in the ascendant. The court faction could still emerge victorious from a confrontation if it could prevent the Yorkists from achieving their full muster, defeating their presently scattered detachments in detail. Warwick's Calais contingent had to run the gauntlet but did so with élan, neatly sidestepping Somerset's attempt to block. The main Lancastrian force, mustering in the Midlands, was commanded by Buckingham, while Queen Margaret had moved to Eccleshall to join the strong detachment under James, Lord Audley – fast approaching Market Drayton. This was a very substantial force; Waurin, our most complete chronicler, puts Audley's numbers at 10,000, most being mounted.

Salisbury was marching for Ludlow. With him were his sons, Sir John and Sir Thomas, together with Sir John Conyers, Sir Thomas Harrington and Sir John Parr. His numbers were considerably inferior to the Lancastrian contingents poised to intercept him; but skilful on the march, he avoided Buckingham. If Margaret was to frustrate a full Yorkist muster she would have to deploy Audley's army to stop Salisbury. By the chill dawn of 23 September the two forces were already jockeying for position, prickers on both sides covering the ground. The subsequent battle resulted in a neat Yorkist win – aside from Lord Audley himself, several knights were slain – Sir Hugh Venables of Kinerton, Sir Thomas Dutton of Dutton, Sir Richard Molineux of Sefton, Sir John Dunne and Sir John Haigh, with perhaps as many as 2,000 of the commons. The Yorkists escaped without the loss of any gentry and only a handful of rank and file.

For the queen this was both a tactical and a strategic setback. She had previously summoned the Stanleys, Lord Thomas and his brother, Sir William. The former was Salisbury's son-in-law and despite protestations of loyalty he avoided the muster. Sir William, however, threw his lot in with the Yorkists. With their available forces concentrated at Ludlow, the Yorkists had successfully frustrated attempts to prevent a full muster. York was at the heart of his dominion with his affinity in numbers and under arms, a notable victory under his belt. He could, therefore, look forward to the outcome of any further standoff with some degree of equilibrium.

Preparing for battle, the Yorkists, on 12 October, deployed in a strong defensive position by Ludford Bridge, their ordnance arrayed before the line. Their situation, in strategic terms, was less secure than their strongly fortified lines might imply. The York/Neville faction was still a minority. In the four years since First St Albans, York had not materially succeeded in widening his power base – support from the magnates was not forthcoming and the deficiency exacerbated when

Buckingham, the moderate, came off the fence and sided with the king. Though York was strong in numbers, the only magnates beneath his banners were his sons, Edward, Earl of March and Edmund, Earl of Rutland, with Salisbury, Warwick and Lord Clinton.[11] This imminent struggle would be no repeat of St Albans. The Lancastrian army was far stronger in terms of magnatial support and had the inestimable advantage of being led, at least in name, by the person of the anointed sovereign.

Taking up arms against the king was not something that the Yorkist affinity had necessarily bargained for, despite a series of elaborate charades aimed at a contrary pretence – the commons quickly became aware they were on the threshold of high treason.[12] Warwick appears to have given the Calais contingent, the cream of the army, bland assurances that such an eventuality would never arise – the men might respect the Earl, even like him, but he was not their lawful king. It was Andrew Trollope who decided the issue at Ludlow. It appears that the burden of his royal oath was too weighty a consideration – he and his detachment simply changed sides there and then, opening a massive breach in the Yorkist line, breaking down floodgates through which others were quick to stream. Despite a desultory cannonade, mere bravado, the game was up for York and the Nevilles, the day lost before it had begun. On the pretext of returning to the castle, the leaders simply took to their heels, abandoning the rump of their affinity and conceding a bloodless victory to the Lancastrians.

The 'Rout of Ludford' was a disaster for the Yorkists: they suffered no losses but their fellowship, all of their matériel, their lands and treasure were given away in an instant. The duke even abandoned Duchess Cicely and his two youngest boys, George and Richard. Their flight was precipitate and chaotic: York and Rutland eventually gained the sanctuary of Ireland, while Warwick, Salisbury and March fled towards the Channel and the refuge of Calais, still held by Fauconberg. John Dinham gave the fugitives shelter at his home by Newton Abbot, then paid for their safe passage.

Their lives might, at least for the moment, be safe, but the Yorkists appeared to have lost everything else. Their forces were scattered, their estates forfeit, their fortunes impounded and, perhaps even more unfortunate, their integrity destroyed. The victors of St Albans had fled from the face of their rightful sovereign. When, on 2 November, the exhausted trio finally disembarked at Calais, it must have seemed their hopes were entirely dashed. Queen Margaret had achieved a great deal: she had rebuilt the court party from the ashes of St Albans, had steadily increased her strength till the time was ripe, and had carefully orchestrated a total collapse of the Yorkist faction.

The Yorkists in Exile

But Queen Margaret's triumph did not render her son's inheritance safe. York was ensconced among friends in Ireland. The Nevilles, with the Earl of March, were secure behind the walls of Calais. Clemency to those implicated, if not fully committed, to the Yorkist faction, was called for. The Lancastrian Parliament that assembled at Coventry in November 1459 inevitably attainted the leading Yorkist peers and their more notable adherents. Lesser fry were dealt with more leniently by fine or censure. York was well received in Ireland, though on paper he was deprived of authority and Wiltshire appointed in his stead, but this had little practical effect – the duke enjoyed great personal popularity, and there was little real possibility of the dilettante Wiltshire taking up his appointment.

Calais was, of course, a wholly different proposition. Had the Lancastrians been sharper they would have tried to seize the place by surprise after Warwick had left for England. As it was, Somerset fitted out a punitive expedition but the queen's government failed both in its efforts to support Somerset's toe-hold in the Pale and in its efforts to isolate Warwick. Attempts at embargo were ineffective and largely ignored by merchants and seafarers as the economic imperative invariably triumphed. The earl had established an accord with the Burgundians and, as ever, his buccaneering won plaudits from the men of Kent, who responded with ample intelligence of the force now being assembled at Sandwich against him. In the creeping winter dawn of 15 January 1460, a Yorkist cutting-out party under John Dinham,[13] almost 1,000 strong and with a posse of citizens from the town, made a lightning descent on Sandwich. The whole fleet, together with its astonished admiral, Earl Rivers,[14] his wife,[15] and their son, Sir Anthony Woodville, were taken and convoyed, in triumph, back to Calais.

The November Parliament had not been asked for a subsidy – a fiscal detail overlooked in the flush of political triumph.[16] While the Court, enfeebled by chronic cash shortages, sought to empower the Sheriff of Kent, Sir Baldwin Fulford, to scrape together a fresh expedition,[17]

Warwick again seized the initiative, boldy sailing from Calais to Ireland to confer with his uncle. Having scooped up more prizes during his unopposed passage, the earl reached his destination without any serious effort to prevent him. He remained a full two months – proof of his confidence in Calais' defences. This development stirred deep unease in London, rightly so, as there can have been little on the Yorkist peers' agenda other than planning a successful descent on England. The Yorkists' intentions were not difficult to fathom – to return and seize power through military action was obvious. But what was the nature of power sought? Did York simply aim to create another unsatisfactory protectorate, where his position would be as assailable as before, or was there a more ambitious plan? Did the duke now propose to seize the throne for himself and his heirs?

It was not until May that Warwick set sail from Ireland, setting in motion events that could have led to a spectacular fight at sea. Although, in the encounter that followed, it was bluff and nerve that decided the day. Exeter proved unequal to the challenge and scuttled into Dartmouth, leaving Warwick to sail into Calais to a hero's welcome.

If this was disappointing for Somerset, who looked vainly for sight of his own reinforcements mustering at Sandwich, then he was doubly discomfited when Dinham, with Sir John Wenlock[18] and Fauconberg, staged a repeat of his earlier spoiling raid. The Lancastrians, ably commanded by Osbert Mountfort and mustering some 400 bows and bills, were not caught totally unawares and gave a good account of themselves before Mountfort, like so many of his comrades, went into the bag. But there was one crucial difference in this second 'descent' – Fauconberg remained in occupation of Sandwich. A beachhead had been secured.

The Road to Northampton

Military preparations were complemented by vigorous propaganda. Warwick's stirring deeds at Calais and at sea had helped win hearts and minds in Kent. Exeter, as the king's admiral, had made a very poor showing. On 26 June Warwick led the main expedition from Calais, accompanied by his father, the Earl of March, and together with the new Lord Audley, who had swapped allegiance. In numbers, the earl's command was no greater than perhaps 2,000, though the men were mainly veterans and the commons of Kent were vociferous in support.

The legitimacy of the invasion received a fillip from the presence of the Papal envoy, who found the Yorkists more congenial than their enemies.[19]

Thomas Bourchier, Archbishop of Canterbury also joined the rebels, adding considerable weight to their manifesto. As the Yorkists advanced towards Canterbury, local Lancastrian commanders, with a keen eye for the weather vane, promptly defected.[20] The march through Kent was unopposed – a triumphal progress with a constant stream of recruits, some of whom, like Lord Cobham, were ancient comrades. In London the government experienced a thrill of near panic. The burgesses were anxious to retain a degree of neutrality, while appearing to remain loyal to the Crown, insisting that they police the city and resisting an attempt by the Lancastrian Lord Scales[21] to act as a military governor.

Warwick cannily refused to be deterred by warnings of armed resistance and continued his inexorable advance, offering the city fathers an escape route by the assertion that he came only to correct failures in the administration – a reformer rather than a rebel. The burgesses were quick to grab the proffered lifeline and sent a party to confirm that the gates would be opened. A wiser, less belligerent man than Scales might have judged this as a propitious moment to withdraw, to retreat into the Lancastrian heart of the Midlands as the court intended; but Scales barricaded himself in the Tower, accompanied by a number of diehards,[22] in the hope that tenure of this great bastion would be a thorn in the Yorkists' flesh.

On 1 July the Yorkists reached Southwark – a muster at St George's Field was swollen by the thousands who'd joined the earl's colours on the march through Kent. The commons of the south-east had amply demonstrated where their sympathies lay. On 2 July the Yorkists entered the city with the host setting up camp by Smithfield. No time was wasted – the bishops, handily meeting in convocation, were canvassed for their support, the burgesses importuned for the supply of baggage wagons and the uplifting of the royal ordnance from Whitechapel. This was clearly intended to be deployed against Scales holding out in the Tower, though the instruction was tactfully phrased as being for the defence of the city.

Warwick skilfully drew the townsmen into the Yorkist web. The burgesses were persuaded to top up the war chest with a 'loan' of £1,000 and the besieged Lancastrians, holding on in the great fortress, were denied resupply. More of the magnates, including Lords Saye, Abergavenny and Scrope of Bolton, Viscount Bourchier and the Duke of Norfolk, came in. On the 4th the van marched from the City; a commanded party was detached by Ware, as there was a rumour the king might be found at Ely. Salisbury, Cobham and Wenlock were left to continue the blockade of Scales' garrison in the Tower. It is unlikely the city fathers regretted their leaving – medieval armies were rapacious and unpredictable guests. Doubtless the burgesses heaved a sigh of relief.

Henry was not in flight, even though his council was in some disarray. The queen and Prince Edward were left in Coventry while the king, with all his available power, marched south as far as Northampton. He had tarried in order to give Northumberland, Clifford and the other northern lords and their affinities time to catch up. None of these, however, arrived in time for the battle about to be fought. The chronicle sources are unreliable in terms of the number of soldiery available to King Henry – perhaps 10,000 men at most. The vestiges of moderate opinion inclined towards some form of mediation but the hawks, including the bellicose Lord Egremont, favoured a further trial of arms. Warwick's prickers would soon have alerted him to the fact the king was neither at Ely, nor in flight and that he was, in fact, marching south from the Lancastrian territory in the Midlands with an army at his back. Fauconberg, leading the detachment towards Ely, was hastily recalled to complete the Yorkist muster at Dunstable, before their combined forces marched on towards Northampton. Any chance for serious talks had by now evaporated. Even Buckingham, hitherto prominent among the doves, was in no mood for compromise with Warwick. Prior to the battle, the earl sent a delegation, led by the Bishop of Salisbury, to seek some ground for negotiation. He got short shrift.

As the royal army lacked a full muster of the northern men, the king's officers had wisely chosen a strong defensive position outside the town walls. Within the fort Buckingham commanded the left-hand division, the king's pavilion to his immediate left rear; Shrewsbury, Egremont, Sir Thomas Percy and John, Viscount Beaumont, held the centre, while the right was taken by Sir Edmund Grey of Ruthyn.

A treacherous pact, negotiated between Warwick and the slippery Ruthyn, undermined the entire position and decided the day in a single stroke. The lines were breached, the Lancastrian left, secure in

Warwick's livery of the black ragged staff, remained as indifferent spectators while their erstwhile enemies dealt with their erstwhile friends. From now on there was no real battle: the Yorkists simply rolled up the flank of their enemy. Warwick had no quarrel with the commons, who might expect full quarter. For the Lancastrian nobles no such clemency was forthcoming. Buckingham, with Egremont, Shrewsbury and Beaumont, formed a final ring around the king's tent and all fell in its defence. King Henry found himself once again in the hands of subjects who protested loyalty to the full, but whose swords were stained with the blood of his magnates. The disaster at Northampton robbed Scales' beleaguered garrison in the Tower of any further purpose. Scales formally surrendered on 19 July, three days after King Henry was towed into the City by the victors. During the campaign Scales' garrison had fired continuously, and at random, into the crowded streets of the city – the Londoners were unforgiving: Scales was murdered by the mob.

The Act of Accord

Warwick held the reins of power; he also controlled the person of Henry VI. His position was very similar to that of his uncle in the aftermath of First St Albans. The difficulties he faced were, equally, not dissimilar: to control the person of the monarch did not suffice to make the puppeteer king. The queen, her son and the Duke of Somerset, were all still at large, the court party was damaged but not destroyed. Those northern lords, keen to avenge the blood of their fathers, were unaffected. What had changed in the Yorkists' favour was that they commanded the sympathies of a much broader constituency of peers. Yet, as the earl divined, this effect could be transient. Henry, however many times he might be bested in the field, was still king – at this stage there was no suggestion the Yorkists enjoyed broad magnatial support for, in the modern idiom, 'regime change'.

Walking a tightrope is never easy, and the depletion of the Calais garrison had been a calculated risk; and Somerset was still holding Guines. In theory, the duke posed a continuing threat but the decision at Northampton had robbed him of prospects. He and Warwick parleyed on Newnham Bridge and Somerset felt constrained to surrender the castle in return for his liberty. He may also have given undertakings, as a condition of parole, that he would refrain from taking up arms against the Yorkist faction. He then withdrew into voluntary exile in France. In England, matters were still finely balanced, the Yorkist grip on London and the south-east was secure, but Lancastrian sentiment remained strong in the north.

What of Richard, Duke of York? He had been no more than a spectator in his own triumphal campaign. If any of the peers had uncertainties as to his intentions these were quickly dispelled when he landed near Chester early in September. His mood had hardened since the days of his Protectorate. He came not to support the Crown but to seize it. His parade through the marches and the West Midlands was akin to a royal progress. If the commons reacted with enthusiasm, there was alarm among the peers – they simply were not ready for this. His entry into London on 10 October resembled a gaudy pageant, his half-a-thousand retainers proclaimed by fanfares, the royal banners floating above, his sword borne upright after the style of the sovereign.

York's state entry into the Palace of Westminster could have been a finely-judged piece of theatre that might have carried all before him but, in failing, appeared farcical. He marched directly up to the vacant throne and laid a proprietary hand on the cushion, allowing the gesture to linger long enough for, as he hoped, loud cheers of approbation to swell through the great hall. None came – the gesture fell flat. What is certain is that York's ill-judged mummery only ended when the Archbishop of Canterbury tentatively stepped forward to enquire if the duke might like to see the king. Despite his rebuff from Parliament York blundered on, breaking into the king's personal apartments and taking over.

Since the debacle at Ludlow, Warwick had been the mainspring of the Yorkist faction; his was the energy, the drive, the dash, the daring and the genius that had transformed their fortunes. It was he who had held Calais and repeatedly humiliated the court party. He who had orchestrated and implemented the skilful propaganda, organised and led the army that, with minimal fuss, transformed the political situation. He had achieved what the older generation had failed to – a wider constituency of peers who were prepared to accept the Yorkists in de facto control of the throne. The duke had blundered, thereby threatening to undo all that had been won. For Warwick this must have been galling.

A factional split was not something the Yorkists could afford – there was nothing to be gained by falling out over the spoils before the prize was won. Warwick had no option but to bite his tongue and try to salvage what he could. As York had now launched a full constitutional challenge, his claim – which, in law, was a strong one – would have to be judged. Lawyers tussled over the central issue: that the seizure of the throne by Henry IV in 1399 was illegal, meaning that Henry VI, as his descendant, had no right to retain it and the crown should pass to Richard II's next legitimate successor – Richard, Duke of York.

The House of Lancaster had held the throne since 1399. Henry was the anointed king. The magnates had sworn to support him, but now they were squirming over their expressed allegiance. Their lordships – even if they had no particular love for King Henry VI – nonetheless could not bring themselves to do away with him. The plain fact was that nobody wanted to make such a momentous decision, with all of the likely consequences. Parliament might be packed with Yorkist sympathisers but the Lancastrians could still command a broad constituency in the shires. Their lordships referred to the King's Bench, who neatly passed the poisoned chalice back, intimating that the matter was so weighty – touching as it did upon the institution of the Crown – that it was above their authority and beyond their competence, 'whereof they durst not enter into any communication thereof . . .'

To dethrone Henry could lead to a renewal of the civil war. The queen, her son, and the rump of her faction, were at liberty and undefeated in the field. Thus the constitutional settlement of 1460 was inevitably a compromise – a solution that tried to please both sides and, in the way of such things, succeeded in pleasing neither. By the provisions of the Act of Accord, passed on 24 October 1460, Henry, for the remainder of his life, would continue to occupy the throne. On his death the crown would pass to York and his heirs, who, in the meantime, were to enjoy an annuity of £10,000. Had Henry been childless, this might just have sufficed, but he was not, and his defiant queen would never acquiesce to a settlement that disinherited her son. It was the Act that charged the failing batteries of the queen's cause. After Northampton she had fetched up in temporary sanctuary in Harlech, narrowly escaping a Stanley ambush, which relieved her of the modest treasure she retained. The Act of Accord, for any Lancastrian, offended against the natural laws of inheritance. It could be strongly argued that the statute, as it appeared, was nothing more than a form of usurpation, with the king in the grip of his enemies. The queen was not without allies and, as the weeks of autumn passed, the threads of her cause began to reunite.

The Road to Wakefield

From Wales, the queen's trusted adherent Jasper Tudor pledged his sword. Somerset ended his brief exile, basing himself at Corfe Castle, from where he could stir mischief. In the west the Courtenays had experienced a change of heart and were willing to defect. To the north, tempestuous young men like Northumberland, Lord Roos and John Clifford were ready for action. The borderers, harrying Neville lands, the westerners, galvanised by Somerset, struck north through the Cotswolds to Coventry, and finally to rendezvous with the northerners at York. Meanwhile, more Lancastrians were said to be mustering in Yorkshire's East Riding.

Despite the reverse at Northampton and the loss of the king's person, Queen Margaret, who had sailed to Scotland to canvass further aid, enjoyed considerable support. The northern kingdom was ruled by James II – 'James of the Fiery Face'[23] – who had ascended the throne as a minor after the assassination of his anglophile father, James I, at Perth in 1437. Such a powerful muster of enemies could not be ignored. On 9 December a Yorkist army, led by York and Salisbury, marched north from London into the dismal mire of the winter roads. Edward, Earl of March, was sent into Wales with a smaller contingent to confront, or at least contain, the Tudors, while Warwick held the capital.

There was logic in this. It was Warwick who had the rapport with the peers. It was he who kept the king close and who could maintain a watch on the south coast, numbering the wardenship of the Cinque Ports among his offices. Warwick still controlled the reins of power; his brother George was Chancellor and Bourchier acted as Treasurer. The governor of the Isle of Wight, Geoffrey Gate, an adherent of the earl, did good service when he captured Somerset's younger brother, Edmund Beaufort – a handy prize and useful pawn.

But, as he marched north, York was embarking on a final miscalculation. His intelligence seems to have been lacking insofar as he failed to detect the weight of opposition being mustered against him. An intimation of what was to follow occurred when his column was ambushed by a commanded party (under the energetic Trollope) near

Worksop, extricating itself with difficulty and some loss. On 21 December the Yorkists reached what appeared to be a secure northern base – York's castle at Sandal[24] on the southern outskirts of Wakefield. In fact, Sandal was more trap than refuge, for the Lancastrians had boxed the place in on three sides.

Ranged against York's slender forces were several enemy columns, all within easy striking distance. York's best chance was to sit behind high walls and pray for early relief. This was well enough in theory but to feed his army in the depths of winter York needed to send out constant foragers, scouring the bleak northern landscape, through necessity ranging farther and farther afield as the area's meagre resources were consumed.

On 30 December, just such a foraging party was active north of Sandal Castle towards the River Calder and the town of Wakefield beyond. An encounter battle thus developed with successive Lancastrian units being thrown into the fight. It was Lord Clifford who finally dealt the death blow. His division was encamped south and east of the village of Sandal Magna, and was thus the final Lancastrian force to arrive on the field – perfectly placed to cut the Yorkists off from their intended refuge behind the walls of the castle. The end was not inevitable: York may have placed Rutland in the keeping of the lad's tutor, Sir Robert Aspall, with an injunction to flee the stricken field. Tradition asserts that the duke, who had ridden out onto the field was unhorsed and suffered a near crippling wound to the knee. With a handful of his household retainers he and those around him fought on till the end.

Perhaps as many as 3,000 Yorkists lay stiffening on the cold ground, including: Sir David Hall, Sir John and Sir Hugh Mortimer, Sir Thomas Neville, Sir Thomas Harrington and Sir Thomas Parr. Salisbury was captured by Trollope's billmen and hauled off to Pontefract, where a hostile mob did him to death. Wiltshire, whose fellowship had not engaged, took possession of Sandal Castle. It was Lord Clifford who captured the luckless Rutland by Wakefield Bridge, killing the seventeen-year-old earl in cold blood. With the heads of their fallen adversaries presently impaled on spikes above Micklegate Bar in York, the Lancastrians could turn their attention to the road south.

Chapter 4

The Parhelion:
Winter 1460–Spring 1461

All the lords of the north they wrought by one assent,
For to destroy the south country they did all their entent.
Yorkist ballad

In early February 1461 a strange meteorological phenomenon occurred – three suns blazed from a cobalt sky. To the superstitious minds of medieval men, this was a very grave and significant event.[1] Edward, Earl of March, had celebrated Christmas in Gloucester. His mission was to suppress Lancastrian sentiment in Wales. Around the middle of January, however, he received the dire news from the north – his father, brother, uncle and cousin were all dead at the hands of enemies, their severed heads food for the crows in York. The shock of this calamity must have been severe, especially for one still in his teens. With the knell of the older Yorkists still sounding, the obvious reaction was to return posthaste to London and link up with Warwick, to rebuild a viable field army with which to defend the city. More bad news followed: a Lancastrian force under Jasper Tudor, Earl of Pembroke,[2] had unfurled its banners in Wales. The danger was obvious – Edward could not afford to ignore this fresh threat, nor could he permit these Welsh adherents to join their victorious comrades in Yorkshire.

Tudor had been reinforced by the elusive Wiltshire, who had raised a contingent of French and Breton mercenaries, stiffened with Irish galloglass.[3] Their combined force, at this point, was marching towards Hereford. Edward did not hesitate. He swung his troops north towards Mortimer's Cross, some 17 miles ahead, in an effort to interdict the

Lancastrians' line of advance. His force was modest – perhaps a little over 10,000, mainly Welsh (raised by the Herberts) plus his own retainers. The road from Hereford to Wigmore (a Yorkist hold) ran more or less due north, veering slightly west. The waters of the river Lugg, swollen by winter rains, flowed roughly parallel on the eastern flank, before angling west, north of the crossing with the Ludlow Road.

On the morning of 2 February that strange meteorological phenomenon – the image of three suns or 'parhelion' – greeted the Yorkist army, 'three suns in the firmament shining full clear'. Many quailed – surely this was a bad omen? Rising to the occasion, Edward declared that the apparition represented the holy trinity – thus God favoured his cause.[4]

As both sides came to contact, the ground was hotly contended and Edward could make no headway against Tudor's Welshmen. The young paladin was everywhere, his great height[5] and prowess providing inspiration for his men, who, yard by yard, began to gain the upper hand. The Earl of Pembroke fought a good fight but, with appalling suddenness, his line snapped and dissolved in precipitate rout. Thus the Lancastrian left triumphed, taking their enemy's ground, but in the centre, the situation was reversed. The honours were virtually even. On the right, the course of the battle had witnessed a rather curious twist. Owen Tudor had led his division on a wide flanking movement – a curious manoeuvre for, in so doing, he left the right flank of his son's brigade very much exposed and 'in the air'. Undeterred, Tudor took his men on a circular ramble towards Kingsland, south and east of the field. Herbert was not slow to profit from his opponent's folly and fell upon the Tudor's exposed left. The Lancastrian right simply gave way.

Wiltshire, commanding his steady mercenaries, appeared to be the final hope. His force was intact and buoyed by victory, but the earl could not persuade them to engage with Edward's central division. Despite Wiltshire's best efforts his men would fight no more, and the earl, once again, turned his thoughts towards escape. With his customary agility, Wiltshire succeeded in evading his foes, as did Pembroke. Owen Tudor was less fortunate: harried the long miles back to Hereford, he, Sir John Throckmorton, and a clutch of other officers were finally taken. The cull of senior Yorkists at Wakefield ensured they would be unwise to expect clemency. Gregory puts the total Lancastrian dead at around 3,000. This seems on the high side; Wiltshire's mercenaries suffered trifling loss and the main blow fell against Pembroke. Owen Tudor's wing broke before any serious loss had mounted, though some would fall in the rout. Mortimer's Cross is, to an extent, neglected by the chroniclers, so our understanding of the course of the fight is limited. However, Gregory gives a brief account:

> Edward, Earl of March, the Duke of York's son and heir, had a gre [good] journey [battle] at Mortimer's Cross in Wales the second day of February next so following, and there he put to flight the Earl of Pembroke, the Earl of Wiltshire. And there he took and slew of knights and squires and of the [missing] to the number of 3,000 etc.[6]

Gregory further relates a particular anecdote from the aftermath, concerning Owen Tudor, who, till the end, refused to believe that defeat would cost him his head. In this, however, he was sadly deluded: mercy had perished in Yorkshire. Along with Throckmorton and another eight Lancastrians, he faced the block:

> This Own Tudor was father unto the Earl of Pembroke, and had wedded Queen Katherine, King Harry the VI's mother, weening and trusting all away that he should not be beheaded till he saw the axe and the block, and when he was in his doublet he trusted on pardon and grace till the collar of his red velvet doublet was ripped off. Then he said 'That head shall lie on the stock that was wont to lie on Queen Katherine's lap,' and put his heart and mind wholly unto God, and fully meekly took his death.[7]

The Lancastrian March from the North

The disaster at Wakefield had robbed the Yorkist faction of their senior commanders and destroyed one of their field armies. It had confirmed the Lancastrians' grip on the north and provided the court party with a clear-cut victory to redress the defeat at Northampton. One particular trump, however – the person of Henry VI – was still in Yorkist hands. Though her western adherents were beaten, Queen Margaret could count on a potent concentration of available forces in Yorkshire. With some Scottish hobilars she had crossed the border after the victory at Wakefield and rejoined the northern lords at York. The road south now lay open. We cannot be sure of numbers but it is reasonable to suppose that Margaret's army was at least 20,000 strong.[8] The northern lords –

Northumberland and Clifford – with Somerset, Neville and Dacre, would be leading many of their own affinity; Trollope his regulars from Calais. These men could be controlled but the army would attract free lances from both sides of the border – those 'roaring northerners' ('Bobinantes Boreales'), so heartily despised by their southern contemporaries. It would have been remarkable if excesses had not taken place, and undoubtedly these did occur – whether such depredations were quite on the biblical scale as depicted by the shrill accounts of contemporary writers is less certain. The Croyland Chronicler probably articulated the fears of the southerners when the Prior, hysterical over the depredations wrought by these wild men from the north, wrote:

> The duke [York] being thus removed from this world, the northmen, being sensible that the only impediment was now withdrawn, and that there was no one now who would care to resist their inroads, again swept onwards like a whirlwind from the north, and in the impulse of their fury attempted to overrun the whole of England.[9]

Actual details of particular horrors are remarkably lacking. Without doubt the northerners plundered as they went – as much through necessity as inclination. To the countrymen and townspeople this apocalyptic vision of a great northern invasion, as murderously rapacious as Tamerlane, would have been terrifying enough. The Prior of Croyland waxed lyrical in his well-rehearsed outrage:

> When the priests and the other faithful of Christ in any way offered to make resistance, like so many abandoned wretches as they were, they cruelly slaughtered them in the very churches or church yards.[10]

Certain locations – particularly towns like Grantham and Stamford, the inhabitants of which were understood to be notably Yorkist in sentiment – were afforded special treatment. In these the army was allowed free rein, as a reminder to citizens of the perils of false allegiance. Defeat at Wakefield had not robbed the Yorkists of their advantage in the ongoing propaganda war – this grand *chevauchée* was a perfect gift. Warwick had, prior to Northampton, proved himself a master of acquiring hearts and minds. The Lancastrians had no such skills and the relentless, ruthless and unchecked advance of their army provided a perfect scoop. The earl, from London, could broadcast and embellish the atrocity stories – the dispute between factions being a lesser issue than the north/south divide, which could be exploited to the full.

When it comes to the action in the next major fight – Second St Albans – we are fortunate that two of the chroniclers were present as eyewitnesses. Abbot Whethamstede was a spectator – understandably nervous – watching the drama unfold from the relative sanctuary of the Abbey itself; while William Gregory marched beneath Warwick's banner. His account, therefore, has the urgency of the participant's view:

> The lords in King Harry's party [he means here the Yorkists] pitched a field and fortified it full strong, and like unwise men brake their array and took another, and ere that they were all sette a – buskyd [fully deployed] to battle the queen's party was at hand with them in town of St Albans, and then all thing was to seek and out of order, for their prickers come not home to bring no tiding how nigh that the queen was.[11]

Warwick had not anticipated the disaster at Wakefield. He had now lost both father and brother and it would be entirely reasonable if he was distracted. The earl, for all his many talents, was not necessarily at his best in a crisis. He was wrongfooted by the Lancastrians' success and disconcerted by the subsequent march south, though, skilled pamphleteer as he was, he was swift to capitalise on and embellish tales of the northerners' excesses. But rather more than a war of words was required to keep Queen Margaret's army from battering at the gates of London. With the Earl of March fully occupied in the west it was up to Warwick to shore the Yorkist position. This necessitated a blocking move north of the capital. There were enough London and Kentish adherents to form a respectable army, but it would not match the northerners in terms of overall numbers.

The Second Battle of St Albans

By 12 February the Earl of Warwick had marshalled all available forces and advanced as far north as St Albans, scene of his triumph six years earlier. Now he would be fighting the sons of those lords whose blood had stained the streets before. It is unlikely that so intelligent a man missed the potential for dramatic irony. Quite why he chose the town is not entirely clear – his enemies were marching straight down the Great North Road; having taken Grantham and Stamford, they now approached through Peterborough, Huntingdon and Royston. As Colonel Burne suggests, it must have been the case that the queen's army veered west and that, informed by scouts, Warwick moved to conform. We know the queen had reached Dunstable by 16 February, which allowed the earl four full days to prepare his position.

To ensure he covered the north and north-west approaches the earl established a line of some 4 miles, stretching from St Albans on the left or west flank, to the aptly named No Man's Land. Warwick had divined the Lancastrians would be moving in a westerly direction towards Harpenden. There they had to decide whether to mount their thrust towards London, down the St Albans road, or that from Hatfield. By covering Barnard's Heath and Sandridge, he blocked both and wisely covered his exposed flanks at St Albans and No Man's Land.[12] This strategy was sound in theory but meant the Yorkists were strung out along a wide front: in an era before wireless communication, this entailed substantial risks. Gregory describes, in some detail, the ingenious, elaborate but ultimately useless, fieldworks the earl had installed to protect his line:

> Also they had nets made of great cords of four fathom of length and of four foot broad, like unto a haye [rabbit net], and at every two knots there was a nail standing upright, that there could no man pass over it by likelihood but he should be hurt. Also they had pavysse [pavises – large wooden shields] bore as a door i-made with a staff folding up and down to set the pavysse where they liked, and loops with shooting windows to shoot out at, they standing behind the pavysse, and the pavysse as full of 3d [1¹/₂p] nail after order as they might stand. And when their shot was spend and done they cast the pavysse before them, then there might be no man come unto them over the pavysse for the nails that stood upright, but if he would mischief himself.[13]

Colonel Burne attributes the flexibility of Lancastrian tactics at this point to the queen herself, though the experienced Andrew Trollope would certainly have been consulted. The queen's army did not take the direct line from Harpenden but chose to move further west in a broad outflanking motion, which Warwick's inertia and extended lines made possible. This was a bold stroke – one that entailed a fast, forced march as far as Dunstable, then through the winter darkness, for the leading formations to arrive at St Albans by dawn on 17 February. Boldness indeed, for, strung out along the line of approach, the Lancastrians would have been at risk of a crushing attack on their exposed flank had Warwick's scouts been more diligent. The perils of a night march, in winter conditions, moving large bodies of men over unfamiliar terrain, were sufficient to deter even the most resolute of commanders. That this could be carried out so efficiently was no mean feat.

The Earl of Warwick has been criticised for relying too heavily on his field works, and perhaps he surrendered the initiative too willingly. On the other hand, his position was an unenviable one: part of the Yorkist strength, including many veterans, had been extinguished at Wakefield; much of the remainder was in the field with Edward to the west and the earl had not had time to weld his scratch-built force into an effective field army. By contrast, his enemies possessed greater numbers and an army that had been successfully welded in battle. A Yorkist outpost at Dunstable, 200 men under Sir Edward Poynings, was easily overrun and silenced by death or capture, before even being able to raise the alarm. The Lancastrian army followed the dead-straight arrow of Watling Street to cover the dozen miles to St Albans, which the head of the column probably reached at around three in the morning,[14] though it was clearly light before they began to infiltrate the sleeping town. Such was the speed and sureness of this daring night march the town was taken completely unawares. That timber gate or barrier, which guarded the point where the road crossed the ancient ditch, a natural blocking position, was undefended. The passage of such large numbers of heavily armed men could not long pass unnoticed. By the time the forward elements, led by Trollope, had penetrated as far as the centre, the startled defenders were under arms and stringing their longbows.

Despite being unprepared and outmatched, the Yorkist bowmen gave a good account of themselves. The attackers, crammed in the narrow street, could not make any headway and, as the clothyard shafts continued to find their mark, the Lancastrians recoiled. The van withdrew in good order to regroup north of the River Ver by the old Roman settlement and St Michael's Church. The solution, as in the earlier fight, was to find some means to outflank the defenders while keeping their attention fixed on the main axis of attack. An opportunity arose when it was discovered the passage over the ditch by Folly and Catherine Lanes was also neglected and unguarded. While the remainder of the Lancastrian detachments were still coming up, passing by St Michael's, the van crept along Catherine Lane to bypass the defence and burst into St Peter's Street. For the Yorkists this was doubly serious, assailed from two sides and their line of retreat effectively severed. These Lancastrians, spilling into St Peter's Street, were also exposed to a flank attack, launched by additional Yorkists, drawn from the main battle line.

From the Yorkist prospect this hard-fought respite could have provided the 'balcony' for a vigorous counter-attack against an enemy whose overall position was by no means entirely favourable. It is likely that the main line of defence ran along the crest of the shallow ridge now crowned by the Sandridge road (Colonel Burne considers whether this was the ground Warwick's forces occupied or whether they deployed by the old Celtic dyke at Beech Bottom[15]). Warwick used the time to prepare for the blow that must soon fall upon his left flank. This necessitated redeploying his men on the threatened left, drawing them from their positions in Beech Bottom and establishing a new line on the higher ground. At the same time the earl had to attempt to reinforce this wing, moving detachments from his centre and right. Given the extended nature of his overall disposition and the difficulties of communications, this would be a difficult exercise.

When complete, the new line had its right anchored in Beech Bottom, stretching over Barnard's Heath, in length just under 1,000 yards.[16] The Lancastrians had secured the town but had not yet achieved any significant tactical advantage. The men were tired from the travail of their night march and those who had fought would be in need of respite. They now faced another tough assault, the new Yorkist line, half a mile or so beyond St Peter's in the town centre. Deprived of the inestimable advantage of surprise but confident in numbers and élan, the attackers advanced towards Warwick's improvised left. A bitter mêlée developed in the afternoon, the roar of battle spreading through the still calm of a winter landscape. The contest was sharp and fierce, both sides locked in the tempest of slashing bills, and for the moment, neither could gain the upper hand. Warwick's various anti-personnel devices certainly impeded the attackers, including the fearsome Trollope, who later reported he had suffered injury by a caltrap: this had pierced one armoured sabaton and held him fast to the spot, obliging his enemies to come to him. Of these he boasted of killing no less than fifteen!

William Gregory, hotly engaged as a participant, observed the great guns did little execution and the handgunners could not deliver effective volleys in the press. The Yorkists here were commanded by Warwick's brother John, Lord Montagu, a brave and highly competent officer. It seemed the contest was locked in stalemate but more and more Lancastrians were being flung into the fight. Warwick's promised reinforcements had still not come up. Where was the bulk of the Yorkist army, which had not yet struck a blow while their comrades, but a short distance away, fought for their lives against lengthening odds? The Earl of Warwick was outflanked and now outmatched.[17] The tactical initiative had been snatched away and the weaknesses of his position were rapidly becoming obvious. Perhaps the earl experienced one of those peculiar crises of confidence that were wont to afflict him in moments of great stress, when his carefully prepared plans started to unravel. It was, perhaps, this uncertainty that now communicated itself to Warwick's officers in the centre: for there was distinct resistance to his pleas for them to advance. This was the crisis point and the delay – as men were bullied and cajoled to march – proved fatal. By the time the main body advanced, the van had been routed. And an army in rout is a terrible sight – men who have fought with valour stampeding like terrified cattle, throwing aside their arms and harness.

The road from Sandridge runs along the line of the Iron Age fosse and then climbs up towards the reverse slope of Barnard's Hill. Now there came this terrified mob of broken men; the flood spilling over the ground.

But Warwick was not yet ready to admit defeat. His right wing, still to the rear, remained intact. If he could bring these fresh soldiers into the fight a total rout might yet be averted. It was at this point that Lovelace and his company broadcast their defection and quit the Yorkists to assume their new allegiance. This fresh blow was too much and robbed the earl of any prospects. Later, a taint of faintheartedness would hang over his reputation on the field. His conduct on that day argues strongly against this.

In spite of these shattering reverses, Warwick managed to weld sufficient men into a creditable rearguard – enough to form a stubborn line along a stretch of higher ground 500 yards south of No Man's

Land. This truncated remnant was adequate to see off a series of probing attacks and keep the ground till dusk offered the cloak of darkness. The earl managed to rally perhaps 4,000 survivors and lead them off the stricken field and out of immediate danger. He probably left as many more dead on the bloody heath. Gregory has left a succinct summary of the defeat:

> And in the midst of the battle King Harry went unto his queen and forsook all his lords, and trust better to her party than unto his own lords. And then through great labour the Duke of Norfolk and the Earl of Warwick escaped away; the Bishop of Exeter, that time Chancellor of England, and brother unto the Earl of Warwick, the Lord Bourchier, with many other knights, squires and commons fled, and many men slain in both parties.[18]

Warwick also managed to lose the person of the king. Dragged in the wake of the Yorkist army like an unwilling mascot, Henry had, once again, been a spectator as the battle for his crown raged around him. He is said to have spent most of the battle seated calmly beneath a spreading oak, in good spirits, much cheered by the sight of his oppressors' rout. So great was the confusion among his retreating enemies that Henry appears to have been overlooked and largely forgotten, till being greeted by his own victorious adherents.

Lord Montagu was among the haul of captives, which included Henry's immediate custodians, Lord Bonville and Sir Thomas Kyrill. This pair had agreed to remain with their royal charge, to safeguard his person, in return for his undertaking that their lives be spared. In this assurance they were misled – not by any deliberate falsehood on the king's part, for he no doubt intended the promise to be honoured. But Henry's word counted for little insofar as his own affinity was concerned. Both Bonville and Sir Thomas were summarily tried and executed.

The Lancastrian Withdrawal to the North

This fresh disaster for the Yorkists was, in some ways, worse than Wakefield. Warwick had been defeated but a short march from the capital, the road to which now lay open and the person of King Henry VI had been lost, returned to the bosom of his family and the victorious mass of his adherents. Final victory appeared to lie within Lancaster's grasp. The obvious move was to advance directly upon and seize the city while Warwick was reeling and Edward, from the west, not yet come up. Fearfully pragmatic, the burgesses indicated they were willing to bow to the inevitable, sending a team of representatives to negotiate the king's access. These included the Dowager Duchesses of Buckingham and Bedford, who could demand an audience by virtue of her husband's blood. The city fathers nervously required that their city be spared the ravages unleashed on Stamford and Dunstable, and that the Lancastrian lords rein in their abominable northerners. An Italian, Carlo Gigli, the London-based representative of one Michele Arnolfini of Bruges, wrote to his principal on 22 February, describing the nature of the negotiations that had taken place:

> They [the envoys] returned on the 20th [of February] and reported that the king and queen had no mind to pillage the chief city and chamber of their realm, and so they promised; but at the same time they did not mean that they would not punish the evildoers. On the receipt of this reply by the magistrates a proclamation was issued that everyone should keep fast to his house and should live at peace, in order that the king and his forces might enter and behave peacefully.[19]

Perhaps it was due to the newly-liberated Henry's wish to secure goodwill but the army was indeed reined in, to the extent the Lancastrians withdrew to Dunstable. This was a fatal error – one that, above all, was to herald ruin. Strategically, the only viable course at this point was for the victors to capitalise on their win and seize London, regardless of the finer feelings of the burgesses. To give Edward and Warwick a respite, to enable them to effect a juncture of their forces, to draw breath and recover the initiative, was cardinal folly. Strong, ruthless action was required – hearts and minds could wait. But in this, the greatest test of their resolve and their single, golden opportunity, the Lancastrians failed. Queen Margaret would be aware of the unenviable reputation of her larcenous army, but this was not the time for a PR exercise, however badly needed. If the city fathers were understandably nervous, the populace appeared more resolute – Yorkist propaganda had bolstered continued support in the streets. As Carlo Gigli continued to relate, with the understandable nervousness of a businessman whose enterprise may, at any moment, be wrecked by an undisciplined mob of rampant soldiery:

But less than an hour later all the people ran to arms and reports circulated that York [the duke was of course, already dead] with 60,000 Irish and March with 40,000 Welsh had hastened to the neighbourhood and would guard their place for them; and they said that the mayor must give them the keys of the gates. They called for a brewer as their leader, and that day this place was in an uproar, so that I was never more afraid than then that everything would be at hazard.[20]

To placate their ire, the burgesses had ordered provisions to be sent out to the Lancastrian army, but the citizens – made of sterner stuff – hijacked the victuals and distributed them through the tenements of the poor.[21] On 22 February Edward and Warwick, who had withdrawn west after the debacle at St Albans, joined forces at Burford in the Cotswolds.[22] On the 26th the pair made a joint triumphal entry into the city. It seemed as though it was the Yorkists who had scored a signal victory. The London chronicler, Robert Fabyan, described the strength of the welcome the joyful citizens afforded the Earl of March:

And upon the Thursday following th'Earls of March and of Warwick with a great power of men, but few of name, entered into the City of London, the which was of the citizens joyously received . . . [23]

As Henry was reunited with his queen and, nominally at least, restored to the command of his faction – the political dynamic had changed. York's taking off had cleared the stage for Edward, as his eldest son and heir, to lay claim to the throne. It was time to slough off any pretence the Yorkists were striving to free King Henry from pernicious counsellors and grasp the dynastic bull by the horns. England was ready for a new king. In the person of the nineteen-year-old earl, the Yorkists had the perfect candidate: of great height, considerable good looks, affable in manner, irresistible to women and the very image of the martial hero. Edward was a complete contrast to the unwarlike Henry. If the Earl of Warwick had failed as a field commander he had not lost his political acumen, nor had his vast energy and powerful charisma declined. While young Edward stood by to claim his inheritance, the earl manipulated and orchestrated the popular mood. The showman in Warwick excelled. In a fine flurry of spectacle, Edward was presented as king. This performance was mainly aimed at the commons, for, besides the Nevilles, his power base was alarmingly thin. Norfolk was with him and ecclesiastical support from Canterbury, Salisbury and Exeter was not lacking. Robert Fabyan described the performance:

> and upon the Sunday following the said earl [March] caused to be mustered his people in St John's Field, where unto that host were proclaimed and shewed certain articles and points that King Henry had offended in, whereupon it was demanded of the said people whether the said Henry were worthy to reign as king any longer or no. Whereunto the people cried hugely and said, Nay, Nay. And after it was asked of them if they would have the Earl of March for their king and they cried with one voice, Yes, Yea.[24]

Having abandoned any attempt on London, the Lancastrian host, like an ebb tide, receded north (doubtless to the heartfelt relief of southerners). Without securing London it was simply not possible to retain such large forces in a land already stripped of provisions. To keep her army intact, the queen now had to retreat, to seek security in the Lancastrian heartlands of the north, where her supply lines were more certain and her affinity more numerous. In so doing, Margaret surrendered the initiative, which her forces had successfully maintained since destroying York and Salisbury at Wakefield. This notwithstanding, the court party's position was by no means hopeless: Edward still had only the slimmest support from the magnates, as Robert Fabyan correctly observed when describing his entry into the city on 26 February, acclaimed by the commons but with few lords in attendance. Even Coppini – that most partisan of foreign observers – was cautious when describing these events to Duke Sforza in Milan, pointing out the Yorkists, despite their defeats in the field, were ahead in the political stakes.[25]

The country was rife with rumour and uncertainty, some of these very extravagant indeed. Prospero di Camulio, official Milanese ambassador, recounted that it was being said Margaret had poisoned her husband, the king, and was replacing him with the Duke of Somerset![26] If Edward wanted to make his throne secure he had to eliminate the Lancastrian field army and, once again, secure or eliminate the person of King Henry. Edward of Lancaster was a further dynastic impediment, who would have to be effectively corralled or removed. What was now proposed was, indeed, regime change. It remained to be seen if Edward was equal to the challenge. With his keen diplomat's eye, di Camulio summed up the situation in correspondence, opining that the new king enjoyed favour, certainly in London:

> As usual in common and great matters, opinions vary in accordance with men's passions. Those who support the claims of Edward and Warwick say that the chances in favour of Edward are great, both on account of the great lordship which he has in the island and in Ireland, and owing to the cruel wrongs done to him by the queen's side, as well as through Warwick and London, which is entirely inclined to side with the new king and Warwick, and as it is very rich and the most wealthy city of Christendom, this enormously increases the chances of the side it favours. To these must be added the good opinion of the temper and moderation of Edward and Warwick. Some, on the other hand, say that the queen is exceedingly prudent, and by remaining on the defensive, as they say she is well content to do, she will bring things into subjection and will tear to pieces these attacks of the people, who, when they perceive that they are not on the road to peace, will easily be induced to change sides . . .[27]

To give his crown any lustre of legitimacy, Edward needed an indication of God's favour. He needed the ultimate validation of trial by battle.

Chapter 5

First Blood

Let him fly that will,
I will tarry with him that will tarry with me.
Richard Neville, Earl of Warwick

The northern party made them strong
with spear and shield,
On Palm Sunday afternoon they met us in the field,
Within an hour they were right fayne to flee,
and eke to yield,
Twenty-seven-thousand The Rose killed in the field.
Blessed by the time that ever God spread that flower.[1]

Having seized the initiative handed to him, Edward, after being acclaimed by a great gathering in St John's Fields, orchestrated by Warwick, did not dally. George Neville asserts that Edward and his principal officers followed differing routes to the north. On 5 March John Mowbray, Duke of Norfolk, was sent into the eastern counties to raise his affinity. Three days later Warwick, furnished with commissions of array, departed. He was empowered to raise forces from Northamptonshire, Warwickshire, Leicestershire, Staffordshire, Worcestershire, Gloucestershire, Shropshire, Nottinghamshire, Derbyshire and Yorkshire. On 11 March Lord Fauconberg led the van north from London. His division was drawn largely from Kent, London and the Welsh marches, stiffened by the presence of seasoned captains, such as the Kentishman, Robert Horne. Edward, King of England, as we may now style him, with the main body, followed two days later.

Fauconberg's van would be a strong party. Boardman suggests that a division of forces on the march would be necessitated partly by recruiting needs and partly to avoid an excessively long baggage train. Using the accepted ratio of men to carts, he calculates that for, say 12,000 men, a train some 33km long would accrue.[2] Whether, as conceded, this ratio would apply to the Yorkist army in 1461 is questionable, as it is probable the troops carried limited rations with them – relying upon paid contractors and advance stores, together with that tricky expedient of living off the land.

Historians have hotly debated the size of the armies mustered for Towton. One thing all are able to agree upon is that these were very large indeed by contemporary standards. Scholars, quite rightly, tend to be sceptical of the figures advanced by chroniclers. Gregory's assertion that the Yorkist forces numbered some 200,000 is patently absurd. Hall, while not strictly contemporary, does claim to have had sight of the muster roll. He claims the Yorkists fielded 48,640 men, the Lancastrians significantly more – as many as 60,000[3], producing a total of over 100,000 combatants on the field. Assuming, for present purposes (and we have no particular reason to doubt that the muster rolls may have been still in existence in Hall's day), the figures given therein will not necessarily represent the number of men participating in the fighting. Sickness, desertion, outpost duty and natural wastage will have reduced these totals, possibly quite significantly.

Colonel Burne[4] adopts the strategy of looking at estimates of total population. He settles upon a likely, if uncorroborated, figure of 3.5 million people. He states the fighting age as being from fifteen to forty, yet we know from the archaeological evidence that some combatants were in their fifties, and that this would produce a pool of half a million men of military age. On this basis, Hall's total of over 100,000 in both armies represents 22 per cent of the total. From these we should subtract non-combatants and allow for wastage, reducing the numbers of Yorkists to say 36,000 and Lancastrians 40,000. On this basis, Burne accepts Hall's figures – a conclusion echoed by Haigh, who offers no further analysis.

Subsequent writers have cast doubt upon Burne's figures. It appears likely the overall population was a good deal under the figure he suggests – perhaps no more than 2.2 million. Boardman suggests the pool would have been depleted by previous losses and the inability of magnates to continually muster fresh forces. Against this is a counter-argument that the very duration of conflict would ensure additional recruits became available as men resorted to the profession of arms for their livelihoods. The wars were not uniformly English – Scots, Irish and Welsh mercenaries would serve. We know Edward had a company of Burgundian handgunners in his train.

Boardman wisely relies upon Edward IV's Act of Attainder to attempt a reconstruction of Lancastrian numbers. He allows each magnate between 2,000–3,000 fighters and the lesser gentry, 300–500 each.[5] This might produce a total of 20,000. To this should be added the urban militias, such as the 1,000 bills sent by York and various foreign mercenaries, including Scottish marchers – he suggests some 5,000 of these. This produces a total force of 25,000 men. Boardman allows Edward, Warwick and Fauconberg some 20,000 soldiers and gives Norfolk a further 5,000, thus producing parity of numbers. These arguments are entirely reasonable. How then do we reconcile these lower figures with the outwardly compelling figures given by Hall?

To begin with, Hall does not enumerate which of those on the roll are combatants and which non-combatants. He does not – clearly cannot – allow for actual wastage on campaign. Bad weather, scarce rations, a long hard winter road, will all have taken their toll. Small outposts will have been left at key locations and supply points. Somerset may have had an easier time. His army had mustered much earlier at the outset of the Wakefield campaign. Even allowing for the shrill protests of southern chroniclers, the host contained many border riders, ancestors of the Steel Bonnets of Elizabeth's day. The rapacity of the riding names cannot be denied, nor should their ability to put men in the field be underestimated. The Liddesdale raiders in the sixteenth century could put 3,000 men in the saddle at very short notice. There is no reason to suppose their grandfathers could not.

Given that the chroniclers seem agreed that the Lancastrians had more men, I am inclined to suggest Boardman's figure may be on the low side. Patrick McGill[6] suggests the following assessment of numbers for Edward's army:

- Edward's force already under arms having fought Mortimer's Cross – 8,000.
- Warwick's survivors from Second St Albans – 4,000.
- Troops mustered from the southern and eastern counties – 5,000.
- Norfolk's muster from East Anglia – 4,000.

- Warwick's additional muster from the Midlands – 5,000.
- Allowing for additional detachments coming up for the final and full muster at Doncaster the Yorkists would have a force some 30,000 strong.

All of the above is entirely speculative, but if we added to such a total second- and third-echelon troops, logistical and ragtag personnel, Hall's figure may not be that far off. Despite the advantages enjoyed by the Lancastrians it does seem incredible that they could put 60,000 combatants into the field. Even allowing for a sizeable rump of *bouches inutiles* ('useless mouths'), this is too many. Many of the marchers, having filled their saddlebags, would have slipped away northwards. Casualties in the two major battles fought may not have been made good – unlikely in that season. Men would have succumbed to cold, hunger and sickness, not to mention faintheartedness. Desertion was a major difficulty for medieval commanders and the hard campaigning since December would have thinned Lancastrian ranks. On a purely arbitrary basis, I would suggest this would have accounted for a third of the original muster, which would shrink Somerset's muster to 40,000. This is probably still too high if we consider the various garrison outposts that would have to be manned. I therefore suggest Somerset commanded a maximum of 30,000–35,000 men, his enemies 25,000–30,000 all told. Nineteenth-century writers, such as Leadman, Markham and Ransome, tend to accept Hall's figures without undue debate. Ramsay, it has to be said, does not. He views Hall's figures as a wild exaggeration and suggests the overall numbers were far less.

Advance to Contact – the March

From London and the Home Counties, Edward's contingents began the long trek north. Many of the towns and villages along the Great North Road would show signs of the recent passing, both ways, of their enemies. Even if accounts of Lancastrian depredations were part-propaganda, the reality would be severe enough. At best, every settlement would have been stripped of provisions, people already hovering on the edge of subsistence reduced to want. This is the face of medieval warfare the chroniclers generally omit. During the middle ages people in rural areas lived largely quiet lives – the very sound of an approaching army would be terrifying in itself. It mattered little whether that army was nominally friend or foe. Indiscipline and plunder were rife, the propensity to inflict violence always tangible.

If we accept a view John Gillingham advances, and Boardman concedes, that the armies marched light, the columns of tramping men and their limited following would crowd the miry roads for a distance of many miles. Each of the Yorkist divisions would probably stretch over 20km of road. We may quickly forget the idealised view of a gaudy pageant of flowing chivalry. These men, lords and commons, were very much warriors for the working day. Gentry and humbler commoners might well ride sturdy garrons or palfreys – proud, stamping destriers, led by grooms, kept fresh for the field. Much heavy harness and tentage would be carried on carts; a cloud of lightly armed mounted prickers forming eyes and ears, positioned on the front, rear and flanks of the column. The whole spectacle formed one great muddied mass, slogging and sliding through the slough in the fag end of a cold winter. Stumbling behind, traders and tapsters, sutlers, whores and pedlars, farriers, carpenters, wheelwrights, bowyers, fletchers, armourers, smiths, cooks and barber surgeons. The artillery train with ordnance carried on carts drawn by protesting, stubborn oxen – as many as three dozen beasts for a heavier piece, sappers toiling beforehand to fill in the worst of the ruts and level the steeper gradients.

Cursing, sweating, stinking, doubtless grousing – thus marched the Yorkist host. Much live flesh would follow on the hoof – cattle, sheep, goats and swine adding their ordure to the slick mess of trodden slush, up through the ravaged lands, black, bare and desolate. Edward was at pains to disassociate his faction from the lawless plunder of his enemies. His troops were ordered on pain of death to abjure the temptations of spoil. What was taken must be paid for and his coffers were well filled with coin of London merchants keen, or at least willing, to back his cause. Warwick's careful managing of Edward's acclamation had profoundly altered the dynamics of conflict. We have seen how the Yorkist affinity stumbled at Ludford when confronted with the majesty of kingship – even in the unimpressive figure of Henry VI.

Throughout, the king remained the Lord's anointed. York's feeble theatre before Members of Parliament had fallen flat and achieved nothing more than stirring the already glowing embers of Lancastrian revival after Northampton, which would end in bloody denouement at Wakefield. After that dire reverse another, even more humiliating, at Second St Albans, yet now the Yorkists had a king to fight for – as yet uncrowned, but acknowledged and certainly cast in heroic mould. Somerset faced the same problem as his predecessors in previous decades: he could determine strategy but could never fill the vacuum at the apex of the pyramid that was Henry VI. The contrast between the two contending monarchs could not be more marked. Henry was to 'sit out' the crucial battle for his throne behind the walls of York. Edward would lead his men in the field and lead them with élan. Here was a king who proved the very epitome of chivalry – an English Achilles. Resplendent in arms, formidable in the field, every inch a warrior – a perfect exemplar of the medieval hero-king.

Edward had, on 6 March, offered amnesty to any former adherent of Henry VI who submitted within ten days. Only those with an income exceeding 100 marks a year were excluded (a mark was equal to 13s 4d or roughly 67p). This, in the modern idiom, would appear to represent a 'hearts and minds' initiative aimed at winning over the commons. As a further incentive, bounties were placed on the heads of certain diehard Lancastrians. Prominent among these was the turncoat Sir Andrew Trollope, valued at one hundred pounds – a significant sum.[7] Given Sir Andrew's reputation and prowess, the fee would likely prove mighty hard in the earning.

Once the Lancastrian leaders decided on retreat from beneath the capital's walls, they surrendered the initiative. All they could do now was garner their resources and await the coming trial of arms upon ground most favourable. They possessed tactical competence but lacked charisma. They possessed no strategy other than to attend upon the convenience of their enemies. Meanwhile, in the north, bitter winter was still biting and the commissariat struggling. The bold revengers had run out of steam; hunters had become the hunted.

As cold and miserable as the northward march would be, the Yorkists would be cheered by the sight of their king in front. They no longer needed to be cajoled by the fiction they strove to rescue the rightful monarch from a cabal of bad advisors. A propagandist verse of the time, *The Rose of Rouen*, lists by reference to livery badges those magnates and gentry who mustered under Edward's banners: the Duke of Norfolk, Earl of Warwick, Lords Fauconberg, Scrope of Bolton, Grey of Ruthyn (the ballad tactfully omits reference to his treacherous volte-face at Northampton), Earl of Arundel, Viscount Bourchier, Lord Stanley, Sir William Herbert, Sir Walter Devereux, Lords Clinton and Audley (son of that Lord Audley who died leading the Lancastrians at Blore Heath),

Sir William Hastings, Sir Roger Corbett, Sir Walter Blount. Edward could also count upon contingents of urban militia drawn from the cities of Gloucester, Leicester, Northampton and Nottingham. Many other knights drawn from magnatial affinities, including the powerful Neville faction, would muster on Palmsunday Field: Sir John Wenlock, Sir John Conyers, Sir John Dinham, Sir Richard Herbert, Sir Robert Ogle, Sir James and Sir Robert Harrington (for a fuller list, please refer to Appendix II).

Edward may initially, according to de Waurin, have been beguiled by tidings that Henry VI was based no further north than Nottingham. His line of march, since leaving the capital via Bishopsgate, had followed the London Road through Barnet and St Albans, the latter still littered with the wreck of Warwick's field works. By 16 March Edward was at Barkway and, next day, entered Cambridge. There was logic in this, for Nottingham, the great Midlands fortress, was a key bastion that allowed the occupier a range of strategic options. Quite why Edward did not pass along the more direct way through Newark is unexplained: possibly recruits and/or supplies were to be found further east. John Benet's Chronicle certainly suggests that he marched via Newark.[8] Fauconberg appears to have pushed straight up Ermine Street.[9] Very probably the Yorkists needed to spread out to conserve precious victuals. When he entered Nottingham on 22 March,[10] Edward discovered his quarry had retreated further north, behind the formidable barrier of the Aire in Yorkshire, where the northern lords would be among their own affinities.

Nonetheless, this was a risky strategy. The Lancastrians were obviously not keen on giving battle, despite the Yorkist muster being incomplete. This suggests some difficulties with supply and/or morale. Yorkshire, with the ancient City of York, was the economic heart of the northern region. Further north, Durham, Northumberland and the wild upland dales simply did not have the resources to maintain so large a host. That great gap between north and south yawned so wide that to retreat into Northumberland would have been akin to disappearing from the map. Yorkshire was economically viable – a Lancastrian heartland containing the second city of the realm. Here Henry could create the semblance of a court while he awaited his general's success in arms. Both sides realised that this must be the decisive throw. Battles had grown bigger and bloodier since the fracas of First St Albans. Neither faction could hope to maintain such large forces in the field indefinitely, even with spring around the corner. For both it was time to do or to die.

King Henry, even if he had surrendered the initiative, still commanded a far more impressive list of peers. Though no Lancastrian poet has left us such a neat summary as to be found in the lines of *The Rose of Rouen*, the subsequent Yorkist Act of Attainder lists those who forfeited their estates in consequence of defeat. The Duke of Somerset was joined by the Duke of Exeter (quarrelsome Henry Holand), the Earls of Devon and Northumberland, Viscount Beaumont, Lord Roos, Lord Clifford, Lord Dacre, Lord Neville, Lord Willoughby, Lord Rougemont Grey. The slippery Earl of Wiltshire is also likely to have been present, along with a host of northern gentry: Sir Philip Wentworth, Sir William Tailboys, Sir Thomas Findern, Sir Nicholas Latimer, Sir Richard and Sir Ralph Percy, brothers of the Earl of Northumberland (all three of whom would perish before peace was restored to the north in 1464).

Sir Andrew Trollope and his brother Sir David were also present. The former, since his defection at Ludford, had performed a chief of staff role for the Lancastrians and informed their subsequent victories at Wakefield and Second St Albans. To his supporters Henry VI – the least martial of monarchs – was still the rightful king, and one whose son was thus rightful heir. The north was, by and large, solidly Lancastrian and the army had a secure base in the northern capital. This array of proud and vengeful lords remained undefeated in the field.

Precise details of the march north, once Edward quit Nottingham, are sparse. It is possible Warwick came up there, as did most of the urban contingents. Fauconberg, with the van, was likely over the Trent, marching past Newark, aiming for Doncaster. At some point on the road north the main elements of the Yorkist army were united. John Benet states that the Earl of Warwick moved via Lichfield to Doncaster. Warwick, at Coventry, had earlier achieved the satisfaction of accounting for at least one notable target of his vengeance – the Bastard of Exeter, whom he held responsible for his father's ignominious taking off after Wakefield. As ever with Richard Neville, justice was swift and summary.[11] As Andrew Boardman points out, this may have served as a useful stimulus for Yorkist recruiting! Both sides could claim to have the weight of legal opinion on their side. The Lord Chief Justice, Sir John

Fortescue, was with Henry VI, though two eminent lawyers – his future successor, John Markham and Sir Guy Fairfax of Steetham – were in Edward's train.[12]

Doncaster was on the fringe of enemy territory. The more comfortable recruiting grounds of the south and east were being left behind. From here the army must be marshalled and made ready for the fight – no easy matter with so large a host comprising so many differing companies. The Duke of Norfolk, with his division, was lagging behind. In the febrile climate of this internecine conflict a taint of treachery would ever linger in the shadows, though clearly the man was desperately ill with an unspecified, terminal illness. Norfolk was not, in fact an old man, being only thirty-seven.[13] Next goal was Pontefract, fortress gateway to the north, which the army entered on 27 March, making camp on Bubwith Heath, off the Knottingly Road.[14]

Never had England witnessed such a vast array. Likely never such ill-tempered confusion, as crimson-faced sergeants bellowed themselves hoarse. It is one thing to organise an army for marching, the complex web of logistics needed to keep such a host moving and fed, supplied and billeted, small beer and rations for the men, fodder for horses and livestock. Generals take credit for victories but battles are as much won by unsung commissaries, whose exertions deliver men onto the ground in a fit state to wield their arms. Dysentery and typhus regularly stalked medieval armies. Sanitation would always be a major problem. Merely ensuring sufficient latrines for say, 30,000 men, would constitute a Herculean endeavour of its own.

In York, Somerset was making his dispositions to meet the inevitable onslaught. Recruiting, after the earlier triumph at Second St Albans, may have been encouraging, though since the march north to the Aire it would have been nigh on impossible to keep so vast a host under arms. Many would have returned home, others remained billeted around the area. The royal family were safely lodged in York. Andrew Boardman[15] feels Lancastrian morale would still be high – I am less certain. They enjoyed superior numbers and would fight on ground of their choosing, in the heart of their affinities, yet the more seasoned would understand the magnitude of their failure before the walls of London. There they could have won back the kingdom in a day. Such gifts are offered but once in war and, once rejected, submerge for good. The initiative, which they'd won and then maintained, had been squandered by a king manifestly unsuited to rule. They would be aware of how compelling, in personal terms, the new contender appeared; for despite his youth, Edward was a proven commander, charismatic and vigorous – it is possible they felt the cold breath of destiny blow upon their faces.

Queen Margaret, in habitual bellicose and bloodthirsty mode, gave thanks there were additional spaces atop Micklegate Bar to accommodate more Yorkist heads. John Gillingham argues[16] that the queen may have felt, as at least one contemporary correspondent confirms, that she could afford to stand on the defensive, maintaining the Lancastrian position till the gloss wore off the would-be usurper and the populace reverted to their established allegiance. Wars, however, are generally won by action rather than merely waiting upon a favourable turn of events. Her officers would be consumed by more pragmatic concerns. They too had an army to marshal. Here, the Lancastrians did have a sure advantage. Their army, for the most part, had already fought as a cohesive force and the sergeants would thus have an easier task. York was a secure base and depot. Supply would probably not present insuperable difficulties, though the northern counties produced little to spare and winter's tentacles still bound fast.

Moreover, the army plainly held elements from both sides of the border marches. These wild hobilars from the upland dales were not inspired by notions of discipline and would heed no orders other than from their chiefs or 'heidmen'. Later accounts from the Flodden campaign in 1513 would confirm that these borderers were usually considered as great a menace to their own side as the foe! Advancing from York to Tadcaster, the Duke of Somerset ordered his muster on the gentle plateau that swells between the villages of Towton and Saxton, tents and bothies crowding behind the formidable barrier of the River Aire. It can hardly have been a congenial billet – bare upland cut by icy winds. The Lancastrians may have slighted the bridge across the Wharfe after they passed over (though this may have occurred later in the rout), following the Old London Road beyond the Cock Beck. We might wonder how many paid this seemingly innocuous burn much heed.

The Battle of Ferrybridge

Safely across the Don, the Yorkists, by Friday 27 March, were drawing close to Ferrybridge. The weather continued inclement but it was imperative to seize a bridgehead over the Aire. John Radcliffe, Lord

Fitzwalter, attempted to take the crossing by a bold coup de main. *Hearne's Fragment* asserts that Fitzwalter sent his 'foreprickers' to lead the assault.[17] It seems clear his assault drove back the defenders, if indeed there were any posted, and though the bridge had been slighted, it was not completely destroyed. By the end of that wet, blustery Friday, planks had been replaced and the Yorkists gained a foothold on the farther bank. Temporary repairs sound more convincing, given the time available, than the construction of a pontoon bridge. George Neville, when writing to the Papal Legate Coppini, does suggest the crossing had been guarded:

> Our adversaries had broken the bridge which was our way across, and were strongly posted on the other side, so that our men could only cross by a narrow way which they had made themselves after the bridge was broken. But our men forced a way by the sword, and many were slain on both sides.[18]

This suggests a hotly contended crossing, but George Neville may be conflating the events of the following day into one description of the overall action. Haigh is of the view that the bridge was defended, though he placed Warwick in charge of the first assault, which does not seem right, unless he merely implies Fitzwalter served within the earl's affinity.[19] If the Yorkists had seen off a body of defenders then this might explain their apparent laxity in failing to send out patrols. It might also explain why Clifford's men were detailed to mount a counter-attack. John Clifford, 9th Baron, has had a poor press. Known at the time as 'Black Faced Clifford' and latterly as the 'Butcher', this pejorative view might derive from a history written by his enemies. His family had a long record of service. From Norman stock, the baronetcy was created in 1299 and the 1st Baron acted as Earl Marshal, doing stout service in the Scottish Wars of Edward I, before falling at Bannockburn in 1314. John Clifford's grandfather, of the same name, was Henry Hotspur's son-in-law and saw much action in the French campaigns of Henry V. The Clifford affinity – 'the Flower of Craven' – were always deemed to be something of an élite force:

> Of hardy mountaineers, the flower and pride
> of Westmorland, and Craven's rough domains
> There by his side, in many a toilsome march
> and furious skirmish, did they win their way.[20]

Now seemingly secure on the northern side, the Yorkist attackers were themselves vigorously assailed in the pallid light of dawn by a commanded party of their enemies, led by Clifford and Sir John Neville with 500 picked troops. Fitzwalter, together with Warwick's bastard brother, Sir Richard Jenny, were cut down in the mêlée. Fitzwalter, on hearing the commotion as the 'Flower of Craven' swirled out of the gloom, thought his fellows were brawling among themselves and dashed from his billet, polearm in hand, intending to restore order. Hall provides a vivid account of the fray:

> The Lord Fitzwalter hearing the noise, suddenly rose out of his bed, and unarmed, with a poleaxe in his hand, thinking that it had been an affray amongst his men, came down to appease the same, but before he could say a word, or knew what the matter was, he was slain, and with him the bastard of Salisbury, brother to the Earl of Warwick, a valiant young gentleman, and of great audacity.[21]

Gregory's Chronicle has Warwick himself in the thick of the fight, leading the rearguard and wounded in the thigh by an arrow. Tactical success, however, rested with Clifford and by noon the earl, with his battered survivors, was explaining the debacle to Edward at Pontefract. It is possible the Kingmaker was distinctly 'wobbly' at this point, suffering one of those crises that beset him when confronted with the unexpected. It is probably at this moment that Hall accredits the earl with the histrionic gesture of killing his horse to indicate there would be no further retreat. This smacks of theatre, though Warwick knew well how to pull an audience. If his lieutenant did waver, the young monarch was made of sterner stuff. Edward's instinctive and sure grasp of tactics, presumably boosted by sage advice from the veteran Fauconberg, dictated an immediate riposte. Hall recounts the earl's conduct in a suitably melodramatic passage:

> When the Earl of Warwick was informed of this feat [the destruction of Fitzwalter by Clifford], he like a man desperate, mounted on his hackney, and came blowing to King Edward saying 'Sir I pray God have mercy on their souls, which in the beginning of your enterprise hath lost their lives, and because I see no success of the world, I remit the vengeance and punishment to God our creator and redeemer' and with that he

alighted down and slew his horse with his sword, saying 'Let him fly that will, for surely I will tarry with him that will tarry with me' and he kissed the cross hilt of his sword.[22]

A question arises as to whether Clifford's raid reflects an element of defined strategy or mere opportunism dictated by individual energy. Hall comments upon this and, for all we should have reservations concerning his account given the three score years and ten which had passed, offers a tantalising insight:

> Let no man think or yet imagine, that either the council of King Henry, or his vigilant queen, either neglected nor forgot to know or search what their enemies did, but that they prepared to their power all the men they either could persuade or allure to their purpose to take their part. And thus thinking themselves furnished, committed the governance of the army to the Duke of Somerset, the Earl of Northumberland and the Lord Clifford, as men desiring to revenge the death of their fathers slain at the first Battle of St Albans. These noble captains, leaving King Henry, his wife and son for their safeguard in the City of York, passed the River Wharfe, with all their power, intending to prohibit King Edward to pass over the river Aire, and for the more expedition and exploit of their purpose (after many comparisons were made between the Earl of Northumberland and the Lord Clifford both being lusty in youth and of frank courage) the Lord Clifford determined with his light horsemen, to make an assault to such as kept the passage of Ferrybridge, and so departed from the great army on the Saturday [28 March] before Palm Sunday and early before his enemies were awake got the bridge, and slew the keepers of the same, and all such as would withstand him.[23]

This suggests a measure of rivalry between the Lancastrian officers – perhaps not unexpected among such ardent exponents of chivalry, but leads us to enquire whether Clifford was acting independently or in pursuit of agreed tactical aims? At the date of the battle he was twenty-six years of age, Northumberland, his alleged rival in arms, fourteen years older – a significant gap[24] and one that places the earl firmly, by the standards of the day, in his middle years. If the bridge had been garrisoned and that force beaten back, then to reassert a Lancastrian grip on the north bank and to continue and deny the crossing to the

Yorkists was tactically sound. If Clifford, as he was to demonstrate, could fight a delaying action and inflict loss upon the enemy, obliging them to waste men and resources at modest cost, this brought clear and tangible gain to the Lancastrians – weakening their enemies by slowing them down, forcing them to fight minor actions at a disadvantage would erode their strength prior to a general engagement. The assertion that Clifford was subsequently 'written off' by his fellow commanders most probably does them a grave disservice. Clifford's end was almost certainly occasioned by the action of a wilier opponent rather than internal jealousies.

Meanwhile, Jean de Waurin offers an alternative scenario and, though scholars have their doubts as to the veracity and reliability of his account, we must recognise him as a contemporary source who should be consulted:

> and as soon as they [the Yorkists] had made camp the Duke of Suffolk [at that point Sir John de la Pole] sent a small company to find out the strength of the enemy, but they went so far forward that a guard saw them and raised the alarm. This small party was in so much danger of being routed that the Earl of March had to send reinforcements for his reconnaissance troops. They managed to push the enemy back to the bridge where they formed a defensive line. When the Earl of March heard about this he ordered all his council and troops to move closer to the enemy, and after he had made a new camp he went to see the situation with his commanders.[25]

De Waurin goes on to relate that after a personal reconnaissance Edward, realising the importance of the crossing, ordered an all out attack on the bridge 'which had been fortified by the enemy'. According to the chronicler the fight raged from noon till 6 p.m. and 3,000 fell, so fierce was the contest. It is possible that both Hall and de Waurin are correct but that the latter has missed the fact the action consisted of two distinct fights. The first on 27 March, when the Yorkists won the bridge (with relative ease) and the second, next day, when the crossing was again denied them by Clifford, who held back the whole of the Yorkist army till evening.

This seems more coherent. With Fitzwalter fatally wounded and his survivors driven out (a classic example on Clifford's part of beating up enemy quarters), Edward, having steadied Warwick and any others who had taken fright, launched a series of planned assaults intended to wrest back the crossing. The Flower of Craven more than lived up to their reputation for toughness and, having barricaded the northern bank, used the ground to good advantage. This was a tactical situation where a few bold, well placed soldiers could hold back an army. The narrow confines of the crossing offered Edward no opportunity to bring weight of numbers to bear. Most chroniclers appear in agreement that the fighting was hard and costly – Yorkist attackers met with keen-edged bills, enfiladed by bows on both flanks. Against such redoubtable opposition frontal attacks would produce only more corpses – the bridge already groaning under the mounting pile of dead and wounded. Many of the latter, falling into the water's icy embrace, would swiftly succumb. Another expedient was required. What could not be won by force might be gained by guile. As reported by Dr Leadman, traces of skeletons and accoutrement were said to have been unearthed around the crossing, yielded by the wet ground of Brotherton Marsh, presumably having been found in the course of early nineteenth-century drainage works. The provenance of these remains is, however, uncertain, as traces may date from a later engagement in the Civil Wars.

Butcher at Bay – Dintingdale

Warwick was ordered to remain at Ferrybridge and continue pinning Clifford to the crossing. Fauconberg would lead a strong flanking movement, bolstered by the support of fellow veterans Sir Richard Blount and Robert Horne, splashing through the swollen but passable ford, 3 miles upstream at Castleford. Clifford might, in turn, be surprised when the Yorkists descended on his right flank. Nonetheless, the 'Butcher' must have known of the crossing at Castleford and the possibility his flank might be turned. That he should be forced to retreat was, at some point, inevitable and he would trust in the steadiness of his men to manage an orderly withdrawal.

Somerset's apparent inertia at this crucial juncture is hard to fathom. Bad weather and poor communications played their part but it was clearly vital to deny the Yorkists passage of the Aire for as long as possible. His failure to reinforce Clifford remains unexplained. As an opinion, I would suggest that Clifford was conforming to orders and that his force was never intended to do more than create a delay. In this they had performed admirably. Once threatened they would withdraw in good order, being mounted this should not place them in undue peril.

Clifford's failing was not one of poor generalship as some writers, notably Cyril Ransome, have asserted. His misfortune was that he was facing a nimble and skilled opponent in Lord Fauconberg who, as Hall confirms, was 'a man of great policy and much experience of martial feats'. This wily old Yorkist got the better of the Lancastrian lord by springing a rather neat ambush of his own. As the two forces scrimmaged along the main route north towards Towton, with the Yorkist van harrying their quarry, Clifford and Neville may have been confident of their ability to stave off defeat till they reached the safety of their own vedettes. The rather enigmatic assertion by Hall that they then 'met with some that they looked not for' suggests something went badly wrong with this assumption and that their destruction was unexpected rather than inevitable. This also goes some way to explaining why the Flower of Craven was not reinforced. Perhaps Somerset was confident Clifford and Neville could hold their own and act out their orders without reinforcement.

What, then, went so badly wrong for the Lancastrians? Here, and once again, we digress into the area of speculation. To afford this a professional gloss we might revert to Colonel Burne's handy theory of 'inherent military probability'. It is possible that on reaching Ferrybridge and setting off after his quarry, Fauconberg detached a party to ride fast along the old Roman high road, running parallel and to the west, then swerving through Saxton to interdict the line of Clifford's retreat at Dintingdale. It was this ambush that finished the Flower of Craven. Such a manoeuvre in the snow-laden dusk of a cold spring evening must have been fraught with peril and brought the ambush party perilously close to the Lancastrian line. How their scouts could have missed such a large formation seems remarkable. Yet this may be what occurred and Clifford was caught completely unawares by so bold an initiative.

At Dintingdale the Westmorland men made their final stand. Clifford fell to an archer when, it is said, he injudiciously removed his bevor to slake a raging thirst. Legend insists the fatal shaft was a headless bodkin, which might have just ricocheted from his harness. Many of Clifford's fellowship died with him. The dead Lancastrian lord left a young heir, barely seven years of age and who lived to fight against the Scots at Flodden over half a century later. Sir John Neville, brother to the Earl of Westmorland, Warwick's great-uncle, who, according to Davies, was credited with misleading the Duke of York prior to the Battle of Wakefield, perished in the extended skirmish. Few of Clifford's affinity seem to have escaped.

> Lord Fauconberg, Sir Walter Blount, Robert Horne with the forward, passed the river at Castleford two miles from Ferrybridge intending to have environed and enclosed the Lord Clifford and his company, but they being thereof advertised, departed in great haste toward King Henry's army but they met with some that they looked not for, and were attraped [*sic*] before they were aware. For the Lord Clifford, either from heat or pain, put off his gorget, was suddenly hit by an arrow, as some say, without a head and was stricken in the throat, and incontinent rendered his spirit. And the Earl of Westmorland's brother and all his company almost were slain, at a place called Dintingdale, not far from Towton.[26]

Andrew Boardman concludes, after a detailed analysis of the sources, that the bridge was broken down by the retreating Lancastrians and left unguarded. I disagree with this. I find the chronicle evidence that the bridge was garrisoned persuasive. Fitzwalter's pioneer company seized the ruined crossing and repaired, at least in part, the damage. They, in turn, were taken unawares the next dawn by Clifford. After Warwick, learning of the reverse, had confirmed the loss to Edward, the king immediately moved strong forces to wrest back the contested crossing. What then ensued was a desperate and hard-fought encounter wherein Warwick and Edward both fought in the mêlée, the former being wounded in the thigh by a chance arrow. Clifford, with the narrow ground in his favour, denied the attackers any advantage for several hours. Realising that his head-on assault was at risk of proving a costly failure, Edward ordered Fauconberg to mount his flank attack via Castleford. Clifford then attempted to disengage, retreating back to his own lines, but was overwhelmed by elements of the Yorkists' mounted van, which had outflanked his line of retreat.[27]

A question arises as to whether Clifford was simply abandoned by his comrades who, depending upon the exact location of the Lancastrian encampment at this stage, may have had a grandstand view of his destruction, or whether his force was wholly out of view. It seems incredible that, whatever jealousies may have obtained between the headstrong Clifford and his fellow commanders, they would allow him to be decimated in front of their lines without raising a finger. The effect on morale may easily be imagined. It seems more likely that, in the fog of war, the danger to Clifford and the Flower of Craven was not immediately obvious to their comrades and that the slaughter was enacted before a relief could be mounted. For the trapped Lancastrians, harried virtually to within sight of safety, this must have been a bitter conclusion. They had fought all day against great odds and held their ground with honour, but now, as the freezing blanket of darkness arrived to cloak their retreat, the Yorkist prickers and mounted archers were swarming around them like vengeful hornets.[28] We may assume the Flower of Craven sold their lives dearly, bunched around the body of their revered leader like the housecarls of old.

With the way cleared, his enemies discomfited and motionless, Edward led the bulk of the army towards Castleford and the crossing there. By dusk the Yorkists were safely over the last significant river obstacle between them and the Lancastrians. A major trial of arms was now imminent and unavoidable. Edward's prickers were as far forward as Saxton but the baggage was left behind at Ferrybridge, so the Yorkist army, as it straggled in tired columns, would be faced with a cold and hungry bivouac. George Neville, in his letter to Francesco Coppini, Bishop of Terni and Papal Legate, confirms that:

> The King, the valiant Duke of Norfolk, my brother aforesaid and my uncle, Lord Fauconberg, travelling by different routes, finally united with all their companies and armies near the country round York [. . .] Our adversaries had broken the bridge which was our way across, and were strongly posted on the other side, so that our men could only cross by a narrow way which they had made themselves after the bridge was broken. But our men forced a way by the sword, and many were slain on both sides. Finally the enemy took to flight, and very many of them were slain as they fled.[29]

Chapter 6

Trial by Battle

For what is in this world but grief and woe?
King Henry VI Third Part; Act 2, scene v

As previously described, the ground past Towton rises gently to form a low plateau, the climb barely perceptible except to the west, where there is a steep decline into the valley of the Cock Beck. This dale was probably more densely forested in the fifteenth century – a tangle of scrub, alder and birch, poorly drained. To the south-west, up beyond Bloody Meadow, the rise becomes more noticeable, still topped by the stand of timber named Castle Hill Wood. The swell is neatly bisected by the lateral depression of Towton Dale, which itself slopes into what was, at that time, a marshy gully. The accepted position adopted by the Lancastrians on the day of the battle was along the crown of the ridgeline, north of the dale, immediately to the south of the present monument. It was necessary, therefore, for the Yorkists to deploy on the higher ground to the south. It has, nonetheless, been suggested that Somerset's men might have advanced some 300 metres south, leaving Towton Dale in their rear. I shall return to this. The duke was certainly not blind to the potential for ambush offered by Castle Hill Wood and concealed a strong party beneath the lee of the trees, still bare and stark against lowering skies. The upland landscape, in this early season, stood desolate – a patchwork of small fields and heath, the sky laden with the promise of yet more snow.

The Eve of Battle

Upon the King! – let us our lives, our souls,
Our debts, our careful wives, our children, and
Our sins lay on the king!
King Henry V; Act 4, scene i

Until Clifford's final and bloody end at Dintingdale, the Lancastrians had done rather well throughout 28 March. The Flower of Craven had successfully beaten up Fitzwalter's detachment, secured the Aire crossing and denied the bulk of the Yorkist army for some hours, inflicting loss. Fauconberg's swift action cancelled out this gain. The Yorkists, by dusk, might be said to have done somewhat better overall. They had forced their way over the Aire and had, at some cost, eliminated a leading opponent with most of his affinity. Throughout the day Norfolk's division had not come up. In part, this must have been due to the poor state of the duke's health. The man had little more than half a year to live. Andrew Boardman speculates that the artillery train may have travelled with Norfolk and the exertion of dragging great guns over bad roads may, and indeed most certainly would have, contributed to a slow rate of progress. This is both persuasive and logical, though we hear nothing from the chroniclers to corroborate it. Indeed, guns are not mentioned at all, nor has any remnant of shot been unearthed from the field. The Lancastrians, with greater leisure and only a nominal distance to march must, we might ponder, have brought guns with them but we find no evidence for their being on the field.

As the Yorkists finally began to filter across at Ferrybridge in late afternoon of the 28th, the three main divisions or battles of their army marched apart following the old dictum *march divided, fight united.* Boardman suggests – and this seems entirely reasonable[1] – that the van, so ably deployed by Fauconberg, sought their bivouac on the gentle ridge upon which the (now deserted) village of Lead stood, extending as far east as Saxton. Here they were no distance from the bulk of their foes at Towton and the rival outposts must easily have been within hailing distance. Did banter and abuse pass between sentinels in that long, cold night? Cold it certainly was and likely the men had little shelter. Such comfortable billets as might be found were reserved, in timeless manner, for the officers. Accounts of other battles, such as the Scots' chroniclers writing of the eve of the main action on the second day of Bannockburn, speak of much drinking in the English lines. It is likely the eve of Towton was very similar.

Cold and apprehension would have prevented many from finding rest, though others would be so exhausted that sleep came on regardless. It is questionable whether Edward and Warwick slept much.

Boardman and other writers have pointed to the great burden resting on the young man's shoulders – leading the largest army his affinity could ever raise. Defeat would be fatal to his cause. He had done remarkably well in a short time, defeating his enemies at Mortimer's Cross and, with his cousin, restoring Yorkist fortunes after the twin disasters of Wakefield and Second St Albans. His coolness during the 28th had overcome a very ticklish situation and this calm decisiveness appears to contrast favourably with Warwick's penchant for histrionics. The Tudor chroniclers no doubt strove to formulate as accurate an account as they could but the fact Edward was Henry VIII's grandfather was not one they could easily afford to overlook.

The young king would have no illusions as to the magnitude of the challenge facing him. Troops were tired and probably hungry, cold and with many dead and wounded during the day's fighting. Through the chill night, surgeons would ply their trade, setting fractured limbs, stitching wounds and providing the solace of drink for those past help. Young men, unaccustomed to war and its attendant horrors, would be seeing sights, hearing sounds that nothing in their previous experience could have equipped them for. Many would suffer unwelcome reactions to their first taste of battle – knees weak and bowels loose. Across the empty upland – civilians, for the most part, having fled – camp fires burned through the hours of darkness, flames swirling in bitter gusts. These men and women on both sides of the plateau were about to write a famous chapter in English history, though they'd certainly be more focused on chilled limbs and empty bellies.

Edward's affinity was very slim compared to the fellowship of peers beneath King Henry's banners. Andrew Boardman[2] feels this conferred a tactical advantage in that the Yorkists were thus less prone to fissiparous tendencies. I am less convinced. That men fought beneath the banner of their lord, to whom they were already tied by feudal obligation or contract, may have had an opposite effect, adding the cohesion of familiarity. The commons might draw comfort from the rightness of Henry's cause to see so many magnates serving. Conversely, Edward had the charisma. Did he, like Henry V on the eve of Agincourt, tour the scattered bivouacs to show the huddled commons a glimpse of his majesty – a 'touch of Harry in the night'?[3] Very possibly he did. Everything we know about Edward shows him to have been the leading captain of his age. Those hedonistic traces that sometimes characterised his attitude during peacetime vanished in the urgency of war. Commanding in the field, he was very much in his natural element – the epitome of chivalry. Whether he could deliver victory remained to be proven.

> Now entertain conjecture of a time
> When creeping murmur and the poring dark
> Fills the wide vessel of the universe.
> From camp to camp, through the foul womb of night
> The hum of either army stilly sounds. That the fix'd sentinels
>   almost receive
> The secret whispers of each other's watch . . .
>
> *King Henry V; Act 3, scene vi*

Early Morning: the Armies Deploy

Six o'clock in the morning, 29 March, Palm Sunday. Cold, dank, pallid sunlight filtered through leaden skies. Soon, sleet and hail were falling, 'and all the while it snew' (snowed).[4]

To marshal the vast Yorkist host, scattered over so many hasty bivouacs, was no simple chore. To drag men from a few hours' fitful rest, cold rations and small beer for those that had the stomach would leave sergeants amply warmed by their exertions, red-faced and bellowing. Simply to move so large a body of men, with all their accoutrement, towards the battleground and order their deployment was an enormous logistical undertaking. This fight would not erupt as a chance encounter, or bickering of outposts drawing in a steady chain of reinforcements, nor would it be swift or sudden. Both armies would marshal and march to the field, shuffle out their deployment and await their enemy.

As sombre priests moved before assembled companies, men knelt to take a scrap of earth in their mouths. Imminence of mortality is a powerful incentive to piety and no medieval soldier would draw steel before making due and proper obeisance. Waurin again provides a distinct view of the events that occurred in the run-up to the battle. The chronicler asserts that it was only after the army had broken camp that Yorkist scouts reported the enemy's advance:

> When the [King] and his lords were told that King Henry was nearby in the fields they rejoiced, for they wished for nothing

more but to fight him. The [King] called for his captains and told
them to put their men in formation and to take their positions
before the enemy came to close. And so it was he organised his
battles, and he sent some men to look around the area because
they were only 4 miles from the enemy.[5]

As the Yorkists toiled up the slope from Saxton they would have
remained out of sight of their enemies deployed on the farther ridge.[6]
While Towton is a battle where most commentators, rather unusually,
are in accord as to the location of the main action, Ramsay advances a
contrary view. He chooses to place the Lancastrian van along the
leading edge of the southern ridge.[7] As Burne observes,[8] this
produces a frontage of no more than 800 yards. This is far too narrow,
and while we can readily accept that Somerset might plant patrols here
for ease of observation, his main line must have lain some 700 yards
further north. It is true that this would not provide so sweeping a
panorama but was strongly posted with flanks well anchored.
Obviously, Lancastrian vedettes would give ample notice of the
enemy's approach. Indeed, the vast noise occasioned by the tramp of
over 20,000 men would be a most powerful intimation in itself. It is
possible these elements of Henry's vanguard formed the ambush party
hiding in Castle Wood – a neat ploy with men well placed to intervene
at a critical point. Ramsay bases his assumption of a more southerly
Lancastrian deployment on a belief there were far fewer combatants
overall than the chroniclers assert and most modern authorities
accept.[9] He has the Yorkists attacking uphill and the Lancastrians
largely motionless, attending upon the southerners' convenience. As
the lines collide, both armies lay on manfully with, in Gregory's words,
'mallys of ledde [lead mauls] [. . .] swyrdys [swords], gleyvys [glaives]
and axys'.[10]

To leave his right resting upon the edge of the steep decline was an
obvious deployment for Somerset. It is likely, as Burne suggests,[11] that
his left reached across the Ferrybridge road towards the other slope, to
a point where encroaching bog and moss provided protection. Burne
notes the lower portion is some 500 yards from the road and he allows
the Lancastrians the top 200, giving them a total frontage of 1,300 yards
or, if the van numbered 10,000–12,000 men, a space of ten men per
yard.[12] The colonel is here applying his theory of inherent military
probability – one that finds little favour with modern academic writers

but, as the chroniclers are vague in the extreme, IMP offers at least a logical variant on speculation.

With Henry's banners planted on the northern ridge, the Yorkists would inevitably deploy along the more southerly. There is debate as to whether the armies marshalled in linear formation or in line astern. Burne argues for the latter[13] and is supported in this by Haigh.[14] It is generally accepted that Fauconberg commanded the Yorkist van or front line with Warwick in the centre and Edward leading the rearward. Across Towton Vale, Trollope with Northumberland took the Lancastrian van. Trollope at some point, however, becomes detached, as it appears he led the ambush party. Dacre and Lord Welles[15] led the middle, Exeter and Somerset the rear. A glance at the map will confirm this must indeed be the case. To bunch the men into dense columns arrayed in line would have been nonsensical – ranked formations would permit fresh men to be rotated through the line. Contrary to what subsequent film depictions may show, a harnessed man can sustain the fight for perhaps ten to fifteen minutes at best: thereafter tiredness will compel him to halt. If we accept the chroniclers view that this battle lasted up to ten hours (or even half that), then clearly such constant rotation was required.

If we look to de Waurin's version, it was by no means certain in the early morning that the armies would fight upon the plateau. Edward was not fully apprised of his enemy's dispositions till prickers returned from scouting:

> They did not go very far before they spotted the reconnaissance party from the enemy, and they quickly returned to the Earl of March to tell him that they had seen large numbers of men-at-arms in the fields and the banners of King Henry. They told him how the enemy was manoeuvring and their position, and when the earl was warned of this, he went to his cavalry, which he had positioned on the wing and said to them 'My children, I pray today that we shall be good and loyal to each other because we are fighting for a good cause!' After they had all echoed this thought a messenger came to tell the earl that the vaward troops of the king had started to move forward and the earl went back to place himself behind his banners.[16]

It may be this that informs Ramsay's view that the Lancastrians had occupied the more southerly ridge, though given the proximity of

Fauconberg's division it is more likely that it was his outposts that gave warning of the advance. Andrew Boardman advances the intriguing possibility[17] that the armies were further apart than suggested. It is possible the Yorkists had pushed no further north than Sherburn-in-Elmet, while the Lancastrians remained at Tadcaster because King Henry was averse to fighting on a holy day.[18] This would mean the gap between Edward's vanguard and main body was considerably greater and the approach march would thus take longer. Both armies would therefore have several hours' march. It seems generally agreed that the opening clashes on the field did not occur till late morning, which allows both some four or five hours of marching time.

Boardman cites Hall,[19] whose account clearly implies the Lancastrians were not in force astride the southern ridge line and the armies were hidden from each other during the Yorkist approach – be this from the immediate vicinity or further back towards Sherburn. As ever, we come up against the difficulty that Hall, writing so long after the event, is not truly a primary source, though we have no specific reason to doubt the veracity of his account. He suggests both armies were deploying on the plateau by 9 a.m. The Lancastrians, if they were bivouacked around Towton, had more time and with such wily professionals as Trollope to advise, Somerset had ample time to choose the best ground. He did not, as we have seen, neglect the potential of Castle Hill Wood on his right.

From wherever they approached it would not be till the Yorkists had ascended this lip of the plateau that they got their first glimpse of the truly formidable array that now confronted them. Even with biting wind and driven flurries, the strength of their opponents would have been immediately obvious. Now there was bright panoply of war – silken banners unfurled and harness gleaming, breaks in the sleet showing the massed rows of bills. It would have been a daunting sight – the most crowded field in England's long catalogue. It was to be a battle, yet also it was a vendetta, a blood feud between the scions of the noble families on both sides of the dale. All had lost fathers, brothers, cousins and friends to the bloodlust of the other. Those rotting skulls of the Duke of York, Salisbury and Rutland still fed the crows, the blood of St Albans and Northampton heavy on the minds of the Lancastrian lords. The commons took their cue from the magnates – many of lesser blood might also have left family dead on earlier fields.

Polydore Vergil[20] suggests the Lancastrians were laggardly in their approach and the Yorkist advance obliged them to move rather more smartly. Boardman, rightly in my view, rejects this. It would have been difficult to slip a strong unit of ambushers into Castle Hill Wood had the Lancastrians been scrabbling to keep pace with their more energetic opponents. Both sides were cramped, so great was the press of men. Outwardly it appears that the Yorkists had the better position, though in fact this was not necessarily so. The drop into Bloody Meadow was effectively dead ground and offered little opportunity for their bows. Assuming we can discern Trollope's vastly experienced eye behind the Lancastrian deployment, he had chosen well. Their line was perfectly sited for defence and if the archers had thrust a line of stakes in front, in the usual way, this would have added a formidable barrier.

The obvious strength of the Lancastrian position may explain why Edward was in no hurry to unleash an offensive. His men were almost certainly outnumbered with Norfolk's division still some distance behind. Boardman suggests the king, with Warwick, took station in the centre, while it seems universally agreed Fauconberg led the van. Other writers place Edward in command of the rearguard – a substantial reserve bolstered by mounted skirmishers. In reality, it is most likely that Edward, surrounded by his household men, formed a strong company that moved across the field to shore up the line wherever pressure was greatest. Fauconberg's was the first Yorkist division to sight the enemy, strongly posted in front to cover the deployment of the main battle and rear. Whether the advancing columns, as they marshalled into line, comprised companies of bows, bills and men-at-arms placed alternately, or whether the archers stepped to the front as distinct missile troops is unclear. Andrew Boardman suggests the van was entirely composed of a mass of bowmen;[21] IMP and the subsequent fall of events would tend to support this view and I wholeheartedly concur.

Late Morning: the Archery Duel

As the hosts were marshalled into line, between ten and eleven in the morning, a brisk shower of dense rain and sleet gusted over the field, chased by a strong southerly wind. This blew hail directly into the faces of the Lancastrians, obscuring their vision. Fauconberg, his veteran's eye quick to discern possibilities, bade his bowmen advance and loose, shooting at extreme range but with the scurrying wind to lend wings to their flights: 'notch, draw, loose . . .' The shafts found their mark and the Lancastrians shot in reply, but they loosed into empty ground some 40 metres short, the Yorkist archers having now smartly stepped back. Capitalising on his success, the wily Fauconberg repeated this tactic, returning his adversaries' shafts back into their own ranks. Hall describes Fauconberg's initiative:

> The Lord Fauconberg, which led the forward of King Edward's battle being a man of great policy and much experience in martial feats caused every archer under his standard to shoot one flight and then made them stand still. The northern men, feeling the shoot, but by reason of the snow, not perfectly viewing the distance between them and their enemies like hardy men shot their sheaf arrows as fast as they might, but all their shot was lost and their labour in vain for they came not near the southern men by 40 tailors yards.[22]

Such an exchange of missiles frequently dictated the outcome of the fight for the losing side: that suffering the greatest loss was left with no alternative but to advance to contact. The arrow-storm was the very essence of terror on the field. Shafts would deluge the Lancastrian ranks and, while a man-at-arms in full plate might escape injury, the lesser protection worn by the commons would leave them horribly exposed – snatched from the ranks to writhe and shudder on the snow, riddled with shafts. As one volley struck home another was whistling behind. Somerset's divisions were deployed for defence – to advance now would be disadvantageous.

For over 120 years 'men of the grey goose feather' had unleashed their deadly skills upon foreign foes, mainly French and Scots. The longbow, paired with the ubiquitous bill, had achieved a decisive tactical advantage, retained almost till the end of the French Wars. On the field of Shrewsbury in 1403 Englishmen had, for the first time, turned this weapon against each other to terrible effect. Fauconberg had the inestimable advantage of the wind but the Yorkists' shooting demanded a very high degree of skill. Happily for Edward, his archers were equal to the task:

> When their shot was almost spent the Lord Fauconberg marched forward with his archers, who not only shot their own sheaves, but also gathered the arrows of their enemies and let a great part of them fly against their own masters, and another part they let

stand on the ground which sore annoyed the legs of the owners when battle was joined.[23]

We have no knowledge as to the duration of the archery duel. In all probability it was very short, perhaps not more than ten minutes. If we allow Fauconberg some 10,000 bows shooting at a rate of ten shafts per minute – which a skilled archer could easily achieve – and accept ten minutes' duration, then the Yorkists must have shot nigh on a million arrows – a staggering total, to which must be added the Lancastrian reply (even if, as we assume, the contest was largely one-sided, King Henry's archers will still have shot a significant barrage). Fauconberg's canny tactics and the fortune of the weather gauge ensured the result of this opening exchange of missiles was swiftly and surely decided in the Yorkists' favour, conferring a crucial advantage. The darkened skies, spitting with sleet, would grow darker still as the fearsome arrow-storm hurtled over the field. Even gentlemen in harness were not invulnerable, for the practised archer, choosing a spot, could strike his bodkin point through a joint in the plate defences. Shooting at some 200 paces, despite the adverse wind and hail, these bowmen excelled at their art.[24] Each volley would strike home with terrible force, pinning men at random, gentleman and commoner alike. No troops, however seasoned, could stand for long against such an onslaught. As there could be no retreat, only the offensive remained.

Late Morning: the Lancastrian Advance

A great shout of 'King Henry!' burst from thousands of throats, rolling over the windswept ground as the Lancastrians surged forward. The tramp of armoured men, slogging over wet slush, drowned the keening of the wind – a great, rolling crash as the opposing ranks collided. The biggest and bloodiest fight in the history of these islands was now fully under way. It was probably sometime before noon.

King Edward would shortly send his horse to the rear, showing he would stand the full hazard of battle with his retainers and live or die accordingly. Such gestures were important. None of the young monarch's fellowship need doubt his seriousness. This was the battle for England. It would appear that the Lancastrian left was the first division to engage, Northumberland, on the flank, lagging somewhat behind. Quite why is uncertain. It is possible his companies had suffered worst from Fauconberg's deluge and he may have needed more time to order his ranks and files. The subject of the Percy's apparent failure on the right to match the momentum of the left would continue to dog Lancastrian deployment on the field. For the whole of their advance the attackers would still be subject to a hail of arrows, men marking targets more closely as the gap narrowed, feeble popping of hand 'gonnes' heralding their imminent approach. As the Percy's strong formation loomed inexorably, Edward issued a final exhortation, as Waurin confirms:

> At that moment [. . .] [the king] saw the army of the Earl of Northumberland coming for battle carrying the banner of King Henry. [The King] rode his horse along his army where all the nobles were and told them how they had wanted to make him their king, and he reminded them that they were seeing the next heir to the throne which had been usurped by the Lancasters a long time ago. He suffered his troops and knights to help him now to recover his inheritance and they all assured him of their desire to help and said that if any wished not to fight they should go their own way.[25]

With the order to advance, surviving Lancastrian archers from the van would have fallen back upon their main body, commanded ostensibly by Trollope and Northumberland. With last-minute adjustments to harness, a final mouthful of water and doubtless many a quick prayer, the ranks stepped out. In such conditions the advance would be sedate rather than rapid. The line was long and the going treacherous, ground already carpeted with dead and dying from the opening exchange, wounded and dying still twitching. Snow was falling steadily now, casting a thickening blanket over corpses. It was essential to maintain cohesion – no easy matter in the dire conditions, and Somerset had hoped to fight on the defensive. Yorkist success in the initial round had robbed him of this advantage and his men were left fully exposed to the deluge of missiles still spitting from Fauconberg's division. The cunning Yorkist, working his advantage to the last, ordered his archers to leave a hedge of arrows still sticking in the ground, an impromptu abattis. The closer the men-at-arms drew, the more galling the bowmen's shooting.

As the Yorkist archers filtered back between companies of their own billmen – no easy manoeuvre in itself – the stage was set for a clash of armoured foot. Until now both sides had seen their enemy at a distance. Now, with the Lancastrian host advancing up the slope towards them, the Yorkists steeled themselves for close combat – a testing time, when the enemy assumes human form, his purposefulness plain and his weapons sharp. But it is unlikely – though the chroniclers are silent on this – that the Yorkists continued to wait passively. As the bows withdrew, the bills would step forward to meet the foe with momentum of their own. Now a murderous, hacking mêlée of points, poleaxes and swords would ensue. In such a fight, however, the number of fatalities would be less than might be expected. The greatest loss of life occurred when one side dissolved in rout and became easy prey for the victors. In spite of the terrible pounding and losses the Lancastrians had endured, the advance allowed them to shake out their line and deploy in such a manner as to bring their greater numbers to bear. Despite the killing done by Yorkist bows, King Henry's men remained far more numerous and there was no sign of Norfolk and his much-needed reinforcement.

As the mêlée erupted many suffered wounds – cuts to the head, body and lower limbs. If a man fell he was lost, snuffed out by a flurry of blows. The noise would be terrific, a mad cacophony of grinding blades, shouts, exhortations, curses and screams. Knots of men would eddy and swirl as with the ebb and suck of the tide, temporarily disengaging as the ranks were thinned or disordered. The very press of dead would form a considerable barrier so that the living must fight atop heaps of slain, adding their blood and entrails to the pile.[26]

Noon and After: the Dogfight

In the dense fog of battle men would stand with comrades in their companies. Telling who was friend and who was foe was no easy matter and there was no recourse to polite enquiry. Men might wear livery jackets, emblazoned with their lord's badge, but this would do little to avert confusion. The standards provided the main anchor and rally point as the mêlée pounded. Commanders would be able to exercise a diminishing level of control, the fight taking on its own momentum. The roar and fury of the red mist were further obscured by the slanting showers that swept over the field as the afternoon wore on. If the Yorkists enjoyed the considerable advantage of having the inspiring persona of their youthful king on the field, they lacked numbers and as the fight continued, this began to tell. At one point Edward was saved by the swift action of a Welsh retainer, Davyd ap Matthew. In recognition of this, and in addition to material reward, the king granted his saviour the honour of standard-bearer and the insertion of 'Towton' into his family arms.

We cannot fully understand, nor perhaps even imagine, the nature of close medieval combat. Most contemporary military actions occur no closer than perhaps a couple of hundred metres. A medieval gentleman was trained in the use of arms from an early age. To be a knight was his profession and, however exalted his status, he would be judged on the field according to knightly virtues. The late Duke of York was regarded by his affinity not because of his political skills, which were limited, but by his prowess and steadfastness as a knight. His death at Wakefield might have been occasioned by poor generalship but the valour of his final stand would suffice for honour. Knights would be taught by their seniors and by professional masters.[27] This was not polite fencing but the art of killing. Survival in battle depended on rendering your foe incapable as quickly as possible – dead for preference. For this reason the head blow would be favoured. Mortal wounds to the body might still afford an opponent the chance for a final lunge of his own.[28] Fighting in harness swiftly leads to dehydration and heat exhaustion, even in a fit young man accustomed to the weight and proficient with his weapons. Wearing a helmet was deemed essential and we have seen what happened to the unwary, such as Clifford or Dacre, who chose to remove their helmet or bevor at an injudicious moment. The penalty for carelessness on the field was often death. The narrow eye-slit of a sallet or armet when closed up greatly reduced the wearer's field of vision. He had to focus on his opponent's eyes and yet judge the movement of his blade. At the same time he had to maintain a degree of spatial awareness as to what was going on around, for threats came not just from the fellow in front.

Even in twentieth- and twenty-first-century eyewitness accounts of battle, participants gain only a limited and often distorted view of events. In the heat of battle, with adrenalin pumping and the senses overwhelmed, it is unlikely any individual would remain so detached as to glean a wider understanding of tactical developments. On the field, courage – like its opposite panic – was collective. Men who had fought steadfastly could give way once fear spread. Often, if not invariably, the rot began in the rear. Those in front were too occupied with the business of survival to contemplate flight. But once ignited, fear spread like wildfire. It was at that point the great killing began. As they fled, men cast aside helmets as they struggled to find breath for flight. The enemy, released from the tension of combat, had leisure to strike at will. Moreover, in battles of this period, where combatants fought on foot, those gaining the advantage, seeing their foe dissolve, would have their horses near enough to hand.

A magnate would have his retainers and household men around him, trained to fight as a unit, weapons honed by long practice. Once battle was joined the higher sentiments were forgotten. What counted on the field was your fellowship or 'mates' – it was they you fought for and they you did not wish to let down. The feudal bond between retainer and lord, knight and magnate was also telling. The social contract bound by oath was important. We have already seen how Sir Andrew Trollope, as an officer of the Calais garrison, was brought by Warwick to fight for York prior to Ludford Bridge. When the knight realised he must choose between sovereign and magnate he judged his oath to Henry VI as king to be absolutely binding. His alleged defection was occasioned by conscience rather than venality or deceit (Trollope was still very much a marked man in Yorkist eyes).

John Waller,[29] a highly accomplished fight-master, reconstructs a hypothetical foot combat in the mêlée at Towton between a Yorkist knight and Lancastrian archer, where he has the former deliver two fast blows to his opponent's head, disabling him and causing him to fall. The knight is being pushed forward by the press of comrades behind. He must therefore brush aside or step over his fallen foe before meeting the next threat. Should the grounded man show any sign of vitality, those coming behind will finish him off, almost certainly with a further blow to the skull. Daggers thrust into armpit or groin might be employed for swift dispatch but, by virtue of the relative shortness of blade, would bring the attacker so close to his victim as to further restrict his already limited vision. Sword or polearm, where the killing blow could be delivered from a greater distance, were safer. The former had the ability to deliver cut or thrust. For a sound killing blow the thrust was always to be preferred, hence the old fighting maxim: 'the point will always beat the edge'. However, the thrust had to be aimed carefully or the point would glance off harness. It needed to be inserted into the gap

This reconstruction gives an impression of the confused, close-quarter fighting at the height of the battle. (Taylor Library)

A portrait of Edward IV, the victor.
(Taylor Library)

Ferrybridge. The nineteenth-century bridge, viewed from the site of Brotherton Marsh on the north bank of the River Aire. This construction is far later than the battle, but marks the earlier crossing and scene of the fighting. (John Sadler)

The 'Leper Pot' just outside Barkston Ash on the A162. A medieval cross base possibly marking the spot where Clifford fell. Overgrown and neglected, locating the pot requires some detective work. (John Sadler)

The only visible memorial to this great battle, the cross possibly incorporates the Dacre Cross, which itself may have originally been mounted on the vanished chapel. (Rachael Tan)

The inscription at the base of the cross. (Rachael Tan)

The weathered cross-head. (Rachael Tan)

The view towards North Acres. (Rachael Tan)

North Acres. (Rachael Tan)

The slope down to the Cock Beck valley. (Rachael Tan)

The slope under snow. (John Sadler)

The view up to the ridge. (Rachael Tan)

Ramshaw Woods, looking north and west. These trees are proof of the ancient woodlands present at the time of the battle. (John Sadler)

Lead Church. Dating from the fourteenth century, the church is all that remains of the settlement. Traces of a medieval manor have been discerned and the church was likely a manorial chapel associated with the Tyas and Skargill families. (John Sadler)

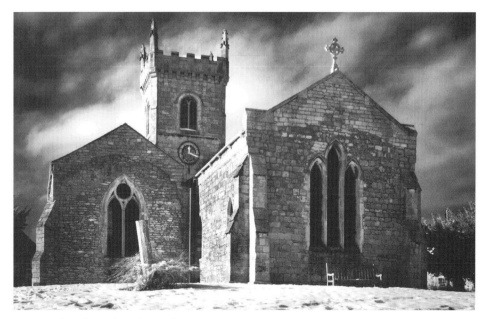

Saxton Church. Although much altered, All Saints stands on its 1461 location, and would have been a natural refuge during the battle. Numerous accounts and visible traces on the ground support the contention that many of the Towton dead were interred here in the immediate aftermath of battle. (Rachael Tan)

Dacre's Tomb. Now much defaced by time, and in rather poor overall repair, the tomb stands within Saxton churchyard. It is said that Dacre's remains were discovered in an upright posture when the tomb was opened and the presumed skeleton of his destrier was located nearby. The inscription reads: 'Here lies Ranulf, Lord of Dacre and Gilsland, a true knight, valiant in battle in the service of King Henry VI. Who died on Palm Sunday, 29th March 1461, on whose soul may God have mercy, Amen.' (John Sadler)

Micklegate Bar, York. On entering the city, the Yorkists would see the rotting skulls of fallen relatives grinning down from the spikes. (Taylor Library)

between plates and driven home far enough to inflict mortal damage without becoming lodged in the victim's torso. The killer did not have the luxury of extended leisure in which to disentangle his blade. Polearm or mace were less sophisticated weapons than blades, but swinging percussive blows would suffice to bring an opponent down without entanglement, shattering bone and tissue. And there would be blood. Men in battle die noisily and messily. The level of bloodletting was almost unimaginable. In this fight they were dying in great numbers and the walls of dead that swiftly arose acted as a barrier to combatants. Of necessity there would have been lulls in the killing frenzy – not any form of ordered truce, but where the lines drew apart as if by tacit consent to clear the dead, order the ranks and, above all, take on water. For dehydration, even in cold weather, is a signal feature of armoured combat. Men could only keep going if they were given drink. Great clouds of steam would rise from the overheated carapaces and the unsung water-carrier was a feature of every fight. Much of this work would be done by women, so the field was by no means an exclusively male preserve.[30] It appears to have been the convention that, as non-combatants, these women were not targeted. They would also act as stretcher-bearers and paramedics. A wounded man's chances of survival would, then as now, be dependent upon how swiftly he could be got off the field. Many of those struck down, despite the best attentions of their enemies, would not be dead and the mounds of fallen would neither be still nor silent but would writhe and moan as though stirred by an invisible hand. And over all hung the smell of blood, ordure and urine, as bowels and bladders emptied.

Andrew Boardman[31] is of the view that the three divisions on each side, which had advanced in line, would bunch up to form two vast phalanxes. I do not believe this to be the case. I think – and here we are entirely in the realm of conjecture – that it is more likely these divisions remained in formation with troops being reinforced or rotated in turn. To maintain so hard a combat the fighting men in front must have been constantly replenished. This could be achieved in lulls, when the lines drew back, but must have been constant during the fight. We know that medieval captains studied their art with care and both factions employed seasoned professionals such as Trollope and Horne. That the battle would be confused is inevitable, but not all was disorder, else the fight could not possibly have lasted. While a commander-in-chief might have limited control over events once the die was cast, it is not entirely true to say he had none at all. This was an enormous battle but it was fought in a relatively confined space. Edward, having harangued his men, sent his horse to the rear, as was his custom, for we know he fought most of his combats on foot:

> Hearing this support the earl thanked them, jumped from his horse and told them, sword in hand, that on this day he would live or die with them in order to give them courage. Then he came in front of his banners and waited for the enemy which was marching forward with great noise . . .[32]

As I have suggested, it seems probable Edward would use his own household men as shock troops to bear the brunt wherever it fell hardest and wherever it seemed the pressure was greatest. Fighting in the mêlée was not confined to men-at-arms. Archers could play their part as they had amply demonstrated in earlier battles such as Agincourt in 1415 where they broke ranks to fall upon the flanks of the French stumbling through the mud. Lightly harnessed, strong and agile, these formidable men made deadly opponents wielding sword or falchion and buckler. Two or three would target an armoured foeman, one would engage his point, the other might seek to hook behind the knee to bring the armoured enemy crashing and floundering onto the slick slush where a dagger thrust to the eye or genitals would suffice.

There is the commonly held view that both sides had given the order that there should be no quarter and, if so, this would add to the terrific fury of the contest. One who cannot hope for safety in surrender, and where no retreat is possible, is bound to fight to the death. And death there was aplenty. It is not possible to assess how many men died in the opening duel, the Lancastrian advance or the initial clashes. That the field was soon congested with piles of dead and dying clearly attests that casualties by this time were already substantial. Although the Yorkists might have had the better of their opponents at the outset, the subsequent balance in that dismal cauldron would have been far more even.

Early Afternoon: the Lancastrian Ambush

Somerset may have chosen this crucial moment to spring his ambush from Castle Hill Wood – the blow falling on the left of the Yorkist line. Evidence for this is largely anecdotal but the lie of the ground admirably suited such a tactic and the frequent snow squalls would act as a further screen. If such an attack could be successfully launched, then the Yorkists would find themselves assailed on two flanks and would very likely give ground – a potentially fatal scenario. Just such a blow delivered from the flank had contributed greatly to the Scottish victory at Otterburn in 1388. Quite possibly, indeed probably, the Lancastrians had retained their mounts and charged as cavalry, adding to their enemy's discomfiture. The assault may well, as Andrew Boardman convincingly asserts, have been of sufficient weight to cause the entire line to alter its alignment, the left flank of the Yorkist army being pushed some way down the line of the present B1217. Part of the army may even have routed, provoking a crisis for the young king and his senior officers. Waurin appears to support this possibility:

> When Lord Rivers, his son and six or seven thousand Welshmen led by Andrew Trollope, following the Duke of Somerset himself with seven thousand men, charged his cavalry who fled and were chased for about eleven miles. It seemed that Lord Rivers' troops had won a great battle, because they thought that the Earl of Northumberland had charged on the other side, unfortunately he had not done so and this became his tragic hour for he Northumberland] died that day. During this debacle many of [King Edward's] soldiers died and when he [Edward] learned the truth of what had happened to his cavalry he was very sad as well as very annoyed.[33]

It may well have been the case that Lord Rivers (Edward's future father-in-law) and Trollope led the ambush party. The latter was a tried exponent of such handy surprises. Once successful, some of the attackers pelted off in pursuit of their beaten opponents, the advantage gained thus diluted. One is reminded of Prince Edward's (Longshanks) horsemen at Lewes in 1263 and Prince Rupert's squadrons at Naseby, nearly four centuries later. Andrew Boardman points out that Edward, a decade later at Tewkesbury,[34] was aware of the risk from woods on his flank. This may have represented knowledge dearly bought, though any experienced commander would be alert to such dangers.

Castle Hill Wood, as any perambulation will show, is still a dense and somewhat tangled tract of woodland. It would simply not be possible to conceal a large force of mounted men-at-arms there, much less launch a cohesive charge. The ambush party must have been concealed in the lee of the trees on the flank, where they would still have been invisible to the Yorkists. That complete surprise was possible seems underlined by the fact there is no suggestion in any of the chronicles that the Yorkists sought to further anchor their flank by occupying this feature. To do so would have conferred no tactical advantage and the potential for ambush seems to have been overlooked. This failure would bear bitter fruit.

None of this can, of course, be proved, thus we are once again, due to the paucity of the primary sources, forced back upon IMP. Trollope is credited with being the architect of the ambush that destroyed York and Salisbury at Wakefield, and if such a tactic could be properly employed once again at Towton, the results might be spectacular. What must follow, if we accept that the ambush developed as suggested, is that Edward would shift any available reserves – and likely his household men – to stem the rot and contain the attack. These measures were clearly effective, for the line did not fold. The very size of his army helped. For a smaller force, as was the case with Hotspur at Otterburn over seventy years before, the shock of an attack rolled up his army and led to certain defeat. At Towton, though, Edward sustained casualties and sections of his rearward division – the mounted contingent – dissolved in rout, but the line held. It was battered and bent but not fatally fractured.

What appears certain is that, for some hours, the outcome hung in the balance, but with the advantage shifting inexorably to the more numerous Lancastrians. Edward may have been saved from a worse catastrophe by a possible failure of command in his enemy's ranks, with Northumberland pushing on too slowly to capitalise on the success of the ambush party. Indeed, his division may have been forced to give ground with Northumberland himself, at this critical point, being struck down. This would now result in the contending battle lines assuming the shape of a shallow 'V' with the apex just east of the Towton road. Northumberland's apparent failure to exploit that initial success of the ambush party appears, at first sight, inexplicable. Faintheartedness was not a Percy characteristic – his father, grandfather and great-grandfather had all died with harness on their backs.

If Northumberland suffered his fatal wounds at this point, then his wing may have lost momentum or, quite possibly, the fog of war and appalling weather frustrated coordination. In any event, Percy's failure was York's salvation. Had the whole line pushed forward the Yorkist position would have been graver still. If the Earl of Northumberland had indeed been incapacitated at this point, his fall would result in a lowering of morale among his affinity. This may have given the Yorkists on that flank fresh heart and enabled them not just to stabilise their position but to win some measure of ground, pushing their opponents back and deepening the 'V'.

Lord Dacre was also among those who fell. Like Clifford, overcome with thirst, he removed his sallet, only to be transfixed by an arrow. Legend insists he fell to a crossbow bolt shot by a youthful sniper carefully concealed in a bur (elderberry) tree, allegedly in pursuance of a blood feud: 'Thou killed my father and I will kill thee.'[35] Dacre probably died in North Acres[36] but despite this loss of a senior officer the juggernaut pressed on, forcing the Yorkists to give ground. As yet there was no rout but perhaps an intimation of panic – a tremor ran through the ranks.

If Edward's right was holding and, indeed, getting the better of their foes on that flank, the situation on the left remained desperate. The Lancastrian ambush had hammered into the rearward division, occasioning some panic and leading certain mounted elements to rout. A clue as to why the ambush failed to be decisive may lie in Waurin's description, for he refers to the fleeing Yorkists being 'chased for about eleven miles'. As I alluded to above, this is reminiscent of other battles where cavalry commanders failed to rally their riders after the initial tactical advantage had been won, thus frittering away the fruits of victory. It appears that this occurred at Towton and we may imagine the experienced Trollope fuming at the indiscipline of Rivers' marchers as they fixed their eyes firmly on loot and dashed off in headlong pursuit. If so, this may have saved Edward. Rivers' indiscipline and folly in thinking the day won, or his simple inability to control his men, squandered the advantage and allowed the Yorkist general time to shore up his flank. The ambush precipitated a crisis rather than a catastrophe.

Overall, however, the tipping point appeared to be at hand. All of the Yorkist reserves, under Wenlock and Dinham, would have been committed. The bulk of Exeter's rearward division would be in the Lancastrian line. Numbers in the slogging match were beginning to tell. As this dreadful day wore on, Edward's men were steadily pushed back towards the lip of the escarpment: disaster loomed. The Yorkists had been shaken and depleted on the left even if they had more than held their own on the right. As the left stumbled the right would have to conform and, in so doing, surrender the momentum they'd briefly enjoyed. If the Lancastrians could maintain their steady, unrelenting pressure, they would sweep their battered enemy from the field and win the day. The stakes could not have been higher.

Edward, his Black Bull banner streaming in the wind, performed prodigies of valour, a paladin and inspiration to his bone-weary soldiers. George Neville, admittedly partisan, refers to the courage and leadership of not only the king, but of his brother and uncle. Personal leadership was the vital element of medieval generalship. The magnate was always a knight, expected to find his place in the thick of the press and there to accomplish chivalric feats. Edward of York perfectly filled this role, his great height, commanding physique, skill at arms and personal courage formed the very stuff of legend. A subsequent chronicle, the *Arrivall*, to which Boardman refers,[37] describes the fighting at Barnet a decade later, when the crisis point was reached and the hero-king, with his strong affinity, battled in the thick of their enemies:

> With the faithful, well-beloved and mighty assistance of his fellowship, that in great number dissevered not from his person, and were well assured unto him as to them was possible, he manly, vigorously and valiantly assailed them, in the midst and strongest of their battle. Where with great violence, he beat and bore down afore him all that stood in his way and then turned to the range, first one hand, and then on the other hand, in length, and so beat and bore them down, so that nothing might stand in the sight of him and the well assured fellowship that attended truly upon him.[38]

While the chronicle is something of a panegyric and plays to the chivalric ideal, there is no doubting Edward was a most formidable knight. His affinity would be young men of similar stamp, well schooled in arms, trained and confident as a team, highly effective as shock troops. Their skills would be needed more than ever at this critical juncture on the bare upland plateau of Towton.

But where was Norfolk? His arrival was now crucial to Yorkist survival. Without his fresh men to redress the balance defeat appeared inevitable. We can only speculate why the duke's progress was so tardy, and it seems reasonable to suppose his deteriorating health was a factor. Possibly he did not lead his division on the field and without the duke at their head, his affinity may have lacked the required degree of urgency.

Mid-afternoon: Turn of the Tide

Locked like punch-drunk fighters in a deadly embrace, the hosts eddied and swayed on the southern rim, behind the Lancastrians a carpet of horrors. Somerset must surely have felt the tang of victory in his nostrils. One last sustained effort would sweep the southern army into chaos and oblivion. Edward and his household men would be shoring up the line wherever a fracture seemed imminent but the Yorkists would sense that time was running out – without Norfolk they appeared doomed.

Desperately ill, the exhausted duke may have been at Pontefract on the evening of 28 March.[39] Nonetheless, he had his men on the move next morning, though whether he was at their head is uncertain. The author of *Hearne's Fragment* certainly asserts he was.[40] Following the Old London Road through Sherburn-in-Elmet, past the field at Dintingdale where the stiffening remains of the fallen were frozen in postures of death; it is possible his division encountered fugitives from the rout sparked by Trollope's ambush party. Undeterred, at some point during the afternoon Norfolk's men began arriving on the field, deploying on their comrades' right flank, propping up the faltering Yorkist line and providing greater parity of numbers.

As these companies arrived at the base of the plateau, details of the mêlée above would have remained obscure. That Norfolk's men deployed on the extreme flank of Edward's right was more accidental than planned. Boardman is the only author to comment on this[41] and I think he must be correct. It was on this flank that the Yorkists had gained their earlier advantage. The enormous impetus of fresh men bolstering the line – permitting surviving Yorkist officers to extend past and overlap their opponents – conferred a significant advantage. This came at a time when those who had been battling so desperately for several hours were utterly exhausted. Vergil maintains the fight continued for ten hours[42] but this is clearly an exaggeration and must include the span of subsequent rout and slaughter. If we assume the archery duel opened hostilities between ten and eleven o'clock, and time Norfolk's arrival for, say, two o'clock, with the final Lancastrian collapse occurring an hour later, this was a fight of around five hours – a prodigious length of time in such circumstances.

Somerset may now have sensed the victory slipping from his grasp, though there was no immediate intimation of panic in the Lancastrian ranks. The duke moved men to shore up the left while trying to maintain pressure on the centre and right. For the moment there was stalemate. Slaughter continued into the wet afternoon, scudding cloud driven by the sharp-edged wind, scattering of hail and snow blinding the combatants and settling a pall over the rising mounds of dead and wounded. Somerset had been within an ace of winning the battle. But now the Yorkists had stopped retreating: it was now their turn to exert pressure, to build up the steady momentum of the advance, fresh blood and untried muscle swelling their ranks. Pressure from Norfolk's fresh troops was causing Somerset's line to bend backwards in response, curving like a flexed bow, but in good order. At some point, however, the Lancastrians began to give way: at first a trickle from the rear that swelled into a stream, then a river in spate – unstoppable. How and precisely when this took place is difficult to assess. Even with Norfolk's men deploying on the right flank of the Yorkist line and the consequential pressure exerted against the Lancastrian left, there was no immediate collapse. Both sides had sustained heavy casualties and these would likely have fallen heaviest on the officers of both sides. Lord Scrope, Sir Edward Jenny and the Kentishman Horne were down on the Yorkist side; Northumberland and Dacre certainly, Trollope perhaps, on the Lancastrian. As they faced stiffening odds and a surge of fresh troops, Somerset's army would need its best men to keep heart in the ranks. Where those ranks were denuded of officers and NCOs the contagion of rout would spread fastest.

It is thus possible that, at this juncture, Lancastrians from the right began to waver. Not all, certainly not a flood, but perhaps a significant defection. The line did not fold but must have given ground, back over the corpse-infested mire of blood-red slush – a withdrawal, fairly steady, over space so dearly gained. Perhaps there was another of those pauses as survivors shook themselves into formations and the newcomers were fully integrated. At this point the honours were probably fairly even, the Lancastrians' overall loss probably greater, their early advantage in numbers dramatically reduced by casualties and offset by Norfolk's arrival. Boardman suggests[43] that the Yorkists, as they now pressed forward, may have been diverted by the lure of spoil – this is entirely feasible. Somerset must, by now, have been thinking in terms of survival rather than victory. If he could fight his adversaries to a standstill, his army, relatively secure in the heart of Lancastrian country, would fare better and enjoy greater prospects for recovery. To fight even a draw upon so contested a field was no mean achievement.

But stalemate was something Edward could not afford. It was time for one last effort. Boardman is openly admiring of the young king, understandably so; few men of his age have ever faced so great a challenge so steadfastly. If we seek a definitive answer as to why the Yorkists, at this juncture, were able to win so decisively, then the answer, as the chronicles do not assist but as IMP would dictate, has to lie in superior leadership. Edward and Warwick drove their men forward, ordered their lines, and by personal example and exhortation, led them on for the decisive push. Norfolk's arrival, however belated, gave them a platform to press home the attack. Ramsay cites Edward's superior leadership as the prime factor in the Yorkist victory: 'Henry's presence usually entailed failure wherever he went.'[44] Somerset was not cast in the same mould as his opponent. His command style had been competent but uninspired. He had neither the majesty of kingship nor the Homeric bravura needed. Put simply, Edward was the better man.

Once morale was gone, rout was inevitable, the collapse swift and terrifyingly sudden as the thinning ranks at the front found themselves deserted. Vergil's account, though it postdates the battle by half a century, does suggest that the collapse, when it came, was quick:

Thus did the fight continue more than 10 hours in equal balance, when at last King Henry [by whom he surely means Somerset] espied the forces of his foes increase, and his own somewhat yield, whom when by new exhortation he had compelled to press on more earnestly, he with a few horseman removing a little out of that place, expected the event of the fight, but behold, suddenly his soldiers gave the back, which when he saw this he fled also.[45]

Now the killing could really begin in earnest.

Chapter 7

Rout

The foe is merciless and will not pity . . .
King Henry VI Third Part; Act 2, scene vi

When Edward IV of England, as he may safely now be called, rode beneath Micklegate Bar, having won the most titanic and hard-fought battle in English history, we cannot readily comprehend the emotions that accompanied his ride. This was no triumphal entry. Above him the skulls of his family grinned – he could so very easily have joined them. Instead he won his kingdom, though the job was not yet completely done: Henry VI, Queen Margaret and her son were still at liberty, fled to the Lancastrian redoubt of Northumberland. Somerset, too, had escaped – another reckoning deferred. The war was plainly not over. The House of Lancaster, though seemingly irretrievably damaged, might rise again. Had not the Yorkists themselves, following earlier disasters, been resurrected by the dynamism of Edward and his cousin? Towton was not the end, for a further three years of hard campaigning remained.

It was on the rim of Towton Dale that the Lancastrian line finally fractured. A few hardy souls determined to form rally points around their banners and sell their lives as dearly as possible, but most joined the deluge. Many scrambled or slid down the slush-covered gradient towards Cock Beck. Bloody Meadow became a vast killing field. Panicking survivors fought each other to gain the narrow span of the bridge – swirling waters below swollen with the frequent downpours. Exhausted men were dragged down by the weight of harness and sodden jacks. It was said the waters were so clogged with corpses, men could cross dry shod over a 'bridge of bodies'. As survivors pelted through the narrow lanes of Towton and on to Tadcaster, they were harried and hacked by cavalrymen, who carried the slaughter virtually to the gates of York.

There are no modern parallels for such a fearful rout. None of those tens of thousands caught up in the horror left accounts. We may get some flavour from later battles. From Culloden, fought in 1746, eyewitness testimony confirms the fury and murderous intensity of a bloody pursuit and where the dead were piled 'after receiving many cuts of the sword on the face, and many stabs of the bayonet'.[1] The cavalry, in this instance, 'pursued vigorously, and killed great numbers without distinction; for being newly raised men they were more willing to exert themselves'.[2] Many of those slain in the wreck of the Jacobite army were mere bystanders come to watch the fight. In an age when public executions were accepted spectacles, battles were a form of bloody entertainment. Indeed, such practice was common throughout history and perhaps Towton had its spectators too. If so, their position in the rout will have been a precarious one. Soldiers have no pity for those who come to watch them die for sport. The celebrated passage from de Commynes asserts that Edward, 'in all the battles which he had won', gave orders that in the pursuit his hounds should 'spare the common soldiers and kill the lords'.[3] The Croyland chronicler provides a suitably vivid account of the Towton aftermath:

> For their ranks being now broken and scattered in flight, the king's army eagerly pursued them, and cutting down the fugitives with their swords, just like so many sheep for the slaughter, made immense havoc among them for a distance of ten miles as far as the City of York.[4]

As this confirms, pursuit was not random. Edward remained with strong forces on the field while flying columns of pursuers mercilessly harried the fleeing Lancastrians. Very likely the king was sincere in his wish to avoid unnecessary bloodshed – even the most fearsome would surely have had his fill that day. Besides, the commons were Englishmen too and did no more than follow their lords. The real quarrel lay between their respective masters and here none could expect quarter. In any rout, terrain dictates the direction of flight plus the impetus and direction of the pursuers. To escape, the Lancastrians would have to overcome three obstacles: the slope of Bloody Meadow, Cock Beck, and perhaps worst of all, the River Wharfe. None would prove easy and each would become a focus for carnage. Evidence from the Towton mass grave reveals that several of those interred probably lost their lives seeking refuge in flight. The blows that rained down upon them came from above and behind, which would suggest a mounted opponent.

As the armies skewed around and the Lancastrians echeloned backwards the slope proved treacherous, the rout spilling in mad confusion. As Andrew Boardman points out,[5] the narrow gutter of Towton Vale was a perfect killing ground. Given the relatively gentle decline here, Yorkist knights and prickers, well mounted on fresh horses, could easily deploy, shepherding their victims towards Cock Beck. Swollen waters, a miry bottom and quick current sucked men to their deaths even before thrusting spears and hacking blades could do their work. Fanning out from the mouth of Towton Vale the Yorkists could cover the banks with ease. Many hundreds would suffocate in the press, so thick that, as previously mentioned, legend insists the beck was spanned by a 'bridge of bodies'. This may be apocryphal but, given the great crush of stampeding fugitives, is all too credible. Hall confirms that:

> the common people there affirm that men alive passed the river upon the dead carcasses, and that the great river of Wharfe, which is the great sewer of the brook, and of all the water coming from Towton, was coloured with blood.[6]

Even those who slogged clear of the deadly bottleneck were far from safe – exhausted, on foot, and pursued by mounted men with the means and leisure to kill. Edward IV was never a vicious or vindictive man, willing wherever possible to forgive his enemies, but he knew this day must prove decisive. He must deal out maximum pain to his beaten foes to ensure they should not rise again. There was no time for squeamishness and the king, if not cruel, knew when to be ruthless. Hundreds of stumbling fugitives were hacked down as the cold spring day drew to a close. How those desperate refugees must have prayed for the sheltering cloak of night. In the darkening glow of dusk more men died – a carpet of dead that covered the ground as far as Tadcaster. The relentless chase continued through narrow streets. Wise men would bolt their doors and close their ears to the screams beyond.

That night the victors would camp on the field, numbed by exhaustion, beset by icy blasts of wind. On the field, those piles of stiffening bodies would shift and shudder as some desperately wounded wretch fought a last, hopeless struggle. For the defeated there were no comrades to care for them, no medical attention – just the cold, blood-soaked ground.

But what of Henry VI, his queen, his son and heir? For, as long as the royal family remained at liberty, Edward's cause was far from secure. Few men of Edward's age can have experienced such a night – part relief, part exhilaration, part uncertainty; total emotional and physical exhaustion.

Counting the Cost

Quite how many men died on the field and in the rout cannot be clearly ascertained. Polydore Vergil later assessed the total as 20,000. Hall gives a more precise but unsubstantiated figure of 36,776. The Paston correspondence mentions a toll of 28,000. Whatever the exact level of mortality, the butcher's bill was very high indeed – England's bloodiest day before 1 July 1916 on the Somme. Of the total number of dead, the majority were Lancastrians. Besides Clifford and Dacre, Northumberland died of wounds, Lords Neville, Morley and Welles with the redoubtable Trollope fell on the field. Thomas Courtenay, Earl of Devon was taken and executed. Micklegate Bar was soon to host a whole new array of heads. The Yorkists had escaped with remarkably few gentry casualties: only Lord Fitzwalter and the Kentish captain Robert Horne. George Neville summed up the day in his correspondence with Coppini:

> That day [Palm Sunday] there was a very great conflict, which began with the rising of the sun, and lasted until the tenth hour of the night, so great was the pertinacity and boldness of the men, who never heeded the possibility of a miserable death. Of the enemy who fled, great numbers were drowned in the river near the town of Tadcaster, eight miles from York, because they themselves had broken the bridge to cut our passage that way, so that none could pass, and a great part of the rest who got away who gathered in the said town and city, were slain and so many dead bodies were seen as to cover an area six miles long by three broad and about four furlongs. In this battle eleven lords of the enemy fell, including the Earl of Devon, the Earl of Northumberland, Lord Clifford and Neville with some cavaliers;

and from what we hear from persons worthy of confidence, some 28,000 persons perished on one side and the other.[7]

Lest he be thought too enthusiastic over the copious shedding of so much Christian blood, the Bishop concluded his missive with a suitable exclamation of piety:

O miserable and luckless race and powerful people, would you have no spark of pity for our own blood, of which we have lost so much of fine quality by the civil war, even if you had no compassion for the French.[8]

The Croyland chronicler was of the view that some 38,000 perished either on the field or in the rout:

Those who helped to inter the bodies, piled up in pits and in trenches prepared for the purpose, bear witness that eight and thirty thousand warriors fell on that day, besides those who were drowned in the river before alluded to [Cock Beck] whose numbers we have no means of ascertaining, the blood, too, of the slain, mingling with snow which at this time covered the whole surface of the earth, afterwards ran down in the furrows and ditches along with the melted snow, in a most shocking manner, for a distance of two or three miles.[9]

Considering the general unreliability of contemporary chroniclers and the dearth of archaeological traces, we cannot expect to arrive at an exact figure for the dead of Towton. That they were very numerous indeed is not open to dispute. Modern commentators have discounted Ramsay's writing down of numbers. Clearly the great numbers committed, the duration of the fight and horrors of the final rout combined to produce a significant tally of dead. It is largely pointless to speculate further. My personal inclination is to discount Hall's figure as being too high and to favour the lower estimate from Vergil. That casualties may have approached the generally regarded figure of 28,000 is nonetheless far from impossible – a very bloody day indeed.

Aftermath

Whence then is the courage of the English vulgar? It proceeds, in my opinion from that dissolution of dependence which obliges every man to regard his own character [. . .] every man that crowds our streets is a man of honour, disdainful of obligation, impatient of reproach. I do not deny that some inconveniences may from time to time proceed but good and evil will grow up in this world together; and they who complain, in peace, of the insolence of the populace, must remember, that insolence in peace is bravery in war.

On the Bravery of the English Common Soldiers – Dr Johnson

If up to 20,000 men died then twice as many would be wounded. Every dwelling, every cottage and bothy in the area would be crammed with hacked and bleeding men; the roads for days, even weeks after the fight, crammed with walking wounded and casualties carried on carts. In a savage close-quarter fight, most of the combatants would expect to sustain some injury – Warwick, as has been noted, was struck in the thigh by an arrow.

As the exhausted victors sat around their camp fires, spectral figures scoured the field, pulling rings from stiffening fingers, scrabbling for purses. Many a wounded man would be sent on his way by the businesslike thrust of a dagger – not from humanitarian impulse but because a dead man is so much less trouble. There is no glory in war and this final act of the Towton drama revealed the business at its worst and human nature at its vilest. Some, of course, came to seek out loved ones. Some, indeed, were moved by compassion. Next day, burial details scoured the wide sweep of the field, heralds making a gruesome tally. The bodies of fallen gentry were removed by consent, express or tacit. The commons were laid in mass graves, perhaps – in so pious an age – with a few words said over each mound.

And what of the survivors? There would be many left permanently disabled by their wounds. Those who suffered skull fractures, abdominal or chest wounds would be lucky to live on. Others, perhaps even with minor hurts, could fall victim to infections, septicaemia or gangrene. Of these uncounted losses we have no possible tally, though we may surmise they were numerous. Much has been written in recent years, rightly so, of the long-term emotional and psychological damage wrought by combat experience. On this subject the chroniclers are silent. Such matters were not considered and it could be argued our fifteenth-century ancestors were less affected. Their way of life was much closer to the daily realities of life and death, that much harsher, more dedicated to routine survival – even in peacetime, when famine and pestilence lurked around every corner. Post Traumatic Stress Disorder (PTSD) was not a recognised condition in the Late Middle Ages.

I have spoken with many who have fought in twentieth-century conflicts, including veterans of the Falklands Campaign of 1982. I was told that the realisation of what war entails does not arise during the heat of battle. For British veterans it arose in the cold light of a following dawn, when they confronted the reality of their night's work. Both sides fought with honour in the Falklands yet the victors were not prepared for such terrible sights as the field displayed. These were professional soldiers, not conscripts. This work was their trade. They were never blinded by a rose-tinted view, yet these horrors never left them. Consequences for some were traumatic to the point of self-destruction – this we now understand as PTSD. Whether their distant ancestors were likewise afflicted must remain a matter of debate. Yet, one suspects the human condition does not really alter that greatly.

Despite harsher realities, there would be many men whose subsequent lives were blighted by the events of Palmsunday Field and perhaps by their own part in them. But for the moment, at least, the killing was done.

> Thou that so stoutly hath resisted me,
> Give me thy gold, if thou hast any gold,
> For I have bought it with an hundred blows.
> But let me see; is this our foeman's face?
> Ah, no, no, no; it is mine only son!
> *King Henry VI Third Part; Act 2; scene v*

James Butler, Earl of Wiltshire had doubtless been one of the first Lancastrian officers to flee the field. The earl possessed a genius for survival, being said to be more concerned for the preservation of his good looks than the maintenance of his royal master's cause. This time his flight merely delayed the inevitable. He was captured far to the west at Cockermouth and subsequently faced the headsman at Newcastle. Though Northumberland, Dacre, Welles, Neville and Clifford perished on the field, several Lancastrian officers – Somerset, Exeter and Roos – galloped free from the rout, pausing only at York to sweep up the royal family. Their only recourse was to reach Northumberland, where fresh support might yet be forthcoming. Edward, on Monday 30 March, rode into the northern capital, now his. The Courtenay Earl of Devon, who lay ill in the city, was not spared. The Yorkist lords, Montagu and Berners, held captive there, were freed and Warwick must have savoured the double boon of victory and a brother's preservation – after all, he had, like Edward, lost a father and one brother.

Andrew Boardman speculates, persuasively, that Somerset, as he withdrew, gave orders for the slighting of the Wharfe crossing at Tadcaster. Such an action would delay pursuit but, as he would clearly have foreseen, must also encompass the ruin of many of his own survivors as they fled. Such ruthlessness could have been justified by the absolute imperative to protect Henry and his queen. Armies could be rebuilt but the fountainhead of the Lancastrian cause, once lost, could not be replaced. Whatever his justification, the consequences for exhausted survivors stumbling after were catastrophic. This crossing became an even greater killing ground than Cock Beck.[10]

Despite the scale of the slaughter the final death toll had not been reached. Despite such high-ranking casualties as Wiltshire and Devon, Gregory asserts that a further forty-two knights were killed in the round of executions that followed. Boardman[11] sees this as proof of Edward's resolve to render Lancastrian opposition impotent. This must surely be correct. Towton might yet turn into a hollow victory if the snake was not scotched. As it was, even with this ruthless winnowing, three more years of hard campaigning and two further battles (Hedgeley Moor and Hexham), remained ahead. The war, or at least this phase, would not be won till a further round of takings-off followed the rout at Hexham in the spring of 1464 (see Appendix IV).

Edward had two clear political objectives: he had to destroy the base of his enemy's power to ensure no further military threat could arise; at the same time his own affinity was so slender that he needed to heal as many wounds as possible to consolidate his position. At present he was dangerously dependent upon the Nevilles and the risks inherent in that relationship would bear very bitter fruit indeed. Furthermore, it was not possible to account for a full tally of his opponents, for every peer cut off left progeny or kin to raise his banner anew. Without a wholesale massacre there was no end to potential opponents. To survive and consolidate his grip on power, Edward needed to wield both stick and carrot. We have already seen he was not a murderous man, nonetheless he could and would, where the need arose, exercise total ruthlessness. No medieval monarch who could not act decisively and, if required by circumstances, bloodily, would rule successfully – the unhappy reign of Henry VI being a notable case in point.

As Coppini confirmed,[12] Edward left the bulk of his forces in the north to fan out across the region and net as great a haul as might be found. The Nevilles were left in charge of mopping up while Edward kept Easter in his newly-won northern capital. This was sound policy, for the king could not long tarry in the north. He had an exercise in nation-building to undertake. Followers must be rewarded and the guilty shorn by Act of Attainder. Gregory gives a neat summary:

> And the king tarried in the north a great while and made great inquiries of the rebellions against his father, and took down his father's head from the walls of York, and made all the country to be sworn unto him and his laws. And then he returned to London again and there he made 18 knights and many lords, and then he rode to Westminster and there he was crowned the 28th day of June in the year of our Lord 1461, blessed be God of his great grace.[13]

Chapter 8

Legacy

And now to London with triumphal march . . .
King Henry VI Third Part; Act 2, scene vi

owton should, in terms of scale and impact, have been the climactic battle, a Waterloo, yet it was not – far from it. For another three long years the conflict spluttered on, mainly in Northumberland – an outpost war of garrisons and skirmishes, with Yorkist control delegated to Warwick and his energetic, capable brother, Montagu. Henry VI, increasingly an anachronism in his own failing cause, remained in Lilliputian splendour, presiding over an impecunious mini-kingdom in Northumberland. Margaret of Anjou, aided by Somerset and Sir Ralph Percy kept the Lancastrian flame flickering, holding the key border bastions of Bamburgh, Alnwick and Dunstanburgh. For those readers interested in a fuller account of subsequent operations in the north, more detail is provided in Appendix III.

Queen Margaret's hope was that the Scots could be bribed and the French persuaded to intervene. The former gratefully accepted the keys to Berwick-upon-Tweed as a down payment,[1] though they were thwarted in taking occupation of Carlisle by an energetic defence and Montagu's report. Possession of the northern bastions was key to defence against the Scots, though the polity of the northern kingdom, unsettled by yet another minority kingship,[2] was never more than lukewarm in its support for Lancaster. To damage the walls of the Northumbrian fortresses by cannon fire was unpalatable, though the king's great ordnance was sent north.[3] Margaret raised some help in France, led by that redoubtable Norman paladin, Pierre de Breze, but the weather, like the odds, was against her, wrecking the Lancastrian ships. After alarms at the abortive Siege of Norham in 1463, fearing for the precious life of her son, she decamped across the Channel, leaving Somerset in command.

He defected, as did Percy, and the Lancastrian cause appeared to collapse. Henry was left skulking in Tynedale while Edward tried hard to integrate the Beaufort family into his affinity – a politic attempt but one that failed: the old allegiance pulled too hard and a legacy of spilt blood could not be ignored. Somerset and Percy, in the spring of 1464, reverted and the former stole northwards to rekindle the flame. For a brief moment it seemed the old king's feeble banner might yet rise but, in reality, the hope was forlorn. Already the Scots were inclined to talk to Warwick, and Somerset's efforts to block Montagu reaching their commissioners at Norham were dashed in the extended skirmish at Hedgeley Moor in April. Next month Montagu marched on Tynedale to finish the business, which he did by Swallowship Hill near Hexham. The battle was brief, the pursuit thorough. Percy had fallen in the earlier fight, Somerset and more than a score of others perished in the ruthless aftermath of this one.

It could be argued that the swing of the headsman's axe in Hexham Market Square and in Newcastle, plus the execution of the turncoat Ralph Grey after the fall on Bamburgh, produced the final casualties from Towton. The three years' seesaw war of siege and skirmish fought in the north might be properly viewed as the natural continuation of the Towton campaign, and that the echoes of Palmsunday Field reverberated until then. For all its dreadful spilling of English blood, Towton was not one of those decisive contests in the manner of Hastings or Culloden. The battle established the legitimacy of the Yorkist dynasty but did not render that dynasty safe. Edward IV would not be firm upon his throne till the outcome of Tewkesbury in 1471. As long as Edward of Lancaster was alive his faction would have a cause to fight for. Even with the Lancastrian prince dead, the rump transferred their loyalty to the yet unheard-of Henry Tudor, who, if not a viable threat in the reign of Edward IV, would emerge to cut short the reign of his successor, and thus create a sea change in English history that was the dawn of another era.

For his labours Montagu became Earl of Northumberland, and Warwick apparent first minister of a Yorkist administration. The Neville star had ascended to giddy heights. Yet, for the Kingmaker this would never be quite high enough. Humiliated by the king's outwardly reckless, lust-fuelled union with Elizabeth Woodville, Warwick saw her rapacious brood gobble sinecures and eligible matches. The rise of the Herberts in Wales added to his mounting resentment. Finding a malleable tool in Edward's brilliant but mercurial brother Clarence, Warwick began to think in terms of a more grateful and obliging sovereign. Edward had blocked the notion of Warwick's two daughters each marrying a royal sibling, but Clarence was betrothed in defiance and plotting turned to rebellion. Initially, Edward was confounded but to rule as king without being king was beyond even the Kingmaker's considerable talents. Warwick had defeated and killed the Herbert brothers[4] and carried out a satisfying though annoyingly incomplete cull of the queen's relatives. Nonetheless, Edward was soon free, turning the tables on cousin and brother, routing their putative forces on 'Losecote' Field at Empingham[5] and harrying them from the realm.

In exile, the Kingmaker was, if anything, even more dangerous. Now abetted by Louis XI, unhappy at the Yorkists' pro-Burgundian stance, Warwick was able to broker a momentous and totally unexpected accord with Margaret of Anjou and the rump of exiled Lancastrians. This rather makeshift alliance, dictated largely by French insistence, was cemented by a further dynastic marriage – Warwick's other daughter wed Edward of Lancaster. Clarence was now one heir-in-waiting too many. What followed was even more remarkable – the 'Readeption' of Henry VI – that sad, largely overlooked pensioner in the Tower. Edward was prepared for an attempt but not for the defection of Montagu, who'd been steadfast previously. The king had found it expedient to restore the Percy heir and compensate the Kingmaker's brother with hollow titles. The king, with his younger brother Gloucester, fled to Burgundy.

Here the exiles proved something of an embarrassment and they received paltry welcome. Edward's subsequent landing in Yorkshire appeared a stillborn thing, but Percy stayed crafty-neutral and the king proceeded on the grounds that he was merely come to recover his father's titles. His forces swelled, he out-faced the Kingmaker before the walls of Coventry and fickle Clarence was persuaded to redefect. The decisive clash took place in the mist of Barnet, armies misaligned and blundering in the fog. The day was hard fought but accident and the whiff of treachery destroyed Warwick's hopes. He and his brother fell on the field.[6] Edward and Gloucester were given no respite. As one star fell another seemed to flame. Margaret of Anjou belatedly landed in the west and raised an army. What followed was a desperate race for the Severn crossings – a campaign of baking heat and forced marches that ended at Tewkesbury.[7] Here Margaret saw her hopes finally dashed as her precious prince was killed, along with most of her affinity. Gloucester, as Constable, refused the defeated Lancastrians sanctuary in Tewkesbury Abbey and paid the headsman's wage.

England now entered into the full flowering of a Yorkist Age, the decade of Caxton and a sumptuous court with the queen, though reviled, the paragon of style – her court rivalling that of glittering Burgundy. Clarence fell from grace once too often, while his younger brother, with whom he was also at odds, inherited Warwick's vast satrapy in the north and most of his dead father-in-law's grand estate.[8] Edward launched an invasion of France in 1475 and though this sat ill with the aggressive Gloucester, allowed himself to be bought off. In 1482 Gloucester campaigned against the Scots and recovered Berwick, championing the cause of James III, brother Albany, Scotland's answer to Clarence.

When Edward IV – still a young man, but corpulent and poxed – died suddenly after a bout of pneumonia in 1483, it seemed as though his young son and heir, Edward V, would accede seamlessly, albeit under the baleful influence of the Woodvilles. Richard of Gloucester, with a ready accomplice in the Duke of Buckingham, snatched the young king, arrested some of the Woodville affinity and carried out a neat coup. Ostensibly, he did so to remove Edward V from the malign clutches of the queen's clan. This proved popular and the dead king's bosom friend and constant companion in debauchery, Lord Hastings – no friend to the Woodvilles – lent support. But matters changed swiftly. Hastings was arrested in the council chamber, dragged outside to a makeshift block and hastily dispatched, as was Earl Rivers and the others taken beforehand. Edward V was never crowned, tainted by sudden allegations of bastardy and consigned to the Tower. There he was joined by his younger brother, dragged from the arms of the queen, who'd fled to sanctuary. The fate of the princes has exercised historians and partisans ever since. One thing is certain: neither was ever seen alive again outside the Tower.

Richard III ruled for two years only – a short reign beset by enemies.

For him the test of battle came at Bosworth on 22 August 1485 and his death marked the passing of the Plantagenets and the accession of the House of Tudor. Later writers were pleased to mark this as the end of the medieval period, though it is unlikely that any of those who fought on that hot summer's day made similar observations. At first, Henry's crown seemed as insecure as that of his predecessor. It was not until he crushed the Yorkist rebels at Stoke, two years later, that the Wars of the Roses, as we now define them, are said to have ended – though increasingly distant rumblings continued well into the sixteenth century.

Towton, for all its horror, fury and bloodletting, was neither an end nor a beginning. It was but one significant chapter in a series of dynastic conflicts that convulsed England from the mid to the late fifteenth century. A.A. Gill observes:

> The reason Towton hasn't come down the ages to us might be in part that it was in the middle of the Wars of the Roses, that complex internecine bout of patrician bombast, a hissy fit that stuttered and smouldered through the exhausted fag end of the Middle Ages like a gang feud.

The Wars of the Roses are undoubtedly, as Gill also notes, best remembered through the medium of Shakespeare's cycle of history plays, which though unquestionably epic in scope, exhibit a fair measure of poetic licence.

To stand by the cross today, to attempt to visualise the pageantry and carnage of Palmsunday Field requires a powerful imagination. I disagree with Gill, as I do not find any echo of the slaughter in the still, pastoral landscape. As though generations of patient farming have somehow exorcised the teeming spirits who might have shadowed the ground that soaked up their lifeblood. If you didn't know what had happened here you probably wouldn't spare the place a second glance. But those who do rush past should perhaps be encouraged to pause, if only for a moment. Like those who pass beneath the Menin Gate at Ypres – as savage as the fighting in the Salient was from 1914–1918, no single day there was ever as costly as Towton Field. Half-forgot or not, Palmsunday Field was England's bloodiest day.

Chapter 9

The Towton Mass Grave
Project

One of the enduring questions concerning the field of Towton has always been: where are the bodies? The remains of, let us agree for present purposes, 28,000 combatants, would require a significant number of grave pits to accommodate them. Tradition maintained that, in addition to burials in Saxton Church, grave pits were located in Bloody Meadow and 'the Graves'. Tumuli, visible towards the south-west corner of the field, adjacent to the Cock Beck, may constitute inhumation or perhaps more likely date from prehistoric times. A preliminary archaeological investigation, initiated by the TBS in 1993, was inconclusive. Trial trenches, sunk to a depth of 0.61 metres, swiftly became waterlogged and yielded no traces of human remains.[1]

In 1889 Dr Leadman, writing on *The English Pharsalia*, describes the traditional site of 'the Graves' – now lost to the plough – as being in the second field from the road between Towton and Saxton, opposite the old Towton Dale Quarry. The pit was described as having been 19 yards wide by 32 yards in length – a very substantial enclosure. No recent traces have been found. High-ranking casualties, such as Lord Welles and the Earl of Northumberland, were permitted burial in family vaults, the former at Methley Church and the latter in a magnificent tomb within St Denys, Walmgate, York. This is described as being executed in fine blue-veined marble, with two effigies and inscribed in brass. It was apparently located in the north choir but vanished during 1736.

Undoubtedly, the most tangible reminder of the battle is Saxton Church itself and Lord Dacre's much defaced tomb. The foundation was originally dedicated to All Hallows – a parochial chapelry within Sherburn parish. One of the bells was donated by the lord of the manor at the time of the battle, who died in 1492. Tradition asserts that local people – who would be in church anyway on such an important day in the ecumenical calendar – took refuge in the church while the fury of battle surged without. It is here, on the north side of the church, that many dead were interred. Dacre's own memorial stands in the north-east corner of the churchyard. Nineteenth-century authors considered this to be a national monument and the damaged sarcophagus was renovated in 1883. Dr Leadman, writing some six years later, refers to an earlier incident, when the monument had been broken into, in order to facilitate a subsequent interment – that of a certain Mr Gascoigne. It was reported that the fallen Lancastrian peer had been buried in an upright posture. This followed a local tradition that further asserted his warhorse had been laid with him. As Dr Leadman continues, a subsequent excavation, carried out in 1861, unearthed an equine skull some 6 feet below the surface. The line of vertebrae extended in a manner to suggest the remainder of the bones lay beneath those of Dacre. In Leadman's day the vicar of Saxton still had the horse's skull in his keeping. The battered inscription, in Latin, reads, as near as can be ascertained:

> Here lies Randolf, Lord of Dacre and Gilsland, a true knight, valiant in battle in the service of King Henry VI, who died on Palm Sunday 29th March 1461, on whose soul may God have mercy, Amen

Geophysical surveys have produced no beguiling anomalies and it appears likely that many graves may have disappeared under the plough during intervening centuries. There was, in 1816, an excavation carried out in the area of Chapel Hill, some 100m east of Towton Hall. Arrow piles, coins of the three Henrys (IV, V and VI) were unearthed, together with a single sword blade and human remains.[2] Dr Leadman reports that, in 1835, while excavations were being undertaken at Dintingdale, adjacent to the line of the present road, human remains, alleged at the time (and presumably identified on the basis of wishful thinking) to be those of Lord Clifford were exposed. Towton Hall dates from at least the reign of Richard II and bones were apparently uncovered during extensions to one of the cellars in the eighteenth century. One antiquary of the early Georgian era, Francis Drake, writing in 1736, referred to bone fragments cast up by ploughing and saw at least one crammed grave pit exposed.

A startling new revelation was to come to light much closer to our own times, in July 1996, when further works were undertaken at Towton Hall. Contractors excavating foundations for a proposed garage extension unearthed a shallow pit that contained nearly two dozen skulls. Once it was clear this was not a crime scene, the archaeologists – mainly from Bradford University and West Yorkshire Archaeological Service – took over and, that September, digging was extended to reveal the full extent of the inhumation. When finally fully investigated the burial chamber was some 3.25m by 2.00m with a depth of 0.65m.[3] The remains of no less than fifty-one males, with ages ranging from sixteen to fifty, were uncovered. Aside from a trio of silver rings and other traces,[4] there was no data from which to identify a date for the burial. However, the remains exhibited significant evidence of serious battle-related trauma. That these are the dead of Towton can scarcely be doubted.

Some of the dead, the shortest being 158.5cm (5 foot 2 inches), were small men. These were typically from the younger age range. Those who were older attained heights of 183.5cm (6 foot) with an average height measurement of 171.6cm (5 foot 8 inches). They were thus a shade taller than the average for this era.[5] The remains, as far as could be determined, showed little signs of disease, though most had lived lives involving hard physical labour.[6] Dietary traces and dental evidence were consistent, though latterly these men had neglected their basic dental hygiene, perhaps due to the strains of campaigning.[7] At least two of the dead, older men, had evidence of previous trauma, suggesting seasoned veterans, perhaps of the French Wars, who had met their deaths at the hands of fellow Englishmen. Three exhibited signs of development associated with the practice of archery and the level of physical evidence clearly indicated numerous others had, as mentioned, undergone prolonged physical labour. Whether this was occasioned by arduous military service or simply by working on the land could not be determined. Others were very much less robust and perhaps represented 'scraping the barrel' in recruiting terms.

That their deaths were shockingly violent was soon obvious. The Towton mass grave tells a very different story from any of our more stylised and glorious views of medieval warfare. In this the bones cannot lie. Given the location of the grave it has been surmised that the dead were adherents of Lancaster, cut down in the rout. Skull injuries strongly suggest the victims were not wearing protective headgear at the point of death. This gave rise to some initial suggestions that these were revenge killings – cold-blooded murder enacted after the fight. This now appears unlikely. Possibly the fleeing men threw aside their helmets as they ran. Dumping kit and harness to facilitate flight is natural. It might be – and this is highly speculative – that some archers fought without steel caps, possibly, as John Waller suggests,[8] preferring soft hats, a steel sallet being a hindrance to the draw.

In medieval conflict, head wounds were generally the most common cause of mortality. Of the twenty-eight skulls that could be successfully examined, twenty-seven had suffered trauma to the head. Interestingly, nine of these had suffered prior wounds to the skull – one individual had no less than five: one lucky fellow whose good fortune, like that of so many others, finally ran out on Palmsunday Field. One particularly unlucky individual exhibited no less than nine injuries,[9] and thirteen in total had identifiable wounds to the body. Obviously, many more such injuries might have been inflicted without leaving archaeological traces. Abdominal wounds, penetrative strikes entering lungs, general damage to soft tissue, would all have occurred; though there is little evidence of damage to ribcages, suggesting the men had been wearing jacks or harness.

Scoring of bones is suggestive of blades rather than blunter weapons, such as the mace or poleaxe. Most prevalent traces were cuts to hands and arms – defensive wounds typically occurring when the victim was attempting to parry or deflect. This would further account for injuries to the left side of the neck and collarbone, inflicted by a right-handed opponent. More wounds to the back of the neck would have occurred while the victim was in flight or already on the ground. The angle of some blows clearly suggests they were inflicted by a mounted assailant.

One victim's skull was so mangled it required a near-complete reconstruction.[10] He was one of those who had survived an earlier injury (a depressive fracture to the left parietal region). Death had resulted from a series of eight wounds, 'multiple penetrating and non-penetrating', sustained in the course of hand-to-hand combat with a right-handed attacker swinging a blade, probably a fair sized weapon, perhaps a hand-and-a-half or 'bastard' sword. One massive swinging cut to the rear of the skull had inflicted catastrophic and probably fatal, certainly disabling, damage. This was delivered with a 'large bladed instrument in a slightly down-to-up motion'. In the frenzy of battle a further two blows were added. It is unlikely our victim noted these.[11]

None of these men died nobly. They fell in a frenzied, hacking mêlée of pure and prolonged horror. The bones show the dire nature of wounds. They cannot reveal the faces of the victims as they died, the sounds of animal cries and screams, the great gushing streams of arterial blood, the stink of sweat and urine and faeces – in short, the reality of war.

On average, each victim had sustained four wounds. One was dispatched with a single stroke, the unluckiest required thirteen. As mentioned, some 65 per cent of injuries were inflicted by cuts of the blade – some sheering along the bone, others biting deep or right through. Most seem to have been inflicted from the front, suggesting combat rather than rout. Although percussive wounds were less frequent, they were more damaging, most delivered against the face or side of the head – crushing blows that smashed bone. Of the skulls, eight had suffered stab wounds, a dozen in all. Delivered to the side or rear of the head these were more surgical in nature, the point of the sword or dagger driven home then twisted free. Sword thrusts accounted for only three wounds, the others were caused by the points or beaks of staff weapons. One unfortunate had been prone when at least two of his three wounds were delivered.[12] The shape of some of the wounds suggested bodkin pointed arrows or chunkier crossbow bolts.

The team was fortunate to include a forensic anthropologist, Shannon A. Novak, who has suggested that, had these Towton dead been exhumed closer to the epicentre of the fight, then more evidence of arrow wounds would have been detected. The logic of this appears unassailable, although we must await further discoveries for confirmation. It is obvious that such a relative handful of remains from so extensive a butcher's bill cannot be said to be wholly representative. It does seem likely that these were victims from the latter stages of the fighting, the rout, who had perhaps cast aside their helmets, which might otherwise have given them protection from these awful blows.

We therefore have a snapshot rather than a panorama, but what a glimpse! Bones cannot speak, but the horror of trauma is eloquence itself. These men died horribly, killed by opponents who were afire with killing frenzy, hacked and battered and trampled, their features obliterated in blood-fury. Whether revenge killing was a factor, we cannot say, most probably not. The implication has to be that these men died in the swirling anonymity of battle, assailed by enemies driven to the very edge of terror and desperation.

Forensic sculpture has provided us with a unique insight into the battle and the men who fought there. One of the faceless dead[13] has been given back his features. An older man and one who had survived previous trauma – in this case a substantial cut across the lower right side of the face, which would have shattered the jaw, he looks like any typical blunt-faced artisan. This treatment of a prior injury hints at a level of battlefield surgery more sophisticated and competent than might be imagined. Such evidence, and his strong physique, suggest a seasoned bowman – one who might have seen much action. Like his fellows in the pit, his luck clearly ran out at Towton, where he sustained a frenzy of eight blows to the head. This skilled and fascinating process has given us something we have not had before – the face of an actual combatant. Not the stylised portraiture or imagery of kings or magnates, but the no-nonsense face of the ordinary footslogger.

As the Towton dead have no epitaph, I shall quote a much later war poet, Henry Reed:

> Things may be the same again; and we must fight
> Not in the hope of winning but rather of keeping
> Something alive: so that when we meet our end,
> It may be said that we tackled wherever we could,
> That battle-fit we lived, and though defeated,
> Not without glory fought.

Chapter 10

The Battlefield Today

D espite its scale and intensity, its crucial place in the study of the English polity and warfare of the second half of the fifteenth century, Towton remains a forgotten field. This is despite the steadfast dedication of the TBS, which has (and continues) to do so much. EH[1] defines the west flank as being defined by the Cock Beck from the Old London Road, southwards to Castle Hill Farm. From the southern rim, the line extends east to Cotchers Lane, Whithill Field and the line of the present A162 to Carr Wood. A generous spread of ground is allowed for the eastern slice of the field – enough for possible deployment of both armies in column and a wide margin of some 400 m beyond the roadway to allow for Norfolk's own belated deployment.[2] South of Towton hamlet the line picks up the A162 again, bisects the buildings, then follows the Old London Road to the Cock Beck. These boundaries do not allow for contacts beyond and indeed, given the overall breadth of the action, it is not possible to do so. The actions at Ferrybridge and Dintingdale may be distinguished and considered separately.

Witnessing the present pastoral calm of Towton, it is difficult to imagine the horrors of battle. Indeed, the lack of any real interpretation or contextual help renders the task nigh on impossible. But at least the site has not been extensively altered or built over. Both Saxton and Towton have spread but not so much as to conceal the village core. To follow the route from Ferrybridge, even if the town now yields little of interest, is rewarding. We can trace Clifford's retreat to the killing ground of Dintingdale by Scarthingwell and the Leper's Pot can (with some difficulty) be located by the roadside, but again we have to rely entirely upon the power of our imagination to conjure the scene.

Saxton Church, with Dacre's sober cairn and other hinted graves is a powerful reminder. If we pass along Cotchers Lane to the T-junction before heading right towards Towton, we may (subject to debate) be following the line of the Old London Road. Castle Hill lies ahead with the mounds or tumuli beneath. Turn left instead, and we pass the former site of Lead village before coming to the Crooked Billet,[3] with Lead Church in the field to our right. Returning to Towton, only the Hall itself is of interest, the track that passes by the gable of the Rockingham Arms public house is a stump of the Old London Road. The Hall is to the left, past the trees, and to the right is the mound upon which the vanished chapel likely stood. As one passes along the track, leaving the pub behind, one comes to Cock Bridge; the steep slope and narrow funnel of the crossing speak for themselves.

Andrew Boardman and other commentators are adamant that a chapel did indeed exist and this seems almost certain. Boardman is also undoubtedly correct when he ascribes the motives of chapel builders to policy rather than piety, though the two could be persuaded to combine quite nicely. The evidence[4] would suggest that a manorial chapel, albeit much decayed, was in existence prior to the battle and may mark the resting place of numbers of the slain. Edward IV may have intended to renovate the place as a fitting memorial but ran out of enthusiasm or, more likely funds, before the process could be completed. The Register of Grants from the Duchy of Lancaster[5] records the intention of Richard of Gloucester, later Richard III, to restore the chapel and a cash grant was forthcoming following his coronation in 1483. The Register entry, intriguingly, refers to the exhumation of dead and their reinterment in Saxton and Towton churchyards. Several of the local gentry and yeomen families were involved in the work. Richard's defeat and death at Bosworth clearly curtailed progress and the work was never finished. The Archbishop subsequently attempted fundraising but likely without success.[6]

Henry Tudor presumably had little interest and his son even less. With the cataclysm of the Dissolution sweeping away the old order, only the stark shell was left standing, sufficient to impress Leland in Elizabeth's reign. There had been attempts at raising funds even after the Dissolution but all must have foundered. In later years the fine masonry would have provided a handy resource for secular builders. Towton Hall, refurbished by Admiral Hawke in 1776, boasted a chapel room and it seems certain the old stones were recycled here. There are no present traces of the original and Ricardian chapels. Chapel Hill remains bare of foundations and only future archaeologists are likely to solve the final riddle of its exact location.

Like many historic battlefields, Towton has left us with few traces. An axe from the period was discovered in the vicinity of the Cock Beck and, in the mid-nineteenth century, came into the ownership of the Dukes of Northumberland. It is still on display in Alnwick Castle – a handy-looking weapon, probably, as Gravett suggests, a footsoldier's tool rather than gentlemanly accoutrement. It remains the only likely arm that can be definitely associated with the fight. Other martial fragments have been putatively identified but are now missing.

In 1792 a decorated rowel spur was unearthed and lodged with the Society of Antiquaries of London. An impressive piece, finished with brass and gilt, bearing the inscription 'en loial amour, tout on cœur' ('all my heart in loyal love'), suggesting a treasured gift from a loving spouse. That the spur was left on the field implies the owner failed to return. Such tantalising fragments reveal a glimpse of the thousands of families affected by the battle and its outcome. But for the most part their stories are mute. Did a lady commission these fine spurs for her lord or lover, and did she weep as his corpse lay stiffening on the field?

Six years previously, the same venerated institution had been gifted with a golden ring, adorned with a lion motif, and thus thought to have belonged to a member of the Percy line. This is now in the British Museum. On its face is the enigmatic inscription, 'Nowe ys Thus', suggesting a signet.[7] As Andrew Boardman points out, the lion was a common motif and the ring cannot be definitely linked to Percy, however compelling the idea. Another ring, known to have been in the keeping of a Dr Whittaker in 1816, has subsequently been lost.

Perhaps the most intriguing find was the 'Towton Dog Collar'.[8] This artefact was unearthed in the last quarter of the nineteenth century on land attaching to Saxton Grange Farm. The finder had employed his treasure as a collar for his retriever. Latterly he came to perceive that the thing was beautifully crafted and studded with gems. Seeking to capitalise on his find, the piece was sold in York for £600 – a significant sum indeed for the time, when a well-paid artisan might earn £150 a year. This was written up in a newspaper article during 1926. The correspondent, a Mrs Davis, had been a girl working on the land when the collar was found. She recalled that after the first sale it had changed hands again for more than double – as much as £1,500 – possibly at Christie's Auctioneers. Since then the trail has gone cold. It seems by no means unlikely this was a gentleman's ornament, possibly the Lancastrian SS collar, which owed its design to the badge of Henry Bolingbroke. If so, then its owner was certainly a Lancastrian and, like the wearer of the rowel spur, probably perished.

Towton is not a field such as Bosworth, where the visitor may glean a fair understanding from the heritage centre alone, without necessarily venturing over the ground. Towton is hidden history, largely devoid of modern aids. The visitor is thus required to understand the ground before he or she arrives, to use this understanding, allied to a decent eye for the map, to unravel the story. It is not, therefore, for the casual tourist, hurrying on to the glories of York. Towton demands patience, attention to detail and imagination. It is, perhaps, most atmospheric in late winter or early spring, when lengthening days cast welcome shadows and a keen-edged wind whips across the open plateau. See it on such a day and visualise grand panoplies of unfurled silk, blazons of livery and the glint of harness. For Palmsunday Field was the cauldron in which our history was made.

Appendix I

Glossary

Abbatis	an obstacle forming part of a field fortification where branches of trees are laid in rows, ready-sharpened with the ends pointing towards direction of the enemy.
Advowson	the lord's right to appoint an incumbent to a living.
Affinity	a magnate's following, comprising not just his own vassals or tenants but his friends and allies.
Annuity	the grant of a pension for life, payable in annual instalments, usually granted by the Crown or magnate.
Appenage	the lands of one of royal blood, with co-existent legal rights and privileges.
Armet	a form of enclosed helmet of the late fifteenth century, possibly of Hungarian origin, the first to combine full-head protection with lightness and compactness.
Attainder	statutory deprivation of one found guilty of treason, forfeiture of all estates, rights and privileges in the context of the Wars of the Roses, the inevitable consequence of failure or defeat. The Act of Attainder was passed by Parliament and did not require a conviction of treason from the courts.
Banneret	a knight who was entitled to carry his own banner, conferred status over more junior knights, likely to be given a command in battle.
Bevor	a section of plate armour, worn with the sallet form of helmet to provide protection to the neck and lower face.
Bill	a polearm, a deadly fusion of agricultural implement and spear with a curved axe-type blade, a spike for thrusting and a hook on the reverse – a formidable weapon in trained hands.
Bombard	a heavy siege gun of the fifteenth century, irregular in calibre but throwing a massive ball, perhaps up to 60 lbs in weight.
Bond	an agreement or contract, confirmed by the pledge of cash as a recognisance – a surety for the act to be performed or for the refraining from an act, obviously forfeit should the contracting party default on the terms of the bond.

Caltrap	a four-pointed iron spike device, which, however it was laid on the ground, ensured one point was always jutting upwards.
Captain	the officer responsible for a particular place or location but whose authority was limited to his charge.
Chamber	the fiscal aspect or operation of the Royal Household; the management of the Royal accounts as distinguished from the Exchequer, then as now the finances of the state as a whole.
Chancery	the executive and administrative function of the Crown.
Chevauchée	a large scale foray aimed at laying waste the territory of an enemy, to belittle the foe and perhaps force him to accept battle.
Commission of Oyer & Terminer	from the French, literally to 'hear and determine'. The commissioners were Crown appointees charged to examine and investigate acts of treason, felonies (serious offences) and misdemeanours (lesser offences) committed in a particular county or locality.
Constable	the official in charge of a magnate's tenantry who might exercise his office within the lord's residence or with his soldiery in the field.
Crenellation	the form of battlements on a castle's parapet, 'licence to crenellate' being required before a castle could be constructed.
Demesne	a lord or magnate's personal holdings, those occupied and managed by him as opposed to being parcelled out to a tenant or tenants.
Destrier	a warhorse, much prized and of considerable value.
Enceinte	the circuit of the walls of a defended castle or town.
Feudalism	the system of government and land-holding introduced into England by William I. The feudal pyramid, whereby land was parcelled out to the tenants-in-chief, together with rights attaching thereto, in return for a complex raft of obligations, inherent among which was military service for defined periods and duration. The system prevailed all the way down the social scale from sub-tenants to the unfree agrarian poor or villeins. 'Bastard Feudalism' is a difficult concept, championed by Stubbs in the nineteenth century but revised by McFarlane subsequently – it embodies the notion of service being undertaken for cash payment rather than as part of a wider obligation.
Fiefdom	a parcel of land, usually substantial, containing a number of manors with rights attached.

Fosse	a defensive ditch.
Garron	a breed of horse recognised in Ireland and Scotland, though generally rather despised, likely to be favoured by the commons rather than gentry.
Gorget	a section of plate armour designed to protect the neck area.
Halberd	a form of polearm with a broad axe blade.
Hand-and-a Half-Sword	the knightly sword of the fifteenth century, often known as a 'bastard sword', the long, tapering, double-edged blade could be used either for the thrust or the cut.
Harness	full plate armour.
Hobilar	lightly mounted cavalry or mounted infantry, associated with the light horse of the Anglo-Scottish border.
Indenture	a form of legally binding agreement, the engrossment of which was, upon completion, cut into halves along an indentation; an 'employee' or retainer could be contracted into service by means of an indenture.
Jack	a form of protective doublet, stuffed with rags and generally sleeveless, worn by the commons. A more sophisticated form was the brigandine, which had metal plates sewn between the facing and lining so that only the rivet heads, in decorative patterns, showed through the fabric covering.
Kettle Hat	a form of iron headgear worn by men-at-arms, with a wide protective brim, similar in appearance to British helmet 'tin hats' of both world wars.
Lance	a tactical unit built around a knight's following, which could therefore vary in size.
Leaguer	a siege or blockade.
Livery	the distinctive coat ('livery coat') worn by the lord's retainers, bearing his badge, thus the expression 'livery and maintenance' – the retainer is clothed and fed by his employer in return, in effect, for wearing his private uniform (and assuming his private quarrels). The Battle of Empingham or 'Losecote Field' refers to the haste with which the panicked rebels cast off the incriminating livery coats of the erstwhile paymasters Warwick and Clarence.
Mainprise	a form of surety or bond.
Manor	a form of landholding, a knightly estate usually comprising the residence of the gentleman, a village or villages, woods, fields, mill(s), wine presses, church etc.
Mantlet	a hinged timber shield or shutter affording protection in the field for archer or gunner.

March	a frontier territory, administered by a warden. 'Marcher' lords were those who held lands along the Anglo-Scottish or Welsh borders.
Matross	a gunner's mate or number two, responsible for loading and sponging, detailed to act as a guard for the train.
Mesnie [meinie] *Knight*	one of a lord's household knights, of his domain or *demesne*.
Palatinate	lands held by a count palatine, who enjoyed exclusive jurisdiction and extensive, quasi-regal privileges. The Bishops of Durham had the secular office of Counts Palatine for Durham and North Durham (Norhamshire in North Northumberland).
Palfrey	a fast horse, from the Latin *paraveredus* – post or courier's mount, not a breed as such, however.
Poleaxe	a polearm, favoured by the gentry for close-quarter combat, consisting of an axe blade, spear head and a hammer for battering an armoured opponent.
Rondel *Dagger*	a fifteenth-century, long-bladed knife, carried by all classes, which could be used as a weapon or implement.
Sallet	a fifteenth-century helmet with a swept neckguard and often fitted with a fixed or moveable visor, worn above the bevor.
Tenant-in- *chief*	magnates who held their lands directly from the Crown, rather than from a superior lord, these were known as sub-tenants.
Vassal	one who holds his land from his feudal superior on terms, which involve an obligation of service as a condition of the tenancy.
Vintenar	a breed of NCO in charge of a platoon of twenty men.
Wapentake	a Norse term, literally 'the brandishing of spears in a popular assembly', long established even by 1086 (Domesday). The expression has the same meaning as the Saxon 'Hundred' and refers to main area sub-divisions within a given county.

Appendix II

The Combatants

Key – 'k' = killed; 'e' = executed

Lancaster

Sir Andrew Trollope (k), Sir David Trollope (k), Sir John Heyton (k), Sir Richard Percy (k), Sir Ralph Percy, Sir John Montgomery (e), Sir Richard Tunstall, Sir John Maulever, Sir John Fortescue, Sir John Tresham, Sir William Catesby, Sir John Heron (k), Sir John Crackenthorpe (k), Sir Henry Narbohew (k), Sir William Harill (k), Sir Philip Wentworth, Sir William Tailboys (e), Sir Edmund Mountford, Sir William Vaux, Sir Edmund Hampden, Sir Thomas Findern, Sir John Courtenay, Sir Henry Lewes, Sir Nicholas Latimer, Sir Gervase Clifton, Sir Ralph Eure (k), Sir William Gascoigne, Sir Ralph Grey, Sir Richard Hammis (k), Sir William Hevill (k), Sir Robert Hillyard (k), Sir Thomas Molyneux, Sir John Bigot (k), Sir Henry Roos, Sir Thomas Butler, Sir John Burton, Sir Baldwin Fulford, Sir Thomas Fulford, Sir Alexander Hody, Sir James Lutterell, Sir William Bertram, Sir Thomas Metham, Sir Thomas Elderton, Sir Richard Carey, Sir Roger Clifford, Sir Thomas Babthorpe, Sir John Dunn, Sir William St Quyntin, Sir John Delves, Sir Henry Bellingham, Sir Robert Whittingham, Sir John Butler, Sir William Hill (e), Sir William Holand (bastard), Sir Symond Hammes, Sir Henry Bokingham, Sir Humphrey Dacre, Sir John Pennington, Walter Nuthill Esq, Everard Dykby Esq, Thomas Philip Esq, Giles Syentlowe Esq (k), Thomas Claymond Esq, John Aldeley Esq, Robert Bellingham Esq (k), William Grimsby Esq, John Doubiggin Esq (k), William Weynsford Esq (k), John Joskyn Esq (k), William Antron Esq, Thomas Stanley gent. (k), Thomas Litley, grocer (k), Henry Spencer, yeoman (k), John Smothing (k), Roger Wharton groom (k), Thomas Carr yeoman (k), Richard Hatecale yeoman (k), Lawrence Hill yeoman (k), Richard Gaitford, gent (k), Richard Cokerell merchant (k), John Hawt, Sir William Fielding, Sir Thomas Hervey, Sir John Marney, Sir Humphrey Neville, Sir Charles Neville, Sir William Newburgh, Sir William Plumpton, Sir William Catesby, Sir Richard Tuddenham, William Joseph Esq, John Myrvyn Esq, Thomas Brampton Esq (k), Thomas Tunstall

Esq, Thomas Crawford (k), John Lenche Esq, John Penycok Esq, Thomas Daniel Esq (k), William Ackeworth Esq (k), Richard Stukely Esq (k), Richard Everyngham Esq (k), John Haydon Esq, Richard Kirkeby gent. (k), John Dauson yeoman (k), Henry Beaumont gent. (k), John Beaumont gent (k), Richard Lister yeoman (k), Robert Bolling gent. (k), Richard Fulmady yeoman (k), Ralph Chernock gent. (k), John Chapman yeoman (k), Thomas Burnby, Thomas Thompson of Guines.

York

Sir Walter Blount, Sir Jon (later Lord) Wenlock, Sir John Conyers, Sir William (later Lord) Hastings, Sir John Stafford, Sir John Dinham, Sir Humphrey Stafford, Sir Nicholas Byron, Sir Richard Jenny (k), Sir Guy Fairfax, Sir Thomas Montgomery, Sir Simon Mountford, Sir Walter Devereux, Sir John Astley, Sir Thomas Lumley, Sir John Bourchier, Sir William Bourchier, Sir Humphrey Bourchier, Sir Richard Croft (elder), Sir Richard Croft (younger), Sir John Clay, Sir Philip Courtenay, Sir Geoffrey Gate, Sir William Herbert, Sir Richard Herbert, Sir Robert Ogle, Sir Richard Hastings, Sir John Pilkington, Sir William Stanley, Sir John Say, Sir Thomas Strickland, Sir Thomas Vaughan, Sir Roger Vaughan, Sir Henry Stafford, Sir Henry Pierrepoint, William Brandon Esq, Ralph Hastings Esq, Thomas Denyes Esq, John Harper Esq, Robert Harcourt Esq, John Milewater (elder), John Milewater (younger), Walter Myton, James Radcliffe Esq, Nicholas Sharpe Esq, Henry Sotehill gent, Sir Robert Clifton, Sir Robert Markham, Sir John Markham, Sir Roger Wolferstone, Sir Henry Ratcliffe, Sir John Howard, Sir Thomas Walgrave, Sir John Asherton, Sir Thomas Fitzalan, Sir Richard Beauchamp, Sir Humphrey Blount, Sir Christopher Conyers, Sir Thomas Burgh, Sir Robert Chamberlain, Sir Roger Corbett, Sir Gilbert Debenham, Sir Robert Green, Sir George Lumley, Sir James Harrington, Sir Robert Harrington, Sir Thomas Parr, Sir William Petche, Sir James Strangways, Sir Richard Strangways, Sir William Stonor, Sir Robert Wingfield, Sir William Norrys, Sir William Tyrell, Sir William Rainford, Thomas Baskerville Esq, James Baskerville Esq, John Harcourt Esq, Richard Hakluyt Esq, Geoffrey Middleton Esq, Gruffydd Ap Henry Esq, Thomas Mornington, Robert Plomer Esq, Richard Salkeld Esq, Fulk Stafford Esq, Thomas Sturgeon Esq, William Tendering Esq, Philip Vaughan Esq, John Fogge Esq, Robert Horne Esq, Sir Henry Lewys, William Sturgeon Esq, John Scott Esq, Ralph Hopton Esq, Sir Thomas Thorpe, Ralph Vestyndon (the bearer on the field of Edward's Black Bull standard, for his good service he was awarded an annuity of ten pounds[1]).

Appendix III

The War in the North
1461–1464

The Act of Attainder, passed by Edward IV's victorious Parliament, attainted all of the northern lords who had fallen in the Battle of Towton: the Earl of Northumberland, Lords Clifford, Neville and Dacre. Many others from the region also found themselves dispossessed: Sir Humphrey Dacre, Sir Thomas Findern, Sir John Heron, Sir Henry Bellingham, Sir Robert Whittingham, Sir Ralph Randolf, Robert Bellingham of Westmorland, Thomas Stanley, John Smothing, Robert Bolling, Robert Hatecale, Richard Everingham, Richard Cokerell (these last five from York), Roger Wharton from Westmorland and Ralph Chernock from Lancashire. Of these attainted a number, including Bellingham, his brother, Randolf and Stanley, had been previously implicated in the disturbances of the early 1450s, though Stanley, at that time, had been of the Neville faction.[1]

The Lancastrians in Northumberland
In his correspondence to Coppini, George Neville had been at pains to stress the magnitude of the victory at Towton:

> The armies having been formed and marshalled separately, they set forth against the enemy and at length, on Palm Sunday, near a town called Ferrybridge, about 16 miles from our city, our enemies were routed and broken in pieces.[2]

Though the Lancastrians had been grievously beaten, the Milanese ambassador to the court of Charles VII, Prospero di Camulio, writing a mere four days after George Neville, sounded a shrewdly cautious note:

> Firstly, if the King and Queen of England with the other fugitives mentioned above are not taken, it seems certain that in time fresh disturbances will arise.[3]

This observation was to prove grimly prophetic as the focus of the war moved north into Northumberland, where it was to fester for the next three years.

The county of Northumberland was a different region from North Yorkshire, where the troubles of the preceding decade and the battles of that phase of the wars, which occurred between 1459 and 1461, had been centred. There is, perhaps, a tendency among historians to point generally to the north as though the land north of the Trent was a single region. This is, of course, not the case, nor was it so in the fifteenth century. The cultural, topographical and social fabric of the north embraced 'a kaleidoscope of overlapping regions and localities'.[4] Northumberland is the most northerly of English counties and shares a long border with Scotland. Northumbrians and Scots had been embroiled in endemic warfare since the late thirteenth century.[5]

To the west, Carlisle, with its great red sandstone Norman keep, had been the gateway to the English west for centuries, defying every effort by the Scots. The city was a flourishing port in its own right, plying the busy routes to Ireland and Man. Naworth and Askerton castles stood along the west march, the Scots' frequent choice of incursion route. A number of these fortifications were to prove significant in the struggles of 1461–1464 but none more than the three great east coast fortresses of Alnwick, Bamburgh and Dunstanburgh. Of these, the first was a jewel of the Percys and much improved by them over several generations.[6] Bamburgh occupies a spur of the whin sill, rising 150 feet from the flat coastal plain: the ancient seat of the Northumbrian kings, said to be the 'Joyous Garde' of Arthurian legend.[7] Begun by Thomas, Earl of Lancaster, Dunstanburgh also occupies a dolerite outcrop, much rebuilt in the later fourteenth century by John of Gaunt, who held the wardenship in the 1380s.[8]

After receiving the dire news of her defeat at Towton, Queen Margaret fled north into Scotland with King Henry, her young son Edward of Lancaster and a scattering of survivors, including Somerset, Roos, Exeter and Sir John Fortescue. Margaret might have shared the view that Northumberland was solidly Lancastrian in sentiment, following the lead of the Percys who 'have the hearts of the north and always have had'.[9] While the Earl of Northumberland found his hegemony challenged in Durham and North Yorkshire by the Nevilles, Salisbury and his affinity had little influence in the most northerly shire. On 22 April 1461, some three weeks after Towton, King Edward IV progressed north to Newcastle where, on 1 May, he attended the demise of James Butler, Earl of Wiltshire, whose happy knack of slipping unscathed from a number of tight spots finally deserted him. With him was John Neville, Lord Montagu, who had previously been held captive in York. He had escaped the fate of the Yorkist lords taken at Wakefield when he himself was captured at Second St Albans. His brother Richard had Somerset's younger sibling Edmund incarcerated at Calais, so a form of quid pro quo had obtained. Having established his authority, however, the king soon tired of the north; pressing matters awaited him in London and he was pleased to delegate mopping-up operations to the Nevilles.

James II, King of Scotland, had led a six-day *chevauchée* through the English borderland in 1456 and had attempted to retake Berwick in the following year. His interest in the dynastic struggle unfolding in England was largely opportunistic and he had petitioned Charles VII of France to launch an assault on the Calais Pale. When James heard of the Yorkist victory at Northampton and the capture of Henry VI, he sat down before Roxburgh, the last bastion of the former Pale. On 3 August, with his batteries sited, he was to be joined by his Queen, Marie de Gueldres. The king ordered a cannonade to herald his consort but one of the great guns burst – a not infrequent peril – and James was fatally wounded when a fragment smashed his thigh.[10] His heir, now James III, was only eight and Scotland was again subject to the uncertainties of a regency council. This body quickly split into factions: the 'Old' lords, led by Bishop Kennedy of St Andrews, and the 'Young', who championed the widowed queen. Margaret of Anjou was desperate for allies, to the extent that she would trade both Carlisle and Berwick. On 25 April the keys of Berwick were handed over but the citizens of Carlisle would have no truck with Scots and grimly barred their gates, refusing the queen's summons.

A joint Scots and Lancastrian expedition was dispatched to besiege the city and the Yorkists perceived the threat sufficiently potent for Edward to bring forward the date of his coronation to 28 June, so he would be free to lead a march north. In the event this proved unnecessary as the resourceful Montagu, raising local forces, saw the besiegers off. Margaret had demonstrated not only the measure of her desperation but an epic disregard for the sentiment of the very northerners she sought to woo, to whom the Scots were a despised and frequent foe. Berwick-upon-Tweed was destined to remain in their hands until 1482, when it was retaken by Richard of Gloucester, at which point it had changed hands no less than fourteen times![11]

There were further disturbances – the French were said to be about to descend on the Channel Islands, led by Queen Margaret's fervent admirer, Pierre de Breze. But with the death, on 22 July, of Charles VII, the likelihood of French meddling diminished. The new sovereign had little time for the gallant de Breze, who was effectively put out to grass.[12] Warwick won the loyalty of a Burgundian captain, the Seigneur de la Barde, who, having succumbed to the earl's charisma and the attractions of his pay chest, led a company of handgunners previously in the service of Duke Philip, joining the Yorkist ranks after the disaster at Wakefield.[13]

In England, the spark of rebellion flared briefly in East Anglia. Wales (where, as in Northumberland, the Lancastrian lords still held several major castles) soon followed suit. By autumn, however, the Welsh adherents had been bested in the field and their strongholds systematically reduced. At the end of the year only mighty Harlech still held out. Feeling themselves relatively secure in Northumberland, the Lancastrian Lords Dacre, Roos and Rougemont Grey launched a raid into Durham, advancing their banners as far as Brancepeth,

King Henry present in their train. True to his fresh allegiance, Lawrence Booth, the prince bishop – previously a staunch supporter, but now converted by the great victory at Towton into an equally enthusiastic Yorkist – mustered the county levies and saw them off:

> The problem here [the north] was a complicated one, Henry VI and his supporters were sheltered and aided by the Scots, and, to a lesser extent, by the French. The region itself was remote, difficult of access and dominated by the great fortresses.[14]

Alarms and Excursions

In July Warwick was appointed as warden for both east and west marches, ably assisted by his brother Montagu. The Nevilles continued mopping up until September, by which time Alnwick surrendered and a garrison of 100 men-at-arms was installed. In early October Dunstanburgh capitulated, the terms of surrender being negotiated by the Lancastrian castellan, Sir Ralph Percy. It might be presumed that the Yorkist triumph was complete, but for as long as the defeated court had a base in Scotland, the border would be troubled. Edward IV, painfully aware of the narrowness of his own affinity and his fragile grip on the sceptre, was prepared to be accommodating and overlook past affiliations – a bold, if risky, strategy in contrast to Warwick's approach, which was considerably more pragmatic. The king was disposed to permit Sir Ralph to remain in charge at Dunstanburgh – a mistake, for the Percy soon reverted. Another Lancastrian, Sir William Tailboys, emerging from Scotland, swiftly recaptured Alnwick, while, in the west, Lord Dacre seized Naworth.[15]

Both Edward and his lieutenant perceived that a diplomatic offensive against the Scots, aimed at depriving the Lancastrians of their foothold in the northern kingdom, was the only sure means of establishing firm control over the English border marches. Warwick thus held preliminary talks with Marie de Gueldres in April 1462, followed by a further meeting in July, but the Scottish council, already divided, seemed determined to sit on the fence and wait on events. In March Somerset and Lord Hungerford had returned empty-handed from a begging mission to the French court. Undeterred, Margaret of Anjou borrowed £290 from the Regent and sailed from Kirkcudbright in April, prepared, as a measure of her desperation, to trade Calais as she had done Berwick.[16]

While Warwick sought an accommodation with Marie de Gueldres, his forces in Northumberland resumed the offensive. By July Montagu had compelled Dacre's surrender and regained Naworth, a vital bastion in the west. In the east, Tailboys surrendered the keys of Alnwick to the Yorkist triumvirate of Lord Hastings, Sir John Howard and Sir Ralph Grey, while Bamburgh was taken by Sir William Tunstall:[17]

The support and sympathy of the local population worked against what was regarded as a hostile government and enabled even small forces of active rebels to defy it for months on end.[18]

Detail on the surrender of Alnwick is somewhat confusing. Worcester is the only chronicler who mentions the event, while the Paston correspondence places Lord Hastings at Carlisle with Warwick in July, though this would not necessarily have prevented him from accepting the surrender. Equally, there is no reason to doubt the appointment of Tailboys as castellan – he remained a staunch Lancastrian till diverted by greed and misappropriated the funds placed in his care.[19]

The Paston Letters also place Sir William Tunstall at Bamburgh in the autumn of 1462. His brother, Sir Richard, sat in the opposite camp and had been in the castle that summer. The collapse of the defensive chain of great border castles and the lack of any material support from either France or Scotland appeared to sound the final knell for Henry's faltering faction. Queen Margaret remained unbowed, however, and proved able still to fan the dying embers of her cause. On 25 October she made landfall, possibly, as Worcester asserts, at Bamburgh. The expedition was led by the faithful de Breze and comprised some 2,000 French mercenaries. The invaders marched inland to Alnwick, which, being poorly provisioned, promptly surrendered. Hungerford and de Breze's son were left in command. Somerset based himself at Bamburgh, where, by the fortune of war, Sir William Tunstall was taken by his brother Richard. Dunstanburgh also changed hands. Though these achievements passed control of the border fortresses back to Queen Margaret, there was no popular upsurge in favour of her house. Whether she intended simply to foment local anti-Yorkist sentiment or whether she was seeking, in the larger game, to open a bridgehead for Scottish intervention, remains unclear.[20]

What is certain is that, having secured these three key bastions, she, with the bulk of her expeditionary force, immediately took ship, presumably heading for Scotland, there to press for significant intervention. Though she and de Breze completed the sea passage, many of the ships were wrecked by adverse weather in the cold North Sea – men were scattered, stores and cash were lost. Some 400 French were stranded on the Northumbrian coast. Foiled in an attempt to enter Bamburgh, they fell back towards Holy Island, firing what remained of their boats. Though they overawed the few defenders they soon found themselves under determined assault from Yorkists, led by the Bastard of Ogle and 'One Maners, a squire'. Falling back and barricading the priory, the French were soon obliged to seek terms.[21]

Though clearly wrongfooted by the queen, Warwick soon recovered and marched his forces into Northumberland by 30 October, with Edward following on 3 November. Though he reached Durham by the 16th, Edward was debilitated by a bout of measles, which enfeebled him for the short remaining span of the year.[22] Meanwhile, Warwick vigorously prosecuted siege operations against the northern castles. Establishing his forward command post at Warkworth, he entrusted the Duke of Norfolk with responsibility for supply and logistics through the port of Newcastle. The Earl of Kent was charged to reduce Alnwick with Lord Scales, the Earl of Worcester and Sir Ralph Grey before Dunstanburgh; Montagu and Ogle leaguered Bamburgh. This was Warwick at his best – a war of attrition, free from the uncertainties and snap decisions necessary in the open field, the earl rode around his outposts on a daily basis, the supply from Newcastle moved smoothly despite the onset of winter conditions and the desperate state of the roads.

The tactical initiative had swung the other way. From Bamburgh, Somerset and the turncoat Percy looked out over the besiegers' lines, Sir Richard Tunstall and Thomas Fyndern held Dunstanburgh. John Paston recorded that William Hasildene, Matilda Walsh and John Carter acted as purveyors for the Yorkists before Bamburgh and the King's Pavilions were erected by William Hill, a servant of the Master of the Tents. Paston goes on to suggest Warwick had mustered some 10,000 soldiers, while Somerset had less than 300 defenders.[23] Thorough as these siege preparations had been, it would appear that the mere show of strength was sufficient to overawe the defenders – there was no bombardment, the great guns never progressed further than the dockside at Newcastle. Even the lighter field pieces were not deployed; these would have been turned against Scottish forces had any intervention occurred. There was a natural reluctance to reduce the vital border castles by gunfire, as, in normal circumstances, they were vital for the defence of the northern shire and borderland. The prospect of campaigning throughout a miserable Northumbrian winter had scant appeal:

> Tough, hardy and used to discomfort as they were, medieval soldiers had a deep distaste for winter campaigning . . . Henry V had forced his armies to maintain winter sieges in Northern France, but no one had yet attempted them in the even bleaker conditions of Northumbria in December.[24]

On Christmas Eve the Lancastrian Lords negotiated the surrender of both Bamburgh and Dunstanburgh: for the abandonment of their allegiance to Henry VI both Somerset and Sir Ralph Percy were to be restored to their titles and property. Both swore fealty to Edward IV. This capitulation may reflect a loss of morale – neither fortress was yet seriously threatened, but there appeared little hope of relief and Somerset may possibly have been resentful of the Frenchman de Breze being given authority over his head. Edward, for his part, was prepared to exercise a fair measure of pragmatism; the feud with the Beauforts ran deep, the blood of his father, brother, uncle and cousin, stained Somerset's hands.[25]

In the meantime, the remaining garrison at Alnwick continued its defiance as the indefatigable de Breze was leading a Scots relief force. Warwick was caught off-balance. He withdrew his forces before Alnwick with such indecent haste that the Scots believed they were being lured into an ambush. This produced a near-farcical denouement as the Scots, in turn, speedily withdrew, leaving only a skeleton force and the discomfited besiegers reoccupied the lines they'd so recently abandoned.[26] The depleted garrison wasted no time coming to terms and Warwick appointed Sir John Ashley to command with Ralph Grey as deputy – a demotion the latter bitterly resented, believing the senior post should have been his. As was so often the case, this personal grudge would bear bitter fruit.[27]

By the end of 1462 the position appeared to have returned to that which had obtained in the summer, prior to Queen Margaret's return, but the Yorkist grip was flimsier than the tactical position would suggest. Percy was at heart a Lancastrian and Grey was nursing his resentment. In the spring of 1463 Percy reverted, opening the gates of Bamburgh while Grey seized Alnwick by a coup de main:

> And within three or four months after that false knight and traitor, Sir Ralph Percy, by false treason, took the said Sir John Astley prisoner, and delivered him to Queen Margaret, and then delivered the castle to the Lord Hungerford and unto the Frenchmen accompanied with him.[28]

Flight of Queen Margaret

Having neatly reversed the position in Northumberland the Lancastrians now concentrated their efforts against Norham, that 'Queen of Border Fortresses' held by the prince bishop and a prize which had, for decades, eluded the Scots. Frustrated by the loss of Alnwick, Bamburgh, and now Dunstanburgh, which Sir Ralph Percy had also gifted, Warwick was constrained to move swiftly and raise the Siege of Norham, with Lord Montagu scattering Queen Margaret and her marchers after a lightning march. So swift and sure was this riposte, both she and Henry were nearly taken. The Lancastrian garrisons made no attempt to interfere. In spite of this success, Warwick did not propose to sit down, once again, before the great walls of the coastal castles. He now preferred to bring further diplomatic pressure to bear on the Scots and thus cut off the Lancastrians' aid at source. Warwick could undoubtedly sense that enthusiasm for the House of Lancaster was waning – the Scots efforts at Carlisle and now Norham had been contemptuously repulsed. Henry, sensing the mood swing of his hosts, transferred his truncated court either to Alnwick or Bamburgh.[29]

Edward had, by now, obtained a further grant of taxation revenues from the English Parliament to be expended against the Scots (though the Commons approved the funds it was some time before the king got the cash). Warwick had, however, precipitated offensive action, with the support of the

Archbishop of York, by launching a destructive *chevauchée* into the Lothians.[30] Margaret and de Breze were both presently engaged in the Siege of Norham, their forces were surprised and scattered by Montagu. After the debacle at Norham, Queen Margaret, fearful for her son's safety and accompanied by de Breze, took ship for Flanders, where she proposed to solicit aid from Duke Philip. These wily Burgundians, the duke and his son, the Count of Charolais (later famous as the mercurial Charles the Bold), were prepared to make encouraging noises and Charles wrote reassuringly to Henry, immured within Bamburgh's stout walls (this correspondence was carried by a John Brown and William Baker, the latter one of Exeter's affinity). No practical assistance was, however, forthcoming.

Gregory[31] asserts that the Lancastrians sailed immediately from Sluys, having escaped from the trap at Norham, pursued, as the chronicler avers, almost to the walls of Bamburgh. Margaret and her shrunken contingent, which included Exeter, Fortescue and the remaining Frenchmen, filled four 'balynggarys' (ballingers – large, sleek, double-ended and oared galleys). Gregory also recounts that a French drummer boy refused to embark and waited calmly on the shore. This disenchanted youth demanded, vociferously, a place in Warwick's retinue and the earl inclined to the request, the renegade doing good service for a number of years.[32]

Unmolested by either Warwick or his brother, King Henry maintained the façade of dominion over his tiny Northumbrian domain. In December 1463 he issued letters of protection to William Burgh, Constable of Prudhoe, seeking to consolidate his faction's grip in Tynedale, where Lancastrian sentiment remained viable. Early in the New Year he issued a charter to the burgesses of Edinburgh. The French ambassador who attended this shadow court was Pierre Cousinot, whom Henry used as a messenger to his wife in Burgundy. Henry's proposed strategy comprised a tripartite alliance between himself, as titular King of England, the Count of Charolais and the Duke of Brittany. He pleaded with the great lords of France to work against any understanding that might be brokered between Edward and Louis. He begged aid from the Burgundians. He begged aid, particularly ordnance, from Rene of Anjou, his father-in-law. He entreated the Bretons to exploit unrest in Wales and join with the Earl of Pembroke.[33] Henry's main difficulty was lack of funds and all of his entreaties included a request for cash. Deprived of parliamentary grants, destitute of lands and treasure, he had no fiscal base to fund aggressive action, his faction had no real leadership and the prospects for 1464 seemed bleak. The single rogue card was Henry Beaufort, Duke of Somerset, the erstwhile champion of Lancaster. His decision, taken in that spring, to revert to his hereditary allegiance, would spark the final, dramatic denouement of the campaigns in the north.

Appendix IV

The Battles of Hedgeley Moor
and Hexham

enry Beaufort, his brother-in-law, Sir Henry Lewis and Sir Nicholas Latimer had all been attainted in 1461 and all three were in Dunstanburgh when the fortress was surrendered on 27 December 1462. In the circumstances they, with Sir Ralph Percy, were treated with extreme leniency. Percy was confirmed as castellan of both Dunstanburgh and Bamburgh; on 17 March the following year he received a commission to accept the submission of other rebels. This clemency reflects an element of realpolitik – Percy was still a name that carried great weight in Northumberland; if Edward could secure the family's allegiance, he effectively kicked away the greatest Lancastrian prop in the north. Somerset fared even better. He appears to have served with some distinction against his former associates, having all the charisma and fortitude of the Beauforts. King Edward made much of him, hunting with his former mortal foe, who even enjoyed the signal honour of acting as a knight of the bedchamber. The duke received cash subsidies and the hefty annuity of 1,000 marks. Tournaments were mounted in his honour and Edward personally intervened to save Somerset from certain death at the hands of an unruly mob in Northampton.[1]

The Road to Hedgeley Moor

Why, then, did the duke defect and resume his former allegiance? He could, presumably, have accepted a safe conduct and withdrawn north of the border, as other members of the Dunstanburgh garrison chose – though whether Warwick would have allowed the former commander-in-chief this option is uncertain. There is a suggestion Somerset already approached Warwick some months before to explore terms. On 10 March, 1463, Somerset's attainder was reversed and yet, by December he and Percy had both reverted. Hicks has asserted, probably correctly, that this was not due to hubris or an unwillingness to accept reality – Somerset was neither fool nor dreamer; he must have known the odds were long and that no second chances would be forthcoming. What occurred, therefore, was a crisis of conscience – the oath to Henry VI was too compelling and it triumphed over expediency. The cause might be hopeless but honour outweighed the odds.[2] Possibly, both Percy and Somerset regarded their earlier compromise as nothing more than a necessary ruse to gain time while matters turned more favourably.

The duke and Sir Ralph were not alone – both Sir Henry Bellingham and Sir Humphrey Neville subsequently defected. Some commentators, particularly Ross, regard Edward's policy of 'hearts and minds' as naïve and culpable – a political blunder.[3] This may be too censorious. Edward had won the crown by the sword, his affinity among the magnates was narrow. To survive and establish a stable regime he needed, urgently, to broaden his platform of support. To achieve this it was clearly necessary to win over former opponents. Simply killing them was not, as recent history showed, an effective policy. The blood spilled on the streets of St Albans had pooled into a legacy of hate and resentment that had led to the carnage of Towton. The effects of this titanic fight should not be underestimated – the Yorkists had won, but only by a whisker. No prince would consider repeating such an epic campaign – the drain on blood and treasure was simply too great, the stakes too high. Edward had judged that suborning his former enemies not only brought new friends but demoralised the remaining diehards and, by the close of 1462, he could have been justified in thinking that the flames of resistance had guttered out.[4]

Edward's contemporaries certainly took the harsher view. Gregory – no friend to Somerset – observed that: 'the savynge of hys lyffe at that tyme causyd mony mannys dethys son aftyr, as ye shalle heyre'.[5] Hicks views Percy's defection as the more serious because of the power of his name in Northumberland, notwithstanding the fact Edward still held both Somerset's brother and Percy's nephew as hostages.[6] Edward's policy of conciliation was at best a gamble and one which, in these leading instances, clearly failed.[7] At the time it seemed a risk worth taking if the prize was a lasting peace – this was not achieved and the Lancastrian cause in the north was to enjoy a final, brief revival in the spring of 1464.[8]

Early in the year sporadic unrest erupted throughout the realm. In fifteen counties, from Kent to Cornwall and as far north as Leicestershire, the disruption was sufficiently serious for Edward to delay the state opening of Parliament. There is evidence from the contemporary record that Somerset might have, mistakenly, perceived that Henry had received some new impetus and supply: 'herynge y King Henry was comynge into the lande with a newe strength'.[9] It is uncertain where these fresh troops were coming from and how they were to be paid – perhaps there was a hope the French or Scots might intervene? Somerset began his reversion by attempting to seize Newcastle – a considerable prize, being the Yorkists' forward supply base. A number of his affinity formed an element of the garrison but the attempt did not succeed; Lord Scrope with some of the king's household knights frustrated the scheme.

The rebel duke was very nearly taken at Durham, where he was obliged to flee from his lodgings in no more than his nightshirt. Gregory reports that a number of his retainers were captured, together with their master's 'caskette and hys harneys [helmet and armour]'.[10] Others attempted to slip through the net and escape Newcastle – any who were caught suffered summary execution.

There is also some further doubt as to the fugitive King Henry's whereabouts. The 'Year Book' claims he was at Alnwick, though this may be incorrect, for the same source claims Margaret and de Breze were with him when we can be certain both were in Flanders at that time.[11] NCH still places his diminished court at lordly Bamburgh and this seems more credible – Alnwick was nearer the Yorkists at Newcastle, while Bamburgh had access to the sea.[12] Somerset may have proceeded directly to Henry or, equally possible, he may have made for Tynedale, where a crop of castles – Prudhoe, Hexham, Bywell and Langley – remained staunch. At some point, either in February or March, he was joined by his former comrades, Ralph Percy and Sir Humphrey Neville of Brancepeth, with their retainers. With Somerset's defection a new sense of urgency infused the faltering cause of the house of Lancaster.

And urgency there was, for the Scots were showing willingness to treat with Warwick, who had detailed his brother Montagu to march north and provide safe passage through the uncertain reaches of the frontier for a team of Scottish negotiators. These talks were initially scheduled to take place at Newcastle on 6 March, but the increasing tempo of alarms caused the start to be delayed until 20 April and the venue shifted south to calmer pastures. Edward, on 27 March, announced his intention to travel north and organise a suitable escort for the delegation waiting at Norham.[13] The success of any such mission would be fatal to Lancastrian hopes, so Somerset was placed in a position where he was bound to take the field, with such forces as he could muster and stake everything. Consequently, he dispatched a commanded body of foot – 'four score spears and bows too'[14] – under Neville, to lay an ambush 'a little from Newcastle in a wood'.[15] Forewarned by scouts or spies, Montagu easily avoided the trap and chose a safer route into the city, where he was reinforced by 'a great fellowship'.[16] He then set out to march north to the border.

Somerset's best chance now lay in forcing a decisive encounter, causing a defeat in the field that would leave the Scots immured and serve to show the Lancastrians still had teeth. By mustering every spear he could and stripping his handful of garrisons, the duke might, as Gregory suggests, have been able to muster 5,000.[17] This seems a very generous estimate notwithstanding he could count upon his own affinity with those of Percy, Neville, Bellingham, the turncoat Grey, Lords Hungerford and Roos. We have no note of the force Montagu was leading north but it would certainly have been the equal of anything his enemies could deploy. As the Yorkists marched north from Morpeth, the Lancastrians sallied from Alnwick, both sides probing with a screen of light horse or 'prickers'. Nine miles west of Alnwick Somerset drew up in battle order, blocking the way north to Norham.

Though the chronicles provide scant details of the battle that ensued, a careful perambulation of the ground, which, save for the spread of cultivation, remains largely undisturbed, indicates the fight took place on the shelf of rising ground just north of where Percy's Cross now stands. This is the area between, to the south, the stand of timber known as Percy's Strip Wood and the monument (Percy's Leap). Here, the ground is slightly undulating, rising towards the northern flank. In the spring of 1464 the land was not under the plough but an expanse of open moor, largely devoid of trees. With the Lancastrians facing south, in front of Percy's Leap, the Yorkists most probably carried out their initial deployment on the line of the present woodland.

As they approached from the south, the main body of the Yorkists would have had no opportunity to view the strength of their enemy until they ascended the slight rise, which swells from the lower ground. The Lancastrians would not have wished to deploy to the south of the position suggested, as this would be to lose the advantages the field conferred. Haigh[18] shows the Yorkists drawn up somewhat to the south of this position and indicates the Lancastrians advanced to contact over open ground. I think this unlikely. Yorkist morale was most probably higher and Montagu may have enjoyed greater strength; he was, by nature, a confident and aggressive commander. This is, however, conjectural, as the chronicles remain frustratingly silent on these initial dispositions and the numbers certainly cannot be assessed with any degree of confidence.[19] Somerset may, like Warwick, have been prone to indecision at key moments (his failure to reinforce Clifford at Dintingdale stands as a clear example).[20]

It could be assumed that the fight commenced with the customary duel of arrows (though there is no evidence) and Yorkist supremacy was swiftly asserted. Before ever striking a blow, the whole of the Lancastrian left or rearward division, commanded by Hungerford and Roos, dissolved in total rout, leaving the centre under Somerset, Bellingham and Grey, together with the right or vaward, under Percy, horribly exposed. Montagu ordered the advance to contact.[21] Most probably the mêlée occurred in the vicinity of Percy's Leap – a short, savage, and largely one-sided encounter. The Lancastrian centre soon joined their fellows on the left in flight, Somerset and his officers swept along, unable to stem the rot. Percy by now was virtually surrounded; fighting bravely, he sustained mortal wounds seeking to break the ring. An enigmatic legend lingers over his last moments – 'I have saved the bird in my bosom,' he is said to have uttered as his mount stumbled the dozen yards between two low outcrops. What was meant by this remains uncertain; perhaps he referred to his true loyalty to Lancaster? Ironic, then, considering he had changed sides with such facility.[22]

Montagu's victory was complete and, though the chronicles give no hint of losses, probably cheaply bought. Aside from Percy and those retainers around him who held their ground, most of the defeated escaped unscathed. Morale was clearly a major factor in the Lancastrian defeat. Despite his humiliation, Somerset was able to rally many of the Lancastrians and retreat in reasonably good order to Tynedale, while Montagu was fully occupied with the diplomatic game. King Henry's kingdom had shrunk further but was not yet extinguished.[23]

With the Scots now in negotiations and the French in talks at St Omer (which had begun the previous autumn), the Lancastrians' diplomatic isolation was all but complete. As Northumberland was no longer viable as a bridgehead, there was little incentive for Somerset to disperse his forces in isolated garrisons – simply holding ground was pointless. With the Scots set to change horses, bargaining chips like Berwick and Norham had no further currency.[24] Henry's prospects appeared brighter in the west, for in March there were some fresh disturbances in Lancashire and Cheshire. Resistance flared briefly in Skipton in Craven, seat of the Cliffords, who, with their local affinity, had bled so liberally for Lancaster. None of these alarms developed into a serious threat.[25] However, King Edward continued to feel insecure in the north and west; commissions of array were sent out to the Midlands and Yorkshire, no writs were issued in Northumberland, Cumberland, Westmorland, Lancashire or Cheshire.[26]

The Battle of Hexham

Both sides were short of cash. Edward had been granted subsidies to prosecute the war in the north, Norham had been relieved but beyond that little achieved bar Montagu's notable success in the field. Parliament's subsidies and a further grant from convocation had been gobbled up by existing commitments, particularly the garrison at Calais.[27] The Yorkist administration was surviving on loans and was substantively in the red – raising taxes built resentment in all quarters and this was exacerbated when there was no tangible gain: so vociferous was this dissatisfaction that Edward felt constrained, in November 1463, to remit some £6,000 of the subsidy granted in the summer.[28] Somerset was under even greater pressure – he had no taxation revenue, no grants nor other subsidies; he was obliged to beg, borrow and steal. Even when cash could be scraped together, it could disappear through misappropriation. For example, when captured, hiding in a coal pit, after the final defeat at Hexham, Lord Tailboys was loaded with pilfered funds:

> He hadde moch money with hym, both golde and sylvyr, that shulde hav gon unto King Harry; and yf it had come to Harry, lat kynge of Ingelonde, hyt wolde have causyd moche sore sorowe, for he had ordynyd harneys and ordenance i-nowe, but the men wolde not go one fote with hym tylle they had mony.[29]

Henry now appears to have moved his lodgings to Bywell Castle, where he was in residence by the latter part of April. After the rout to come the victors found evidence of a hurried departure, the king's helmet or 'bycoket' (a coroneted cap), 'richly garnysshed wt ij crownys, and his followers trapped wt blew velvet'.[30] There was a suggestion that the Lancastrians might have been bolstered by 'a great power out of Scotlade'[31] but likely these were riders from Liddesdale and Teviotdale, drawn by the scent of booty. Bywell was not a significant castle and possessed no strategic value.[32] Both Tynedale and Redesdale were administered as 'Liberties' – franchises where the Crown sub-contracted the business of local government to franchisees, which led to a fair measure of autonomy. The Lancastrians still had a foothold in Tynedale,[33] holding Hexham, Prudhoe and possibly other centres.[34]

How much local support the Lancastrian cause enjoyed is questionable. The northern lords, Percy, Dacre and Clifford, had all bled freely, their affinities thinned and leaderless. Much had changed since the halcyon days of 1459–1460; even then, Queen Margaret had offered free quarter and plunder as incentives – now her cause was depleted by the disaster at Towton and three more years of attrition.[35]

There is no indication of how long King Henry remained at Bywell. In all probability he shifted west to Hexham, then fled deeper; he was likely gone before the battle and, therefore, the story of a precipitate flight from Bywell is almost certainly fanciful. Somerset would have been a fool to leave the king so exposed: Henry, however diminished, was his only trump. Montagu left Bywell undisturbed on his approach march. He would not have done so had he entertained any notion of Henry's presence there. Hexham was a larger castle and further west. In the fifteenth century the enceinte comprised the Moot Hall and Gaol, linked by a strong curtain wall.[36]

Montagu, by the end of the first week in May, had returned from York to Newcastle and, being aware (through scouts and agents) of Lancastrian activity in Tynedale, resolved to take the offensive. On this occasion he would not be hamstrung by diplomatic duties and could concentrate his considerable abilities on achieving a decisive outcome. Thus: 'on xiii of May, my lorde Mountague toke his jornaye toward Hexham from Newcastelle'.[37]

Advancing with Montagu's forces strung along the north bank of the Tyne, Hexham was his immediate tactical objective, his strategy being to expunge the Lancastrian presence, once and for all. Somerset would have been aware of this and though some Tudor chroniclers assert King Henry was present on the field, this is clearly fanciful. Gregory avers he fled north to Scotland, but as this was no longer safe, it is more probable he slipped further into the west, to Lancashire. Montagu crossed the Tyne either at Bywell or Corbridge – only the line of the Devil's Water now stood between him and the Lancastrian base of Hexham.[38] Devil's Water follows a meandering course from the high ground of the Shire towards the Tyne. From Hexham the ground shelves markedly towards the crossing at Linnels Bridge, some 2 miles distant; then, on the south side, rises steeply in the direction of Slaley. The traditional site for the Battle of Hexham – challenged by Dorothy Charlesworth – lies south of the present B6306, on low ground by the banks of the Devil's Water, and as featured on the OS 1:25000 map.

As the best contemporary source, the Year Book describes the actual field as 'un lieu appelle Livels sur le ewe Devyls' ('a spot called the Levels on the Devil's Water').[39] Worcester refers to a hill 1 mile from Hexham.[40] Ramsay, who had visited the location or talked to someone who had, observes tellingly that '[the site] is a nice, sheltered camping ground [. . .] but a very bad battlefield'.[41] The Year Book, which also states the fight occurred on 15 May, merely points to Linnels as a general area. Dorothy Charlesworth observes that the low ground is indeed most unsuitable.[42] It appears clear from a perambulation that the traditional location for the battle is badly flawed. To the rear it is hemmed by the water and to the front by steeply rising ground, which impedes visibility and inhibits manoeuvre, making a gift of the heights above to the attacker.

Later writers have accepted this view[43] without re-examining the topography and considering the implications. Dr Charlesworth argues, compellingly, that while Somerset may have camped on the Levels he did not deploy for battle there on the morning of the 15th, but drew up his forces on the higher ground along the crest of Swallowship Hill. Had he not done so, Montagu could have outflanked him and gained Hexham from the ford over the Devil's Water directly below the hill. The chroniclers do not really give us any assistance here,[44] so we are in the area of 'inherent military probability' as advanced by Colonel Burne. If, as Dorothy Charlesworth supposes, the defenders occupied the rise of Swallowship Hill, no such outflanking move would have been possible – with the stream circling the base, the crest of the hill commands all of the viable crossings. As the ground on both elevations drops quite sharply towards the Devil's Water, it would be possible for Somerset to refuse both flanks and channel the attacking Yorkists against his centre. It may, therefore, be that his line was curved to conform to the contours – Grey and Neville commanded on the left, Hungerford and Roos the right.

The Lancastrian left thus dominated the ford that lay below them and that to the north by Earl's Bridge; from the right it was possible to cover Linnels and the more southerly ford by Newbiggin. This is conjecture but the nature of the ground clearly favours Dr Charlesworth's view. This was the deployment that confronted Lord Montagu, who then made his own dispositions accordingly. While he probably fielded more troops, with higher morale, both his flank commanders, Lords Greystoke and Willoughby, were former Lancastrians. Greystoke, on the left, had fought at Second St Albans, where Willoughby, on the right, had served with him, losing his father Lord

Welles in the wreck of Towton. Willoughby had made his peace with Edward at Gloucester in September 1461 and had done good service since.[45]

Whether this fight began with a duel of arrows is not recorded; the Yorkists may have advanced quickly to contact and the mêlée was both swift and certain of outcome. Hungerford and Roos, on the Lancastrian right, were the first to give ground, and the line dissolved in precipitate rout. Somerset may have tried to cling to the crest and rally but he was swept away in the confusion of panic, the fords soon choked with fleeing men. With the brief fight over, only the business of pursuit remained.[46] Casualties in the combat were most likely light, the chroniclers do not mention any knights killed on the field – more noble blood by far was spilt by the executioners in the killing spree that followed. Worcester argues that Montagu fielded 10,000 men against Somerset's 500[47] but no commander would accept battle against such odds – perhaps the duke could count on no more than 500 retainers of his own immediate affinity.

Conversely, Warkworth argues that the Lancastrians had 'gathered a great people in the north country' and that the Yorkists were outnumbered, having no more than 4,000.[48] Looking at the ground, the position on Swallowship Hill covers a front of around 1,000 yards, allowing one man per yard and a gap between divisions; a force of at least 4,000 would be needed to give substance to the deployment. For his part, Montagu would surely have been less enthusiastic to engage had not his army been equal to or greater than that of his opponent.

Unlike the immediate aftermath of his previous victory, Montagu was not encumbered by distractions and was fully able to harry the fleeing Lancastrians. Somerset, Hungerford and Roos were all taken, captured 'in a wood faste by'.[49] Henry Beaufort, 2nd Duke of Somerset could not anticipate any further clemency; Montagu, like his brother, was not interested in reconciliation. It was now time for retribution and Somerset was executed the following day in Hexham. Hungerford and Roos were conveyed to Newcastle, where they, too, faced the axe 'behedid at Newcastle'.[50]

Others, including Sir Philip Wentworth, Sir Edmund Fitzhugh, John Bryce, Thomas Hunt and a reiver called 'Black Iaquys' ('Black John' or 'Black Jack'), were given appointments with the headsman at either Hexham or Middleham, 'after some writers'.[51] At least one captive, Sir Thomas Hussey, was executed at York.

The Siege of Bamburgh

Lancaster in the north was ruined; Somerset and the rebel lords hunted out, their retainers scattered. Humphrey Neville managed to escape the hounds; like Beaufort, his attainder had followed on from Towton but he, too, had been subsequently pardoned. Previously he'd escaped from the Tower and possessed a genius for survival, with Sir Ralph Grey and the odd remnant he regained Bamburgh, where the reduced garrison maintained a show of defiance. The embezzling Lord Tailboys was also netted and his hoard provided a handy bonus for Montagu's soldiery:

> the sum of 3,000 mark. And the lord's meinie of Montagu were sore hurt and sick, and many of his men were slain before in the great journeys, but this money was departed among them, and was a very wholesome salve for them.[52]

Tailboys was executed at Newcastle on 20 July, the last of the crop of prisoners to face the axe.

Barely two weeks after Hexham, John Neville, Lord Montagu – before king and court at York and in the presence of both of his brothers – was elevated to the Earldom of Northumberland. This was the high-water mark of his house, the zenith of the Nevilles. While at his northern capital Edward ratified the treaty with the Scots, concluded on 11 June, which secured a truce of fifteen years. Warwick, as the king's lieutenant, was charged once again with the recovery of the three border fortresses. To assist in these operations, Edward had assembled a formidable siege train, 'the great ordnance of England' – the bombards 'Edward', 'Dijon', 'London', 'Newcastle' and 'Richard Bombartel'.[53] The sight of these great guns was sufficient to overawe the shaken defenders at Alnwick, which capitulated on 23 June, followed next day by Dunstanburgh. Bates, however, maintains that the latter was, in fact, stormed and that the governor, John Gosse of Somerset's affinity, was taken and sent south to York to face execution.[54]

Bates continues to assert that Warwick maintained the feast of St John the Baptist at Dunstanburgh, while Henry VI was still within the walls of Bamburgh. He further claims that Henry made good his escape with the aid of Sir Henry Bellingham. NCH concurs and suggests Sir Thomas Philip, William Learmouth, Thomas Elwyk of Bamburgh, John Retford of Lincolnshire – all described as gentlemen – together with John Purcas of London, a yeoman, Philip Castelle of Pembroke, Archibald and Gilbert Ridley, from Langley, Gawen Lampleugh of Warkworth, also a gentleman, John Whynfell of Naworth, yeoman and Alexander Bellingham from Burneside in Westmorland, were all in the king's reduced household during this episode.[55]

This is most certainly inaccurate – none of those mentioned appears to have fought at Hexham and, if so, definitely avoided capture. It is more likely that these individuals were in Henry's service before the debacle on Devil's Water and fled west at the same time. Bates, with the NCH, suggests Sir Ralph Grey also escaped back to Bamburgh before the rout, rather than after.[56] Once again this seems unconvincing – Grey and his retainers would be needed on the field. Bamburgh was very much a last resort for a defeated captain who was all too aware that his duplicity excluded him from amnesty.

Though perhaps the greatest of the Northumbrian fortresses, Bamburgh was not built to withstand cannon and the deployment of the royal train before the massive walls gave ample notice of deadly intent. The Earl of Warwick dispatched his own and Edward's herald, Chester, formally to demand the garrison's surrender. Quarter was offered to the commons but both Grey and Neville were excluded from any terms, 'as out of the King's grace without any redemption'.[57] Grey, with nothing to lose, breathed defiance; he had 'Clearly determined within himself to live or die in the castle'. The heralds responded with a stern rejoinder and one can perhaps hear the words of the Earl of Warwick resonating through the chronicler's account:

> The King, our most dread sovereign lord, specially desires to have this jewel whole and unbroken by artillery, particularly because it stands so close to his ancient enemies the Scots, and if you are the cause that great guns have to be fired against its walls, then it will cost you your head, and for every shot that has to be fired another head, down to the humblest person within the place.[58]

Thus began the only siege bombardment of the wars. The bombards 'Newcastle' and 'London' were emplaced, sighted, loaded and began firing – the crash of the report like the crack of doom, with a great sulphurous cloud of filthy smoke drifting over the embattled ramparts. Whole sections of masonry were blasted by roundshot and crashed into the sea.[59] A lighter gun, 'Dijon', fired into the chamber where Sir Ralph Grey had established his HQ in the eastern gatehouse: he was injured and rendered insensible when one of these rounds brought down part of the roof.[60]

Humphrey Neville, ever the survivor, seized the moment of his ally's fall to seek terms, securing clemency for the garrison and, cleverly, for himself. The dazed Sir Ralph was tied to his horse and dragged as far as Doncaster to be tried by Sir John Tiptoft, Earl of Worcester and Constable of England. One of the indictments lodged against him was that he 'had withstood and made fences against the king's majesty, and his lieutenant, the worthy lord of Warwick, as appeareth by the strokes of the great guns in the king's walls of his castle of Bamburgh'.[61] Grey was executed on 10 July – the war in the north was finally over.

Notes

'The Rose of Rouen'
1. Edward IV as Earl of March – born in Rouen.
2. The dead Duke of York.
3. Cecily Neville ('The Rose of Raby') – Edward's mother.
4. The Earl of Warwick.
5. The Duke of Norfolk.
6. Lord Fauconberg.
7. Lord Scrope of Bolton.
8. Lord Grey of Ruthyn.
9. Sir William Herbert.
10. Viscount Bourchier.
11. The Earl of Arundel.
12. Sir Walter Devereux.
13. Lord Stanley.
14. Lord Clinton.
15. Edward IV as Duke of York.
16. Sir William Hastings.
17. Lord Audley.
18. Sir Roger Corbett.
19. Sir William Blount.
20. City of Gloucester.
21. City of Leicester.
22. City of Nottingham.

Introduction
1. Hall, p. 255.
2. See Towton Battlefield Society website: http://www.towton.org.uk
3. Leland, *Itinerary*.
4. RP pp. 277–478.
5. English Heritage, *Battlefield Report, Towton 1461* (1995), p. 2.
6. Ibid. A lynchet is defined as 'a bank formed by ploughing for a long period on a slope where a field has a fixed boundary while below it the soil is cut away to form a negative lynchet', http://www.netserf.org/glossary/l.cfm
7. English Heritage Report, p. 2.
8. Towton Spring, suggests coppicing, *see* English Heritage Report, p. 2.
9. Ibid. Carr Wood suggest heavy and frequently waterlogged ground.
10. Leland, *Itinerary*.
11. Boardman, A. W., *Towton, The Bloodiest Battle*, p. 80.
12. Ibid., p. 81.
13. Gregory, p. 217.

Chapter 1: The Art of War in the Fifteenth Century

1. Of those who took part in the apparently bloodless fracas at Heworth, Lord Egremont was killed at Northampton in 1460; Sir Thomas Neville and his father, the Earl of Salisbury, fell at Wakefield at the end of that year; Richard Percy died at Towton in 1461; John Neville, Lord Montagu, later Earl of Northumberland, was killed at Barnet in 1471.
2. Philip de Commynes 'The Memoirs for the Reign of Louis XI, 1461–1463' transl. M. Jones, 1972 p. 187.
3. P. A. Haigh, *The Military Campaigns of the Wars of the Roses* (London, 1995), p. 59.
4. T. Wise, *The Wars of the Roses* (London, 1983), p. 22.
5. Ibid., p. 23.
6. Sir Charles Oman, *The Art of War in the Middle Ages* (London, 1924), vol. 2, p. 408.
7. Wise, op. cit., p. 27.
8. Ibid., p. 27.
9. In *Henry IV Part One* act IV scene i – [Falstaff] 'If I be not ashamed of my soldiers, I am a soused gurnet. I have misused the king's press damnably.'
10. Wise, op. cit., p. 27. The Stonor correspondence is that of an Oxfordshire family in the middle ages, *see* C. L. Kingsford (ed.), *The Stonor Letters and Papers 1290–1483*, C. S. 3rd Series 29, 30m (London, 1919).
11. Wise, op. cit., pp. 27.
12. Ibid., p. 27.
13. A. W. Boardman, *The Medieval Soldier in the Wars of the Roses* (London, 1998), p. 173.
14. Wise, op. cit., p. 29.
15. Boardman, op. cit., p. 167.
16. Ibid., p. 167.
17. When a lord sent his horse to the rear and took his place amongst the foot, this was perceived as having an effect on morale as the gentleman was placing himself in equal peril.
18. C. Blair, *European Armour* (London, 1958), p. 77.
19. A. V. B. Norman and D. Pottinger, *English Weapons and Warfare 449–1660* (London, 1966), p. 114.
20. R. E. Oakeshott, *A Knight and his Weapons* (London, 1964), p. 51.
21. C. Bartlett, *The English Longbowman 1330–1515* (London, 1985), pp. 23–30.
22. 'Edward' is featured in an inventory of 1475; the Master of Ordnance, John Sturgeon, handed into store at Calais 'divers parcels of the king's Ordnance and artillery, including a bumbardell [bombard] called "The Edward"', *see* H. L Blackmore, *The Armouries of the Tower of London*, Ordnance (HMSO 1976), p. 33.
23. Norman and Pottinger, op. cit., p. 137.
24. A survivor from this period and still to be viewed in Edinburgh Castle is 'Mons Meg', which may be considered not untypical of the heavy guns of this period, cast in Flanders, around 1460.

25. H. C. B. Rogers, *Artillery through the Ages* (London, 1971), p. 19.
26. Norman and Pottinger, op. cit., p. 141.
27. P. Warner, *Sieges of the Middle Ages* (London, 1968), p. 198.
28. H. T. Riley (ed.), *Registrum Abbatis Johannis Whethamstede*, 1872, vol. 1 pp. 388–392.
29. Boardman, op. cit., pp. 181–183.
30. Bartlett, op. cit., p. 51.
31. S. L. Thrupp, *The Problem of Replacement Rates in Late Medieval English Population*.

Chapter 2: The House of Lancaster and the Path to Conflict 1400–1455

1. Carpenter, C., *The Wars of the Roses – Politics and the Constitution in England c. 1437–1509* (Cambridge, 1997), p. 27.
2. Carpenter, p. 35.
3. Pollard, A. J., *The Wars of the Roses* (England, 2001), pp. 53–54.
4. Ibid.
5. Ibid.
6. York was four at the date of his father's attainder.
7. Carpenter, p. 97.
8. Carpenter, p. 95.
9. Ibid., p. 57.
10. Fougères was a key Breton fortress.
11. Ross, C., *The Wars of the Roses* (London, 1976), p. 26.
12. The leaders adopted colourful pseudonyms, see Gillingham p. 62.
13. Jack Cade is a shadowy figure – possibly he'd seen military service.
14. Carpenter, p. 117.
15. Neillands, R., *The Hundred Years War* (London, 1992), pp. 281–283.
16. Carpenter, p. 121.
17. Thomas Young, the Bill's proposer, was an ally of the Yorkist Oldhall.
18. Gillingham, p. 72.
19. Oldhall sought sanctuary in the Church of St Martin-le-Grand, Dover.
20. Gillingham, p. 74.
21. Griffiths, R. A., 'Local Rivalries and National Politics; the Percys, the Nevilles and the Duke of Exeter 1452–1455' in *Speculum*, vol. XLIII 1968 p. 589.
22. Weiss, H., 'A Power in the North? The Percys in the Fifteenth Century' in *Historical Journal* 19. 2 1965 pp. 501–509.
23. Griffiths, p. 589.
24. Ibid., p. 590.
25. Griffiths, p. 592.
26. Ibid., p. 591.
27. Ibid., p. 592.
28. Ibid., p. 594.
29. Ibid.
30. Ibid., p. 595.
31. Ibid.
32. Griffiths, p. 602.

33. Ibid., p. 603.
34. Ibid., p. 604.
35. Ibid., p. 605.
36. Ibid.
37. Ross, p. 28.
38. Ibid., p. 29.
39. Ibid., p. 608.
40. Ibid., p. 609.
41. Ibid., p. 610.
42. Ibid.
43. Ibid., p. 611.
44. Ibid., p. 612.
45. Ibid., p. 613.
46. Ibid., p. 616.
47. Ibid., p. 620.
48. Ibid., p. 621.

Chapter 3: By the Sword Divided 1455–1460

1. Haigh, P., *The Military Campaigns of the Wars of the Roses* (London, 1995), p. 8.
2. Ibid., p. 8.
3. Warwick claimed credit for the initiative which may have been suggested by a subordinate.
4. Wiltshire assumed the guise of a monk and thus slipped through the Yorkist lines.
5. Calais had come into English hands at the conclusion of a successful siege in 1347.
6. The city was dubbed 'brightest jewel in the English crown', so vital was the trading connection.
7. Lord Privy Seal was an important post within the household.
8. Durham was a County Palatine.
9. Buckingham, though a noted moderate was nonetheless personally at odds with Warwick.
10. Andrew Trollope, Master-Porter of Calais, commanded the detachment.
11. John, 5th Lord Clinton of Maxstoke (1410–1464).
12. Gillingham, p. 105.
13. Lord Dinham (1443–1501) of Hemyhock Castle, Hartland in Devon.
14. Earl Rivers was a Woodville, father of the future Queen.
15. Jacquetta of Luxembourg, widow of John of Bedford.
16. Gillingham, p. 108.
17. His assertion was that this could be achieved for no greater outlay than 1,000 marks (a mark = 13s 4d or *c*.67p), *see* Lander, p. 71.
18. Sir John, later Lord Wenlock (1400–1471).
19. Coppini had been sent by Pope Pious II in February 1459 to drum up support for a fresh crusade, *see* Lander, p. 73.
20. John Fogge, John Scott and Robert Horne, *see* Gillingham, p. 111.
21. Thomas, Lord Scales (*c*. 1400–1460).

22. Lords Hungerford, Lovell, de la Warr, de Vesci and the Earl of Kendal.
23. James was so named on account of the large fiery birthmark which covered half his face.
24. Sandal Castle was originally associated with the de Warennes, beginning as a timber motte in the thirteenth century.

Chapter 4: The Parhelion: Winter 1460–Spring 1461
1. A parhelion is a phenomenon which produces the effect of three suns in the sky.
2. Owen Tudor had married Henry V's widow, Queen Catherine.
3. Galloglass – Norse Hiberean mercenaries from the Western Isles.
4. Edward's banner of 'the Sunne in Splendour' is said to have been inspired by the parhelion.
5. Edward was a very tall man, perhaps as tall as 6 feet 4 inches.
6. Gregory, p. 211.
7. Ibid., p. 211.
8. The Lancastrians numbered perhaps 8,000 *see* Haigh, op. cit., p. 42.
9. Croyland, p. 531.
10. Ibid., p. 531.
11. Gregory, pp. 211–214.
12. Colonel Burne echoes Sir Mortimer Wheeler in commenting on Iron Age earthworks.
13. Gregory, pp. 211–214.
14. Burne, op. cit., p. 86.
15. For a commentary on the nature of the ground, *see* Burne, pp. 88–89.
16. Burne, op. cit., p. 86.
17. Warwick seems to have been poorly served by his scouts.
18. Gregory, pp. 211–214.
19. CSPM i, 49–50.
20. Ibid.
21. Sir John Wenlock's cook apparently acted as instigator.
22. Lander, op. cit., p. 89.
23. GCL, pp. 194–196.
24. Ibid.
25. Ibid.
26. CSPM i, 58.
27. Ibid., pp. 58–59.

Chapter 5: First Blood
1. Extract from *The Rose of Rouen*.
2. Boardman, A. W., *Towton, the Bloodiest Battle*, p. 47.
3. Burne, op. cit., pp. 104–105.
4. Ibid., p. 105.
5. Boardman, op. cit., pp. 47–48.
6. McGill, P., *Battle of Towton 1461* (privately printed Lincoln, 1992), pp. 35–36.
7. Gillingham, op. cit., p. 131.

8. Boardman, op. cit., p. 59.
9. Ibid.
10. Ibid.
11. Ibid.
12. Markham, C., *The Battle of Towton*, vol. 10, Yorkshire Archaeological Society, 1889, p. 27.
13. Ibid.
14. Boardman, op. cit., p. 49.
15. Ibid., p. 61.
16. Gillingham, op. cit., p. 131.
17. *Hearne's Fragment*, p. 9.
18. CSPM, p. 61.
19. Haigh, op. cit., pp. 58–59.
20. See the very useful website of the Red Wyverns, the Clifford Household re-enactment society – www.red-wyverns.org.uk
21. Hall, pp. 254–255.
22. Ibid. The earl was mounted on a hackney, much cheaper to replace than a precious destrier; theatre comes on a budget!
23. Ibid.
24. Markham, p. 5.
25. Waurin, pp. 337–338.
26. Leadman, A. D., *The Battle of Towton*, vol. 10, Yorkshire Archaeological Society, 1889, p. 290.
27. Ransome, C., *The Battle of Towton*, vol. 4, English Historical Review, 1889, p. 461.
28. Hall, p. 255.
29. CSPM, p. 61.

Chapter 6: Trial by Battle
1. Boardman, op. cit., p. 76.
2. Ibid., p. 78.
3. Burne, op. cit., p. 99.
4. *Hearne's Fragment*, p. 9.
5. Waurin, pp. 338–340.
6. Boardman, op. cit., p. 108.
7. Ramsay, Sir. J. H., *Lancaster and York* (Oxford, 1892), p. 278.
8. Burne, op. cit., p. 105.
9. Ramsay, op. cit., p. 278.
10. Gregory, p. 214.
11. Burne, op. cit., p. 106.
12. Ibid.
13. Ibid., p. 99.
14. Haigh, op. cit., p. 60.
15. Leon (Lionel) Lord Welles was married to the late Duke of Somerset's widow Margaret, Rot. Parl. v. 310.
16. Waurin, pp. 338–340.

17. Boardman, op. cit., p. 97.
18. Ramsay, op. cit., p. 271.
19. Hall, p. 104.
20. Vergil, pp. 110–111.
21. Boardman, op. cit., p. 108.
22. Hall, pp. 255–256.
23. Ibid.
24. Boardman, op. cit., p. 113 – I have assumed a rather closer range: he says 300 yards, I suggest nearer 200.
25. Waurin, p. 340.
26. Many contemporary illustrations show the field heaped with piles of dead.
27. John Waller in Fiorato, V., A. Boylston & C. H. Knusel (eds) *Blood Red Roses – the Archaeology of a Mass Grave from the Battle of Towton* (Oxford, 2007), p. 148.
28. Ibid.
29. Ibid., pp. 149–50.
30. There is anecdotal evidence from the field of an earlier Scottish battle, the 'Red Harlaw' of 1411, where there is a tradition that separate grave pits were dug for female dead killed during the battle.
31. Boardman, op. cit., p. 120.
32. Waurin, pp. 338–340.
33. Ibid.
34. Boardman, op. cit., p. 125.
35. Leadman, op. cit., p. 297.
36. Boardman, op. cit., p. 133.
37. Ibid., p. 131.
38. Quoted in Boardman, p. 131.
39. Whether the duke was present remains a matter of debate even though certain chroniclers assert this was the case, *see Hearne's Fragment*, p. 9.
40. Ibid.
41. Boardman, op. cit., p. 133.
42. Vergil, p. 111.
43. Boardman, op. cit., p. 134.
44. Ramsay, op. cit., p. 273.
45. Vergil, p. 111.

Chapter 7: Rout

1. Prebble, J., *Culloden* (London, 1961), p. 119.
2. Ibid.
3. De Commynes, p. 87.
4. Croyland, p. 425.
5. Boardman, op. cit., p. 136.
6. Hall, p. 256.
7. Quoted in Lander, op. cit., pp. 92–93.
8. Ibid.

9. Croyland, p. 425.
10. Boardman, op. cit., pp. 142–143.
11. Ibid., p. 145.
12. CSPM, p. 66.
13. Gregory, p. 218.

Chapter 8: Legacy
1. Berwick-upon-Tweed had changed hands more than a dozen times during the border wars.
2. James II had been killed when one of his own cannon exploded at the Siege of Roxburgh.
3. Ordnance was brought from London to Newcastle upon Tyne by ship, then transported by carts to the siege lines.
4. Both were executed after being captured by Warwick on the field of Edgecote on 26 July 1496.
5. Empingham was dubbed 'Losecote Field' when the fleeing rebels cast off their telltale livery.
6. Warwick fought on foot at Barnet, sending a message of solidarity to his troops, possibly at his brother's urging. It proved a fatal decision.
7. The battle was fought on 4 May 1471.
8. Richard of Gloucester married Anne Neville, widow of Edward of Lancaster.

Chapter 9: The Towton Mass Grave Project
1. Fiorato, V., A. Boylston & C. H. Knusel, op. cit., p. 7.
2. Ibid., p. 33.
3. Ibid., p. 29.
4. Aside from the aforementioned rings the principal finds were a series of copper 'aiglets' – these are the tips of the laces called points and used to fasten clothing and perhaps, as in one instance, sections of harness.
5. Fiorato et al, op. cit., p. 55.
6. Ibid., p. 74.
7. Ibid., p. 88.
8. Ibid., p. 153.
9. Ibid., skeleton 41.
10. Ibid., skeleton 25.
11. Ibid., p. 100.
12. Ibid., skeleton 41.
13. Ibid., skeleton 16.

Chapter 10: The Battlefield Today
1. EH Report, p. 6.
2. Ibid., p. 7.
3. The 'Crooked Billet' is said to be on the site of an ancient inn which provided the Earl of Warwick with a comfortable night's lodgings prior to the battle, with some solace for his wounds in the day's fighting. The

name, it is said, derives from an association with the Kingmaker's White Ragged Staff badge, though this cannot be verified nor is there any evidence for an older structure.

4. Boardman, op. cit., p. 166.
5. Ibid., p. 166.
6. Ibid., p. 166.
7. Ibid., p. 151.
8. Ibid., p. 188.

Appendix II: The Combatants
1. Markham, op. cit., p. 10.

Appendix III: The War in the North 1461–1464
1. Rot. Parl. 1st Edward IV 1461 vol. v fo. 477–478.
2. Calendar of State Papers and Manuscripts existing in the Archives and Collections of Milan ed. and transl. by A. B. Hinds 1912 pp. 61–62.
3. Ibid., pp. 74–77.
4. A. J. Pollard, 'Characteristics of the Fifteenth Century North' in *Government Religion and Society in Northern England 1000–1700*, ed. C. Appleby & P. Dalton (England, 1977), p. 131.
5. L. W. Hepple, *A History of Northumberland and Newcastle upon Tyne* (London, 1976), pp. 14–15.
6. N. Pevsner & I. Richmond, 'Northumberland' in *The Buildings of England* (London, 1992), pp. 135–136.
7. Pevsner & Richmond, op. cit., pp. 155–156.
8. Ibid., pp. 258–259.
9. D. Charlesworth, 'Northumberland in the Early Years of Edward IV' in *Archaeologia Aeliana* (4th Series 1953), p. 70.
10. M. Lynch, *Scotland: A New History* (London, 1991), pp. 146–151.
11. R. Lomas, *Northumberland – County of Conflict* (East Lothian, 1996), pp. 45–50.
12. P. Murray Kendall, *Warwick the Kingmaker* (New York, 1957), p. 86.
13. Ibid., pp. 202–203.
14. Ross, op. cit., p. 56.
15. Gillingham, op. cit., pp. 140–141.
16. Scottish Exchequer Rolls, vii Ramsay ii, p. 290.
17. Gillingham, op. cit., p. 141.
18. Ross, op. cit., p. 60.
19. Worcester 'Annales', p. 470.
20. Ibid., p. 480.
21. NCH, vol. I, p. 48.
22. Worcester 'Annales', p. 480.
23. Paston Letters, no. 464.
24. Ross, op. cit., pp. 62–63.
25. *Gregory's Chronicle*, p. 219.
26. Ibid., p. 219.

27. Ibid., p. 220.
28. Ibid., p. 221.
29. 'The year Book de Termino Paschae 4 Edward IV' in *Priory of Hexham*, Surtees Society, p. cviii, gives Alnwick as the location but NCH vol. 1 p. 46 claims Bamburgh – the latter seems more likely being on the coast and closer to Scotland.
30. Ross, op. cit., p. 65.
31. *Gregory's Chronicle*, p. 222.
32. Ibid., p. 222.
33. NCH 1, p. 46.

Appendix IV: The Battles of Hedgeley Moor and Hexham

1. M. A. Hicks, 'Edward IV, the Duke of Somerset and Lancastrian Loyalism in the North' in *Northern History*, vol. xx, p. 24.
2. Ibid., p. 25.
3. C. Ross, *Edward IV* (London, 1974), pp. 51–52.
4. Hicks, op. cit., p. 31.
5. *Gregory's Chronicle*, pp. 221–223.
6. Hicks, op. cit., p. 32.
7. Ibid., p. 33.
8. Ibid., p. 34.
9. *Fabyan's Chronicle*, p. 683.
10. *Gregory's Chronicle*, p. 224.
11. *Year Book of Edward IV*, p. cviii.
12. Gillingham, op. cit., p. 180.
13. *Gregory's Chronicle*, p. 224.
14. Ibid., p. 224.
15. Ibid., p. 224.
16. Ibid., p. 224.
17. Ibid., p. 224.
18. Haigh, op. cit., p. 80.
19. *Gregory's Chronicle*, p. 224.
20. Boardman, op. cit., p. 75.
21. Haigh, op. cit., p. 80.
22. G. Brenan, *The House of Percy* (England, 1898), vol. 1, p. 93.
23. Gillingham, op. cit., p. 152.
24. Ross, op. cit., p. 56.
25. Sir J. H. Ramsay, *Lancaster and York* (Oxford, 1892), vol. II, p. 302.
26. Paston letters, no. 252.
27. Ramsay, op. cit., vol. II, p. 302.
28. Ross, op. cit., p. 55.
29. Ibid., p. 56.
30. *Gregory's Chronicle*, p. 226.
31. *Fabyan's Chronicle*, p. 654.
32. *Chronicles of London* ed. C. L. Kingsford, (Oxford, 1905), p. 178.

33. B. Long, *The Castles of Northumberland* (Newcastle upon Tyne, 1967), p. 76.
34. Lomas, op. cit., p. 136.
35. Ibid., pp. 154–155.
36. Boardman, op. cit., p. 38.
37. Charlesworth, op. cit., p. 62.
38. *Gregory's Chronicle*, p. 224.
39. Ibid., p. 232.
40. Charlesworth, op. cit., p. 63.
41. *Worcester's Chronicle*, p. 779.
42. Ramsay, op. cit., vol. II, 303.
43. Charlesworth, op. cit., p. 64.
44. Haigh, op. cit., p. 84.
45. *Gregory's Chronicle*, p. 224.
46. Ramsay, op. cit., vol. II, p. 303 n.
47. Ibid., p. 303.
48. *Warkworth's Chronicle*, p. 4.
49. *Fabyan's Chronicle*, p. 654.
50. *Chronicles of London*, p. 178.
51. *Fabyan's Chronicle*, p. 654.
52. *Gregory's Chronicle*, p. 219.
53. 'Edward' is later listed in an inventory of 1475; the Master of the Ordnance, John Sturgeon, handed into store at Calais, 'divers parcels of the King's ordnance and artillery including a bumbartell called "The Edward"'; *see* Blackmore, op. cit., p. 33.
54. C. J. Bates, *History of Northumberland* (London, 1895), p. 202.
55. NCH vol. 1, p. 47.
56. *Worcester's Chronicle*, p. 280 (note) – the assumption may be based on a misreading of the Latin text: 'Radulfus Gray fugit de Hexham ante bellum inceptum ad castrum Bamburghe et post bellum de Hexham multi ex parte Regis Henrici fugerunt in eodem castro'. It is more probable the chronicler is describing Grey's flight as the battle opened rather than beforehand.
57. NCH vol. 1, p. 48.
58. *Warkworth's Chronicle*, pp. 37–39.
59. NCH vol. 1, p. 48.
60. *Warkworth's Chronicle*, pp. 37–39.
61. NCH vol. 1, p. 49.

Bibliography

Primary Sources

A Chronicle of London from 1089–1485 (eds H. Nicholas and E. Tyrell), London 1827.

'A London Chronicle of 1460' (ed. G. Baskerville) in *English Historical Review*, XXVIII, 1913.

Adam of Usk, *Chronicon Adae de Usk* (ed. E. M. Thompson), London 1904.

An English Chronicle of the Reigns of Richard II, Henry IV, Henry V and Henry VI, ed. J. S. Davies, 1856.

Benet J., 'John Benet's chronicle for the years 1400 to 1462' (eds G. L. Harriss and M. A. Harriss), *Camden Miscellany*, vol. XXIV, London 1972.

Brut Chronicle, 2 vols., ed. F. W. D. Brie, 1906.

Calendar of Documents relating to Scotland, vol. IV, 1357–1509 (ed. J. Bain), London 1888.

Calendar of Fine Rolls: Edward IV; Edward V; Richard III, 1471–1485, London HMSO, 1961.

Calendar of Patent Rolls, Edward IV 1467–1477, Edward IV, Edward V, Richard III, 1476–1485, London 1899–1901.

Calendar of State Papers and Manuscripts existing in the Archives and Collections of Milan, ed. and transl. A. B. Hinds, 1912.

Chastellain G. 'Chronique des derniers Ducs de Bourgoyne' in *Pantheon Literaire*, IV.

'Chronicles of London' ed. C. L. Kingsford, Oxford 1905.

'Croyland Abbey Chronicle' ed. H. T. Riley, 1854.

'The Croyland Chronicle Continuation 1459–1486' (eds N. Prona and J. Cox), England 1986.

The Cotton MS in the British Library.

Davies R. 'York Records of the Fifteenth Century'.

Edward Hall, 'The Union of the Two Noble and Illustre Famelies of Lancastre and York 1548'.

'English Historical Documents' vol. 5 1327–1484 (ed. A. R. Myers), London 1969.

'Froissart's Chronicles' ed. G. Brereton, 1968.

Furnivall F. J. and H. W. Hales eds 'Bishop Percy's Folio Manuscript' vol. 3, London 1868.

Hammond P.W. and R. Horrox 'The Harleian Manuscripts' 4 vols. British Library Harleian Manuscript 1979–1983.

'Hearne's Fragment' in 'Chronicles of the White Rose' ed. J. A. Giles, 1834.

'Historie of the Arrivall of King Edward IV in England and the final Recoverye of his Kingdomes from Henry VI A. D. 1471', (ed. J. Bruce) Camden Society 1838.

'John Benet's Chronicle for the years 1400–1462' eds G. L. Harriss & M. A. Harriss in 'Camden Miscellany' 24 1972.

John Warkworth 'A Chronicle of the First Thirteen Years of the Reign of Edward IV 1461–1474' ed. J. O. Halliwell C. S. Old Series x 1839.

'Knyghthode and Bataile' (eds R. Dyboski and Z. M. Arend) Early English Texts Society 1935.

Mancini Dominic ed. C. A. J. Armstrong 'The Usurpation of Richard III' Oxford 1969, reprinted Gloucester 1984.

More, Sir Thomas ed. R. S. Sylvester 'The History of Richard III' Complete Works vol. II Yale edn. 11 1963.

Philip De Commynes 'The Memoirs of the Reign of Louis XI 1461–1463', transl. M. Jones 1972.

'Plumpton Letters' ed. T. Stapleton Camden Society 1839.

Polydore Vergil 'Three Books of Polydore Vergil's English History' ed. H. Ellis 1844.

H. T. Riley (ed.) 'Registrum Abbatis Johannis Whethamstede' 1872.

Robert Fabyan 'The New Chronicles of England and France' ed. H. Ellis London 1809.

'Rose of Rouen' Archaeologia XXIX. pp. 344–347.

'Rotuli. Parliamentorum' eds J. Strachey & others 6 vols. 1767–1777.

Rous J. 'Historiae Regum Anglicae' (ed. T. Hearne) Oxford 1716.

Rous J. 'The Rous Roll' (eds C. Ross and W. Courthope) England 1980.

Scottish Exchequer Rolls vii Ramsay ii.

'Short English Chronicle' ed. J. Gairdner C. S. New Series xxviii 1880.

Hans Talhoffer 'Manual of Swordfighting' (transl. & ed. M. Rector) facsimile edn. 2000.

'The Household of Edward IV' (ed. A. R. Myers) 1959.

'The Great Chronicle of London' (eds A. H. Thomas and I. D. Thornley) London 1938.

'The Paston Letters 1422–1509' ed. J. Gairdner 3 vols. 1872–1875.

'The Priory of Hexham' vol. I Surtees Soc. 1864.

'The Year Book de Termino Paschae 4 Edward IV' in Priory of Hexham, S. S. 1 1864.

'Three Fifteenth-Century Chronicles' (ed. J. Gairdner) Camden Society 1880.

Waurin Jean de 'Recueil des Chroniques D'Angleterre' eds W. Hardy & E. L. C. P. Hardy 1891.

Whethamstede J. 'Registrum' in 'Registra quorandum Abbatum Monasterii S. Albani' 2 vols (ed. H. Riley) Rolls Series 1872–1873.

William Gregory's 'Chronicle of London' in Historical Collections of a Citizen of London in the Fifteenth Century ed. J. Gairdner C. C New

Series xvii 1876.

William of Worcester 'Annales Rerum Anglicarum' in Liber Niger Scaccarii ed. J. Hearne 2 vols. Oxford 1728.

Secondary Sources

Allen, K., *The Wars of the Roses* (London 1973).

Allmand, C., *Henry V* (London 1992).

Archer, R. E. C., *Government and people in the Fifteenth Century* (Stroud 1995).

Archibald, E. H. H., *The Wooden Fighting Ship* (London 1968).

Arthurson, I., *The Perkin Warbeck Conspiracy 1491–1499* (Stroud 1977).

Attreed, L., (ed.) *York House Books* (London 1991).

Bagley, J. J., *Margaret of Anjou, Queen of England* (London 1948).

Bain, J. (ed.) *Calendar of Documents Relating to Scotland 1108–1509* (1881–1884).

Barbour, R., *The Knight and Chivalry* (London 1974).

Barnard, F., *Edward IV French Expedition* (London 1975).

Bartlett, C., *The English Longbowman 1313–1515* (Oxford 1995).

Bates, C. J., *History of Northumberland* (London 1895).

Bean, J. M. W., *The Estates of the Percy Family* (Oxford 1958).

Bennet, M., *The Battle of Bosworth* (New York 1985).

Bennet, M., *Lambert Simnel and the Battle of Stoke* (Stroud 1987).

Bennett, H. S., *The Pastons and Their England* (Cambridge 1932).

Bingham, C., *The Stewart Kings of Scotland 1371–1603* (London 1974).

Blackmore, H. L., *The Armouries of the Tower of London*, Ordnance (HMSO 1976).

Blair, C., *European Armour* (London 1958).

Boardman, A. V., *The Battle of Towton* (Stroud 1994).

Boardman, A. V., *The Medieval Soldier in the Wars of the Roses* (London 1998).

Brenan, G., *The House of Percy* 2 vols. (London 1898).

Burne, Colonel A. H., *Battlefields of England* (London 1950).

Burne, Colonel A. H., *More Battlefields of England* (London 1952).

Carpenter C., *The Wars of the Roses: Politics and the Constitution in England c. 1437–1509* (Cambridge 2002).

Charlesworth, D., 'Northumberland in the Early Years of Edward IV' in *Archaeologia Aeliana* (4th Series, Newcastle upon Tyne 1953).

Charlesworth, D., 'The Battle of Hexham' in *Archaeologia Aeliana* (4th Series 1952, Newcastle upon Tyne).

Chrimes, S. B., *Henry VII* (London 1952).

Clive, M., *The Sun of York, Edward IV* (London 1973).

Cole, H., *The Wars of the Roses* (London 1973).

Cook, D. R., *Lancastrians & Yorkists, The Wars of the Roses* (London 1984).

Coward, B., *The Stanleys, Lord Stanley and Earls of Derby 1385–1672* (Stroud 1983).

Dockray, K. R., 'The Yorkshire Rebellions of 1469' in *The Ricardian* vol. 6, no. 82 (December 1983).

Dockray, K. R., *Chronicles of the Reign of Edward IV* (Stroud 1983).

Ducklin, K., & J. Waller, *Sword Fighting* (London 2001).

Falkus, G., *The Life and Times of Edward IV* (London 1981).

Fiorato, V., A Boylston & C. Knusel (eds) *Blood and Roses: The Archaeology of a Mass Grave from the Battle of Towton AD 1461* (Oxford 2000).

Foss, P. J., *The Field of Redemore Plain: The Battle of Bosworth* (Stroud 1990).

Gairdner, J. (ed.) *The Paston Letters*, 6 vols. (London 1986).

Gillingham, J., *The Wars of the Roses* (London 2001).

Goodman, A., *The Wars of the Roses* (London 1981).

Grant, A., 'Richard III in Scotland' in *The North of England in the Reign of Richard III* (ed.) Pollard (Stroud 1996).

Grant, A., *Henry VII* (London 1985).

Gravett, C., *Medieval Siege Warfare* (Stroud 1990).

Green, V. H. H., *The Later Plantagenets* (London 1955).

Griffiths, R. A., *King and Country: England and Wales in the Fifteenth Century* (Stroud 1991).

Griffiths, R. A., *Kings and Nobles in the Later Middle Ages* (Stroud 1986).

Griffiths, R. A., *Local Rivalries and National Politics: The Percys, the Nevilles and the Duke of Exeter 1452–1455* in Speculum, vol. XLIII (1968).

Griffiths, R. A., *The Making of the Tudor Dynasty* (Stroud 1985).

Griffiths, R. A. (ed.) 'Patronage' in *The Crown and the Provinces in Later Medieval England* (Oxford 1981).

Griffiths, R. A., *The Reign of King Henry VI* (London 1981).

Haigh, P. A., *The Battle of Wakefield* (Stroud 1996).

Haigh, P. A., *The Military Campaigns of the Wars of the Roses* (London 1995).

Hallam, E. (ed.) *The Chronicles of the Wars of the Roses* (London 1988).

Hallam, E., *The Plantagenet Encyclopedia* (London 1990).

Hammond, P. W., *Richard III – Lordship Loyalty and Law* (Donington 1986).

Hammond, P. W., *The Battles of Barnet and Tewkesbury* (New York 1990).

Hammond, P. W., & A. Sutton, *Richard III – The Road to Bosworth Field* (London 1985).

Harvey, J., *The Plantagenets* (London 1948).

Hepple, L. W., *A History of Northumberland and Newcastle Upon Tyne* (London 1976).

Hibbert, C., *Agincourt* (London 1964).

Hicks, M. A., Edward IV, 'The Duke of Somerset and Lancastrian Loyalism in the North' in *Northern History* (vol. xx).

Hicks, M. A., *False, Fleeting Perjur'd Clarence, George Duke of Clarence* (London 1980).

Hicks, M. A., 'Warwick; The Reluctant Kingmaker' in *Medieval History* vol. 1 no. 2 (1991).
Hodges, G., *Ludford Bridge and Mortimer's Cross* (London 1988).
Horrox, R., *Fifteenth Century Attitudes* (Cambridge 1994).
Horrox, R., *Richard III – A Study in Service* (Cambridge 1989).
Horrox, R., *Richard III and the North* (Cambridge 1986).
James, M. E., 'The Murder at Coxlodge on 28th April, 1489' in *Durham University Journal* VII (1965).
Johnson, P. A., *Richard, Duke of York 1411–1460* (London 1988).
Jones, M. K., *Bosworth 1485 – The Psychology of a Battle* (Stroud 2002).
Keegan, J., *The Face of Battle* (London 1976).
Keen, M., *English Society in the Later Middle Ages 1348–1500* (London 1990).
Keen, M. (ed.) *Medieval Warfare – a History* (Oxford 1999).
Kendall, P. Murray, *Richard III* (New York 1955).
Kendall, P. Murray, *The Wars of the Roses* (New York 1957).
Kendall, P. Murray, *Warwick the Kingmaker* (New York 1957).
Kightly, C., *The Dukes of York and their Duchesses* (York 1987).
Lander, J. R., *Crown and Nobility 1450–1509* (London 1976).
Lander, J. R., *The Limitations of English Monarchy in the Later Middle Ages* (Ontario 1989).
Lander, J. R., *The Wars of the Roses* (London 1990).
Leadman, A. D., *The Battle of Towton* Yorkshire Archaeological Journal vol. 10 (1889).
Lomas, R., 'North-East England' in *The Middle Ages* (Edinburgh 1992).
Lomas, R., *Northumberland – County of Conflict* (East Lothian 1996).
Long, B., *The Castles of Northumberland* (Newcastle upon Tyne 1967).
Lynch, M., *A New History of Scotland* (London 1991).
Macdougall, N., *James III: A Political Study* (Edinburgh 1982).
McFarlane, K. B., *England in the Fifteenth Century* (ed.) G. L. Harris (London 1981).
McFarlane, K. B., *The Nobility of Late Medieval England* (Oxford 1975).
McFarlane, K. B., 'The Wars of the Roses' in *Proceedings of the British Academy* (50 1964).
Markham, C., 'The Battle of Towton' *Yorkshire Archaeological Journal* vol. 10 (1889).
Meade, D. M., *The Medieval Church in England* (Worthing 1988).
Mortimer, I., *The Greatest Traitor* (London 2003).
Myers, A. R. (ed.) *The Household of Edward IV: The Black Book and the Ordinance of 1478* (Oxford 1950).
Neillands, R., *The Hundred Years War* (London 1990).
Neillands, R., *The Wars of the Roses* (London 1992).
Nicolle, D., *Medieval Warfare Source Book* (London 1999).
Norman, A. V. B. and D. Pottinger, *English Weapons and Warfare 449–1660* (London 1966).

Northumberland County History (Newcastle upon Tyne).

Oakeshott, R. E., *A Knight and his Weapons* (London 1964).

Oman, Sir Charles, *The Art of War in the Middle Ages* vol. 2 (London 1924).

Pevsner, N. & I. Richmond, 'Northumberland' in *The Buildings of England* Series (London 1992).

Pollard, A. J., 'Percys, Nevilles and the Wars of the Roses' in *History Today* (September 1992).

Pollard, A. J., 'Characteristics of the Fifteenth Century North' in *Government, Religion and Society in Northern England 1000–1700* (eds) C. Appleby and P. Dalton (Oxford 1977).

Pollard, A. J., *North-eastern England during the Wars of the Roses: War, Politics and Lay Society, 1450–1500* (Oxford 1990).

Pollard, A. J., *The Wars of the Roses* (London 1995).

Prestwich, M., *Armies and Warfare in the Middle Ages* (London 1996).

Ramsay, Sir J. H., *Lancaster and York* 2 vols. (Oxford 1892).

Ransome, C., 'The Battle of Towton' *English Historical Review* vol. 4 (1889).

Ridpath, G., *The Border History of England and Scotland* (Berwick-upon-Tweed 1776).

Roberts, D., *The Battle of Stoke* (Stroud 1987).

Rogers, Col. H. C. B., *Artillery Through the Ages* (London 1971).

Rose, A., *Kings in the North* (London 2002).

Ross, C., *Edward IV* (London 1974).

Ross, C. (ed.) 'Patronage, Pedigree and Power' in *Later Medieval England* (England 1979).

Ross, C., *Richard III* (London 1981).

Ross, C., *Wars of the Roses* (London 1976).

Rowse, A. L., *Bosworth Field and the War of the Roses* (London 1966).

Runciman, Sir Stephen, *The Fall of Constantinople* (Cambridge 1965).

Sadler, D. J., *Battle for Northumbria* (Newcastle upon Tyne 1988).

Sadler, D. J., *War in the North – The Wars of the Roses in the North East of England 1461–1464* (Bristol 2000).

Sadler, D. J., *Border Fury – The Three Hundred Years War* (London 2004).

Simons, E. N., *Reign of Edward IV* (London 1966).

Scofield, C. L., *The Life and Reign of Edward the Fourth* 2 vols. (London 1967).

Seward, D., *Henry V as Warlord* (London 1987).

Seward, D., *Richard III – England's Black Legend* (London 1983).

Seward, D., *The Wars of the Roses* (London 1995).

Seymour, W., *Battles in Britain* vol. 1 (London 1989).

Smurthwaite, D., *The Ordnance Survey Guide to the Battlefields of Britain* (London 1984).

Stapleton, T. (ed.) *The Plumpton Correspondence* (Stroud 1977).

Storey, R. L., *End of the House of Lancaster* (London 1966).

Storey, R. L., 'The Wardens of the Marches of England Towards Scotland 1377–1489' in *English Historical Review* (72: 1957).

Summerson, H., 'Carlisle and the English West March in the Late Middle Ages' in *The North of England in the Reign of Richard III* (Durham 1996).

Sunday Times Magazine 24 August, 2008.

Thrupp, S. L., *The Problem of Replacement Rates in Late Medieval English Population* ECHR 2nd Series (1965–1966).

Tomlinson, W. Weaver, *A Comprehensive Guide to Northumberland* (Newcastle upon Tyne 1863).

Tough, D. L. W., *The Last Years of a Frontier* (Oxford 1928).

Trevelyan, G. M., *A History of England* (London 1926).

Tuck, A., *Crown and Nobility, 1272–1462* (England 1985).

Wagner, P. and S. Hand, *Medieval Sword and Shield* (San Francisco 2003).

Warner, P., *Sieges of the Middle Ages* (London 1968).

Watson, G., *The Border Reivers* (Newcastle upon Tyne 1974).

Weiss, H., 'A Power in the North? The Percys in the Fifteenth Century' in *The Historical Journal* (1965).

Williamson, A., *The Murder of the Princes* (England 1978).

Wise, T., *Medieval Heraldry* (Oxford 1980).

Wise, T., *The Wars of the Roses* (London 1983).

Wolffe, B., *Henry VI* (London 1981).

Woolgar, C. M., *The Great Household in Late Medieval England* (London 1999).

Websites

http://www.brad.ac.uk/aced/archski/depart/resgrp/archpros/Towton/landscape

http://www.brad.ac.uk/acad/archsci/depart/resgrp/archpros/Towton

http://mysite.wanadoo-members.co.uk/TowtonBattlefield

http://www.towton.org.uk

http://www.battlefieldstrust.com/resource-centre/warsoftheroses/battleview.asp?BattleFieldId=46

http://www.red-wyverns.org.uk

Index